Prentice Hall LITERATURE

PENGUIN EDITION

Unit Four
Resources

Grade Seven

PEARSON

Upper Saddle River, New Jersey
Boston, Massachusetts
Chandler, Arizona
Glenview, Illinois

BQ Tunes Credits
Keith London, Defined Mind, Inc., Executive Producer
Mike Pandolfo, Wonderful, Producer
All songs mixed and mastered by Mike Pandolfo, Wonderful
Vlad Gutkovich, Wonderful, Assistant Engineer
Recorded November 2007 – February 2008 in SoHo, New York City, at
Wonderful, 594 Broadway

ISBN–13: 978-0-13-366439-3
ISBN–10:   0-13-366439-2

3 4 5 6 7 8 9 10   12 11 10 09

CONTENTS

For information about the Unit Resources, assessing fluency, and teaching with BQ Tunes, see the opening pages of your Unit One Resources.

BQ Tunes

Listen & Learn, performed by Nina Zeitlin

Listen, can you hear me?
Learn what you need to know

We **speak** to the listener
We **communicate** the information
We're **enriched** by knowledge (makes us better)
And when we share, we contribute to communication

Each and every minute
That passes by
Someone's **producing** a new gadget
Made for people to buy
Each and every minute
That passes by
This new **technology**
Enters someone's mind's eye

Listen and **learn**
Listen and learn
For information people yearn
Listen and learn
Listen and learn
Listen and learn
Listen and learn
For information people yearn
Listen and learn
Listen and learn
Then your words will make the world turn

Continued

To play our favorite music

To **transmit** the words we say

Show an **entertaining** movie, or my favorite TV show

On whatever media we chose today (we chose today)

Teach ourselves how to use it

To learn and to be **informed**

To speak and to **express** ourselves

Choosing one from the other, we might be torn but

Listen and **learn**

Listen and learn

For information people yearn

Listen and learn

Listen and learn

Listen and learn

Listen and learn

For information people yearn

Listen and learn

Listen and learn

Then your words will make the world turn

There will always be something new

People **react,** they respond to the next big thing

Who's **producing** the greatest **media** toy? (**media** toy)

No matter what form of communication this year brings, ya gotta...

Listen and **learn**

Listen and learn

For information people yearn

Listen and learn

Listen and learn

Listen and learn

Listen and learn

Continued

x

For information people yearn

Listen and learn

Listen and learn

Then your words will make the world turn

Song Title: **Listen & Learn**

Artist / Performed by Nina Zeitlin

Guitar: Josh Green

Drums/Bass: Mike Pandolfo

Keys: Mike Pandolfo & Nina Zeitlin

Conga: Vlad Gutkovich

Lyrics by Nina Zeitlin

Music composed by Mike Pandolfo & Nina Zeitlin

Produced by Mike Pandolfo, Wonderful

Executive Producer: Keith London, Defined Mind

Name _____ Date _____

Unit 4: Poetry
Big Question Vocabulary—1

The Big Question: What is the best way to communicate?

communicate: *v.* to exchange information with others; other forms: *communication, communicating, communicated*

entertain: *v.* to amuse or interest others in a way that makes them happy; other forms: *entertainment, entertaining, entertained*

listen: *v.* to pay attention to what someone is saying; other forms: *listening, listened, listener*

react: *v.* to respond to; act with respect to; other forms: *reacted, reacting, reaction*

speak: *v.* to say words; talk; other forms: *speaking, spoke, spoken*

A. DIRECTIONS: *Read each sentence carefully. Each one describes an action that is the* **opposite** *of the action that a vocabulary word describes. Identify each vocabulary word. Write it on the line following the word* **Opposite***.*

| **Example:** He wanted to *open* the door.   Opposite:_____shut_____ |

1. I decided to *ignore* what he said.   **Opposite:** _____

2. She learned to *show no response* to any situation.   **Opposite:** _____

3. He will *bore* the audience with that performance.   **Opposite:** _____

4. She wanted to *conceal* her ideas.   **Opposite:** _____

5. He wanted us to *keep silent* about our *ideas*.   **Opposite:** _____

B. DIRECTIONS: *Complete each sentence by adding the correct vocabulary word.*

1. Lucy's parents knew she would _____ favorably to the news of her baby brother's arrival.

2. If you don't _____ to the students about the new reading programcarefully, you won't hear the beautiful, soft call of the Baltimore oriole.

3. The school principal planned to _____ to the students about the new reading program.

4. To _____ with each other effectively, you must speak clearly and listen carefully.

5. Using rich, vivid words and humorous situations will help you to _____ your readers.

Name _____ Date _____

Unit 4: Poetry
Big Question Vocabulary—2

The Big Question: What is the best way to communicate?

contribute: *v.* to share or give something of value to others; other form: *contribution*

express: *v.* to use words or actions to show thoughts and feelings; other forms: *expression, expressing, expressed*

learn: *v.* to gain knowledge and understanding of information; other forms: *learning, learned*

produce: *v.* to create something; other forms: *production, producing, produced, producer*

teach: *v.* to help someone learn by giving them information; other forms: *teacher, taught*

DIRECTIONS: *List three things as instructed. Then, use the vocabulary word in a sentences about one of the things. You may use one of its other forms, as shown above.*

1. List three ways that a person might use to *express* happiness.

   _____   _____   _____

   Sentence: _____

2. List three things that grandparents and other older people can *teach* young people.

   _____   _____   _____

   Sentence: _____

3. List three things that a person might *produce* with a pencil and paper.

   _____   _____   _____

   Sentence: _____

4. List three ways that a person might *contribute* to his or her neighborhood or community.

   _____   _____   _____

   Sentence: _____

5. List three things that you consider to be the most important things for a young child to *learn.*

   _____   _____   _____

   Sentence: _____

Name _____ Date _____

Unit 4: Poetry
Big Question Vocabulary—3

 The Big Question: What is the best way to communicate?

enrich: *v.* to improve the quality of something; other forms: *enrichment, enriching, enriched*

inform: *v.* to share facts or information with someone; other forms: *information, informed*

media: *n.* institutions or items that present news and other information, including newspapers, magazines, television programs, and Internet sources; other form: *medium*

technology: *n.* machines and equipment that are based on modern knowledge about science; other forms: *technological, technologies*

transmit: *v.* to send a message or signal, through such sources as radios, televisions, or the Internet; other forms: *transmission, transmitting, transmitted*

A. DIRECTIONS: *Give an example of each of the following.*

1. a *technology* that you use at school: _____

2. something that you *transmitted* to someone electronically: _____

3. a way to *enrich* a friendship: _____

4. a fact that you'd like to *inform* people about: _____

5. a specific form of the *media* that you respect as a news source: _____

B. DIRECTIONS: *Imagine that you are a scientist who just discovered life on another planet. On the lines below, write a summary of your findings, telling how you made your discovery, what messages the people sent to you and how they sent them, and why you feel your discovery might improve life on Earth. Use each of the vocabulary words.*

_____

_____

_____

_____

_____

_____

_____

_____

Name _____ Date _____

Unit 4: Poetry
Applying the Big Question

What is the best way to communicate?

DIRECTIONS: *Complete the chart below to apply what you have learned about communication. One row has been completed for you.*

Example	Type of communication	Purpose	Pros	Cons	What I learned
From Literature	Writing about meaningful family lessons as in the poem "Mother to Son."	To share an important life lesson.	Conveys a personal story to a broader audience.	The audience for poetry is smaller than current media forms, like television.	A poetic metaphor can contain a meaningful life lesson that applies to many people.
From Literature					
From Science					
From Social Studies					
From Real Life					

Unit 4: Poetry Skills Concept Map—1

What is the best way to communicate?

Words you can use
to discuss the
Big Question

Literary Analysis:
Poetry

Poetry — has → different forms — and → **figurative language**

(demonstrated in this selection)
Selection name:

(demonstrated in this selection)
Selection name:

Basic Elements of Poetry
- Figurative Language
- Sound Devices
- Stanzas

Forms of Poetry
- Narrative
- Haiku
- Free Verse
- Lyric
- Ballads

Reading Skills and Strategies:
Conclusions

You can draw **conclusions** — by → **asking questions** to help you identify details — and by → **connecting the details**

Informational Text:
Technical Directions

You can use a **checklist** — to → **follow technical directions**

(demonstrated in this selection)
Selection name:

Comparing Literary Works:
Narrative Poetry

Narrative Poetry — combines elements of → **poetry** / **fiction**

(demonstrated in these selections)
Selection names:
1.
2.

Student Log

Complete this chart to track your assignments.

Writing	Extend Your Learning	Writing Workshop	Other Assignments

Vocabulary Warm-up Word Lists

Study these words from the poetry of Pat Mora. Then, complete the activities that follow.

Word List A

blend [BLEND] *v.* to combine or mix so that the separate parts cannot be distinguished
  If you <u>blend</u> blue and yellow paint, you'll get green.

cactus [KAK tuhs] *n.* a desert plant with a green pulpy trunk covered with spines or prickles instead of leaves and often having showy flowers
  The saguaro is a type of <u>cactus</u> found in the southwest region of the United States.

glare [GLAIR] *n.* a strong, steady, dazzling light
  The sun's <u>glare</u> bounced off the pool.

spiked [SPYKT] *adj.* with long, slender, pointy parts or projections
  The yard was surrounded by a <u>spiked</u> iron fence.

sprinkles [SPRING kuhlz] *v.* scatters in small drops
  Before ironing her clothes, Hazel <u>sprinkles</u> water on them.

tease [TEEZ] *v.* to pick on or fool with (another) for fun, in order to annoy or provoke
  Jen would often <u>tease</u> her sister, saying, "You can't catch me!"

Word List B

melody [MEL uh dee] *n.* a meaningful succession of musical tones in a single part or voice; tune
  Claire sang the <u>melody</u> while Allan accompanied her on piano.

partners [PAHRT nuhrz] *n.* one of two or more people who perform an activity together, as dancing or playing a game
  Of all her dance <u>partners</u>, Alicia dances best with Enrique.

strummed [STRUMD] *v.* played (as a stringed instrument or a tune) in a careless or unskilled way
  Carlos <u>strummed</u> the guitar and hummed a tune.

swaying [SWAY ing] *v.* moving from side to side
  The reeds were <u>swaying</u> in the wind.

trio [TREE oh] *n.* a group of three
  We listened to a jazz <u>trio</u> as we enjoyed our dinner.

village [VIL ij] *adj.* having to do with a country settlement smaller than a town but larger than a hamlet
  The <u>village</u> market is open every day from ten to five.

The Poetry of Pat Mora
Vocabulary Warm-up Exercises

Exercise A *Fill in each blank in the paragraph below with an appropriate word from Word List A. Use each word only once.*

Dustin's favorite plant in his entire garden is an exotic purple orchid. He and his sisters take good care of it. They keep it in a shady spot to shield its delicate petals from the sun's [1] _____. They even [2] _____ several kinds of fertilizer to keep the soil healthy for the plant. Sometimes, Dustin [3] _____ water on the plant by hand, to make sure it gets enough. To further protect the plant, Dustin has considered putting a [4] _____ fence around it. His sisters [5] _____ him, saying he's much too fond of that orchid. They suggest that, for his birthday next year, Dustin get a plant that requires almost no work at all, a big, prickly desert [6] _____.

Exercise B *Answer the questions with complete sentences or explanations.*

1. If you <u>strummed</u> a guitar, would you be likely to win a contest as the best guitar player?

   _____

2. What <u>melody</u> would you probably sing before someone blows out the candles on a birthday cake?

   _____

3. If you were forming a musical <u>trio</u> with two friends, what instruments would you most like to have?

   _____

4. If an audience were <u>swaying</u> to the music, would they be dancing fast?

   _____

5. Would two squeamish students make good laboratory <u>partners</u> in science class? Why or why not?

   _____

6. Would you wear formal clothes to a <u>village</u> square dance?

   _____

The Poetry of Pat Mora
Reading Warm-up A

Read the following passage. Pay special attention to the underlined words. Then, read it again, and complete the activities. Use a separate sheet of paper for your written answers.

What do you think of when you imagine a desert? Most people think of deserts as hot, dry, and empty. It is true that some deserts get as hot as 130 degrees Fahrenheit during the day. Other deserts, such as the polar deserts in the Arctic regions, are very cold. The one thing all deserts have in common is that they are dry. Most scientists agree that a desert is a place where very little rain sprinkles down. Deserts get ten inches or less of rain every year.

Because living things in deserts must get along with very little water, they have developed various ways to save it. A spiked cactus, for example, stores water in its trunk and branches. The saguaro, a cactus found in the southwest United States, can store hundreds of liters of water.

The dryness of the air is one thing that makes desert living so difficult. Because there is so little water vapor in the air, clouds do not form. Because there are no clouds, the glare of the sun's rays beats down on the land. The ground then heats the air. Sometimes, this hot air rises in waves that you can see. These heat waves distort the images people see. These distorted images, called mirages, sometimes tease people into thinking water is near.

At night, the temperature can drop very quickly. This is because the desert lacks the humidity and clouds that protect other areas. It might get as cold as 40 degrees Fahrenheit at night.

Desert areas are increasing because of human activity. Overgrazing of animals has done some damage. In addition, cutting trees for firewood has caused many grasslands to become deserts. Areas that once supported human settlements are now covered with sand. They just blend into the desert landscape.

1. Circle the words that tell what sprinkles down. Use *sprinkles* in a sentence.

2. Underline the word that is described as spiked. Define *spiked*.

3. Circle the words that tell where the saguaro cactus is found. What is a *cactus*?

4. Underline the words that further explain glare. Use *glare* in a sentence.

5. Circle the words that tell what a mirage can tease people into thinking. Describe a situation in which one person tries to *tease* another.

6. Underline the words that tell what things now blend into the desert landscape. Use *blend* in a sentence.

The Poetry of Pat Mora
Reading Warm-up B

Read the following passage. Pay special attention to the underlined words. Then, read it again, and complete the activities. Use a separate sheet of paper for your written answers.

Have you ever <u>strummed</u> a guitar or just enjoyed listening as someone else did? If so, you might have wondered about the history of this remarkable instrument. Historians are not sure about the origin of the guitar, but they think it was invented in Malaga, Spain. It can be traced back as far as the fifteenth century. The first guitars were much smaller than the ones we use today. They had four pairs of strings.

It took many years before the guitar became popular. During the Renaissance (the 1300s through the 1500s), the lute was the favored instrument. Minstrels used it to accompany themselves as they sang one <u>melody</u> after another. Slowly but surely, however, the guitar became more and more popular.

By the Baroque period (about 1600 to 1750), an extra pair of strings was added to the guitar. Soon after, two important changes were made: The double strings were changed to single ones, and one extra string was added. This guitar looked more like our modern six-string guitar, although it was still smaller and narrower.

The Classical period (about 1750 to 1830) saw a surge of interest in the guitar. People played it at home, at <u>village</u> get-togethers, and in city performances. Dance <u>partners</u> enjoyed its sound as they moved around the floor.

Francisco Tarrega, who was the first to play with the fingernails, influenced many guitarists. One of them was Andrés Segovia, a famed musician who traveled and performed all over the world. Audiences, <u>swaying</u> to the Spanish rhythms in his music, would enjoy the flamenco music he played. Before Segovia's time, people thought the guitar was not suitable for a performance in a large concert hall. Segovia proved them wrong when he performed at Madrid's most important concert hall.

Today, guitar music is performed everywhere, whether played as a solo instrument, or as part of a <u>trio</u> or larger group.

1. Underline the word that tells what might be <u>strummed</u>. What does *strummed* mean?

2. Explain what minstrels did as they sang one <u>melody</u> after another. Name one *melody* that you enjoy humming.

3. Underline the word that is described by <u>village</u>. Describe what a *village get-together* might have looked like in pioneer days.

4. Circle the words that tell what dance <u>partners</u> did. What qualities do people need to become good dance *partners*?

5. Underline the words that tell what the audience was <u>swaying</u> to. What does *swaying* mean?

6. Circle the words that tell two other ways in which people perform using guitars, other than as part of a <u>trio</u>. What is a *trio*?

Pat Mora
Listening and Viewing

Segment 1: Meet Pat Mora
- Why does Pat Mora use both English and Spanish when she writes?
- What are some reasons that it is important to read literature by or about people of many different cultures?

_____

_____

_____

_____

Segment 2: Poetry
- Why does Pat Mora write the last line of "The Desert Is My Mother" in Spanish?
- What effect do the Spanish lines in this poem have on you as a reader?

_____

_____

_____

_____

Segment 3: The Writing Process
- How does Pat Mora prepare to begin writing?
- Which one of her writing strategies would you use, and why?

_____

_____

_____

_____

Segment 4: The Rewards of Writing
- How are poetry readings particularly rewarding to Pat Mora?
- Has a certain piece of literature had a strong impact on you as a reader? Explain.

_____

_____

_____

_____

Learning About Poetry

Poetry is the most musical, and often the most imaginative, of all literary forms. A common characteristic of poetry is **figurative language,** which is writing or speech that is not meant to be taken literally, or as though it is realistic.

FIGURATIVE LANGUAGE	• **metaphor:** describes one thing as if it were something else *(You are the sunshine of my life.)*
	• **simile:** uses *like* or *as* to compare two unlike things *(Your smile is as bright as the sun.)*
	• **personification:** gives human qualities to a nonhuman thing *(The sun smiled on our picnic.)*
	• **symbol:** something that represents something else *(The flag is a symbol of our country; a dove is a symbol of peace.)*

A. DIRECTIONS: *On the lines, write the letter of the type of figurative language used in each line of poetry.*

___ 1. bubbly and bright like a mountain stream   **A.** simile

___ 2. a bright lantern that welcomed me home   **B.** metaphor

___ 3. your eyes are moonlight to my earth   **C.** symbol

___ 4. the apple pie that means "home"   **D.** personification

B. DIRECTIONS: *Follow each direction by writing an original phrase or sentence.*

1. Use a metaphor to write about the moon.

_____

2. Use a simile to write about a dog.

_____

3. Use personification to write about a clock.

_____

4. Write a sentence containing a symbol.

_____

The Poetry of Pat Mora
Model Selection: Poetry

In addition to figurative language, Pat Mora's three poems contain examples of **sound devices,** or writing or speech that adds a musical quality.

SOUND DEVICES	• **alliteration:** repetition of consonant sounds at the beginning of words (*a busy bee*)
	• **repetition:** use of a sound, word, or group of words more than once (*the beat of the drum and the beat of my heart*)
	• **onomatopoeia:** use of words that imitate sounds (*quack, bang*)
	• **rhyme:** repetition of sounds at the ends of words (*sit, lit, hit*)
	• **meter:** arrangement of stressed and unstressed syllables (*The day began at eight o'clock.*)

A. DIRECTIONS: *Answer these questions about the characteristics in Pat Mora's poems.*

1. In the first stanza of "Maestro," what verb is an example of onomatopoeia?

   _____

2. What example of repetition appears in the first five lines of "Bailando"?

   _____

3. What type of sound device is represented by the word *whispers*?

   _____

4. What type of sound device is represented by the phrase *the snow's silence*?

   _____

B. DIRECTIONS: *In these poems, Pat Mora speaks of family members. On the lines below, write your own short poem about a family member or friend. Include at least two examples of figurative language and sound devices.*

   _____

   _____

   _____

   _____

   _____

   _____

Name _____   Date _____

The Poetry of *Pat Mora*
Open-Book Test

Short Answer *Write your responses to the questions in this section on the lines provided.*

1. A poet writes about "the key that unlocks the meaning of the universe." Is the poet talking about a real key? Use your understanding of figurative language to explain your response.

_____

_____

2. You read this line in a poem: "the sun, that great big yellow balloon." Which poetic device is being used in the poem? Explain your answer.

_____

_____

_____

3. You have written a poem in which you used the words *buzz, clang,* and *whirr.* What do these words have in common, and why do poets use this poetic device?

_____

_____

_____

4. Reread line 3 from "Maestro." What is happening during the moment at which line 3 occurs? Support your explanation with other lines from the poem.

_____

_____

_____

5. Reread lines 4, 15, 17, and 19 from "The Maestro." Cite the poetic device Mora uses in these lines, and explain why she might be using this device. Consider what connection the lines might have to a musician.

_____

_____

_____

6. How does the first stanza of "Maestro" help you understand the meaning of the word *maestro?*

_____

_____

_____

7. In "The Desert Is My Mother," certain words are repeated. Choose one example of repetition, and explain why it is important to the meaning of the poem.

_____

_____

8. Use the graphic organizer below to list three examples of how the desert behaves like a mother in "The Desert Is My Mother." On the lines, explain why you think the poet chose to compare the desert to a mother instead of to another person.

Line number	How the Desert Behaves Like a Mother

_____

_____

9. In "Bailando," the poet is speaking directly to someone. To whom is she speaking, and why? Use information from the poem to support your response.

_____

_____

_____

10. In the final line of "Bailando," the poet's aunt is laughing. Why? Explain your answer, using support from the poem.

_____

_____

_____

Essay

Write an extended response to the question of your choice or to the question or questions your teacher assigns you.

11. In "The Desert Is My Mother," the poet uses personification to have the desert take on the characteristics of a mother. Do you think the poet's use of personification is effective? Support your opinion in a brief essay. Provide examples of the poet's use of personification.

12. In many forms of communication, repetition can be tiresome. However, repeating words, ideas, or phrases can also have a forceful impact. Choose "Maestro," "The Desert Is My Mother," or "Bailando." In an essay, explain whether you think the poet has succeeded in using repetition to make the poem more powerful. Include examples of repetition from the poem.

13. Suppose you were asked to continue writing the poem "Bailando." What poetic device or devices would you use to extend the description of the aunt and her relationship with the speaker? In a brief essay, describe what your approach would be in creating additional stanzas. Support your ideas with details from the poem.

14. **Thinking About the Big Question: What is the best way to communicate?** In her poems "Maestro" and "Bailando," Pat Mora shows two ways to communicate. The maestro uses music. The aunt uses dancing. Do you think either of these is the "best" way to communicate? Explain your answer in a brief essay. Use support from the poems to strengthen your response.

Oral Response

15. Go back to question 4, 5, 7, or 10 or to the question your teacher assigns you. Take a few minutes to expand your answer and prepare an oral response. Find additional details in Mora's poems that support your points. If necessary, make notes to guide your oral response.

Name _____ Date _____

The Poetry of Pat Mora
Selection Test A

Learning About Poetry *Identify the letter of the choice that best answers the question.*

____ 1. Which of the following is an example of <u>rhyme</u>?
   A. A big white cat is round and fat.
   B. A big brown bear lives in a den.
   C. "Ruff, ruff," the dog replied.
   D. May your pride soar like the eagle.

____ 2. Which of the following is a <u>simile</u> that uses "like" or "as" to make a comparison?
   A. My mother is a great cook.
   B. My aunt sings like a sparrow.
   C. My bedroom is a disaster.
   D. My alarm clock likes to ring.

____ 3. <u>Onomatopoeia</u> is the use of words that imitate sounds. Which of the following is an example?
   A. The alarm clock woke me up.
   B. The alarm clock was set for 7 o'clock.
   C. The alarm clock sits right by my bed.
   D. The alarm clock let out a horrible buzz.

____ 4. People sometimes wear flag pins. Which statement *best* describes this type of action?
   A. It is a metaphor of support for their nation.
   B. It is a symbol of support for their nation.
   C. It is a simile of support for their nation.
   D. It is a form of personification.

____ 5. <u>Alliteration</u> is the repetition of consonant sounds at the beginning of words. Which of the following is an example?
   A. a cat and a rat
   B. a bright yellow sun
   C. back on track
   D. a bright blue bow

____ 6. Which of the following is the best definition for <u>meter</u>?
   A. the repetition of sounds at the ends of words
   B. the arrangement of stressed and unstressed syllables
   C. the use of a sound or word more than once
   D. something that represents something else

Critical Reading

___ **7.** Read the following lines from the opening of "Maestro":

Rows of hands clap
again and again

What is the maestro doing during these lines?
A. He is playing guitar music with his parents.
B. He is dancing with his aunt while others watch.
C. He is bowing on a stage while the audience claps.
D. He is playing his violin for a large audience.

___ **8.** In "Maestro," what does the maestro remember when he hears the applause?
A. his mother's voice
B. the desert wind
C. to thank the conductor
D. a dance he likes

___ **9.** "Maestro" ends with the metaphor, "the last pure note sweet on the tongue." With what is a note of music being compared?
A. a beautiful violin
B. a thoughtful letter
C. a nice memory
D. a sweet taste

___ **10.** Whom does the poet address in "Bailando" when she says, "I will remember you dancing . . ."?
A. the speaker's aunt
B. the speaker's father
C. the speaker's daughter
D. the speaker's son

___ **11.** The phrase *round and round* appears twice in "Bailando." What characteristic of poetry is this?
A. meter
B. simile
C. repetition
D. onomatopoeia

_____ **12.** How are "Maestro" and "Bailando" alike?

    A. In each poem, the speaker talks about memories.

    B. Each poem is about a great musician.

    C. Each poem mentions a birthday celebration.

    D. In each poem, the speaker talks about dancing.

_____ **13.** What characteristic of poetry occurs in the title "The Desert Is My Mother"?

    A. rhyme

    B. simile

    C. metaphor

    D. symbol

_____ **14.** In "The Desert Is My Mother," the speaker says that the desert caresses, sings, and teaches. What characteristic of poetry does this represent?

    A. alliteration

    B. personification

    C. simile

    D. meter

_____ **15.** What do "Maestro," "Bailando," and "The Desert Is My Mother" all contain?

    A. Spanish words

    B. a Mexican village

    C. a sad theme

    D. a respect for nature

Essay

16. What feelings does the speaker in "The Desert Is My Mother" have for the desert? How do these feelings lead her to compare the desert with a mother? Support your answers with details from the poem.

17. Think about "Maestro," "Bailando," and "The Desert Is My Mother." Which poem did you like best? Explain why, using examples for the poem you prefer.

18. Thinking About the Big Question: What is the best way to communicate? In her poems "Maestro" and "Bailando," Pat Mora shows two ways to communicate. The maestro uses music. The aunt uses dancing. In an essay, explain which of these activities is a better way to communicate. Support your answer with specific examples from the poems.

The Poetry of Pat Mora
Selection Test B

Learning About Poetry *Identify the letter of the choice that best completes the statement or answers the question.*

_____ 1. What type of poetic sound device contains repetition of a consonant sound at the beginning of words, such as <u>brave brothers</u>?
A. onomatopoeia
B. alliteration
C. rhyme
D. meter

_____ 2. Which is the best definition of <u>rhyme</u>?
A. the arrangement of stressed and unstressed syllables
B. the use of words that imitate sounds
C. the repetition of sounds at the ends of words
D. the repetition of sounds at the beginnings of words

_____ 3. Which of the following is an example of a <u>metaphor</u>?
A. The moss was a blanket for the forest floor.
B. He was as steady as a rock of granite.
C. The rain washed away my sadness.
D. The clang of the gong awakened us.

_____ 4. Which term names an object that represents something else, such as peace or courage?
A. onomatopoeia
B. simile
C. personification
D. symbol

_____ 5. Which of the following is an example of <u>personification</u>?
A. The crows were as black as coal.
B. My dad is a fountain of knowledge.
C. The clouds and winds told us to go inside.
D. The glass smashed when it hit the floor.

_____ 6. Which of the following is an example of <u>onomatopoeia</u>?
A. silver stars in a silent sky
B. the ticking of the tall clock
C. a night in June with a silver moon
D. I saw a man, a quiet man

Critical Reading

_____ 7. The first two lines of "Maestro" contain the sentence "He hears her when he bows." What characteristic of poetry do these lines contain?
A. rhyme
B. personification
C. onomatopoeia
D. alliteration

Name _____ Date _____

____ 8. What is the meaning of the word *maestro,* as it is used in "Maestro"?
   A. grandfather
   B. master of music
   C. guitar player
   D. audience member

____ 9. In "Maestro," what memory does the applause bring to the maestro?
   A. He remembers how helpful his violin teacher was.
   B. He remembers good advice from his grandmother.
   C. He remembers leaving his home in Mexico.
   D. He remembers playing music with his parents.

____ 10. Which is the best description of the family in "Maestro"?
   A. hard-working and courageous
   B. affectionate and supportive
   C. proud and defiant
   D. determined and fortunate

____ 11. To whom does the speaker in "Bailando" speak?
   A. her mother
   B. her father
   C. her grandmother
   D. her aunt

____ 12. The phrase *years later* appears twice in "Bailando," in lines 10 and 12. What characteristic of poetry is this?
   A. alliteration
   B. repetition
   C. metaphor
   D. simile

____ 13. What does the speaker in "Bailando" mean when she says that the woman is "white-haired but still young"?
   A. The woman is old but likes to dance with her friends.
   B. The woman is old but still has the spirit of a young person.
   C. The woman's white hair makes her appear younger than she is.
   D. The woman's white hair has a new, younger look.

____ 14. In "Bailando," the speaker says that the woman is "tottering now" when she walks. What does this expression mean?
   A. She is unsteady on her feet due to old age.
   B. She is light on her feet, like a great dancer.
   C. She makes a clicking noise when she walks.
   D. She walks everywhere very quickly.

____ 15. In "The Desert Is My Mother," the speaker says that the desert "shouts thunder." What poetic characteristic is this an example of?
   A. alliteration
   B. personification
   C. repetition
   D. simile

____ 16. The speaker says that the desert wind is a song. What is this comparison an example of?
   A. simile
   B. personification
   C. metaphor
   D. onomatopoeia

____ 17. In "The Desert Is My Mother," which statement best expresses the poet's feelings about the desert?
   A. She fears the desert because of thunder and unbearable heat.
   B. She respects the desert for its changes over the seasons.
   C. She respects the desert for its beauty and resources.
   D. She is puzzled by the desert's ability to rain on a sunny day.

____ 18. Which statement is true about all three of Pat Mora's poems?
   A. Each speaks about her mother.
   B. Each contains Spanish words.
   C. Each contains personification.
   D. Each one mentions a desert setting.

____ 19. Which statement is true about "Maestro" and "Bailando"?
   A. Each mentions a beloved aunt.
   B. Each involves dancing and singing.
   C. Each involves a birthday celebration.
   D. Each involves childhood memories.

Essay

20. In "The Desert Is My Mother," the speaker mentions a rainstorm, thunder, and the wind. Each of these natural elements can make specific sounds. Describe some of the sounds of each one, using onomatopoeia.

21. Select "Maestro," "Bailando," or "The Desert Is My Mother." What is the main idea of the poem you have selected? Is it about a person, a place, or an experience? Use examples from the poem to help you answer the questions.

22. **Thinking About the Big Question: What is the best way to communicate?** In her poems "Maestro" and "Bailando," Pat Mora shows two ways to communicate. The maestro uses music. The aunt uses dancing. Do you think either of these is the "best" way to communicate? Explain your answer in a brief essay. Use support from the poems to strengthen your response.

Vocabulary Warm-up Word Lists

Study these words from the poetry of Naomi Shihab Nye, William Jay Smith, and Buson. Then, complete the activities that follow.

Word List A

darts [DAHRTZ] *v.* moves suddenly and quickly
   The hummingbird quickly <u>darts</u> from flower to flower.

deep [DEEP] *adj.* located far back or down in something
   We went camping <u>deep</u> in the backwoods of Colorado.

flick [FLIK] *n.* a quick, snapping motion
   With a <u>flick</u> of her finger, Martha chased away the fly.

float [FLOHT] *v.* to stay on the surface of the water or another liquid
   Mark watched the model sailboat <u>float</u> on the pond.

plunges [PLUNJ ez] *v.* throws oneself or rushes into something
   The newspaper reporter <u>plunges</u> into her weekly assignment.

watery [WAW tuhr ee] *adj.* containing or full of water
   When the ship sank, the pirates went to their <u>watery</u> grave.

Word List B

bicycles [BY si kuhlz] *n.* vehicles with two wheels on a metal frame, handlebars, and pedals
   We rode our <u>bicycles</u> along the flat streets near the beach.

champion [CHAM pee uhn] *n.* a winner
   The Olympic <u>champion</u> worked out every day.

departs [dee PAHRTZ] *v.* leaves or sets out for somewhere
   Anna <u>departs</u> on a jet for Paris tomorrow.

desperately [DES puhr it lee] *adv.* with intense need
   The survivors <u>desperately</u> paddled the lifeboats away from the sinking ship.

panting [PANT ing] *v.* breathing heavily and quickly due to shortness of breath
   After the dog ran across the field, it was <u>panting</u>.

victory [VIK tuhr ee] *n.* a win or triumph
   The debate team celebrated its <u>victory</u>.

Name _____ Date _____

Poetry Collection: Naomi Shihab Nye, William Jay Smith, and Buson
Vocabulary Warm-up Exercises

Exercise A *Fill in each blank in the paragraph below with an appropriate word from Word List A. Use each word only once.*

Did you ever watch people at the beach? This sandy and [1] _____

playground is a good place for people of all ages to have fun. One person

[2] _____ headlong into the water and begins to

[3] _____ on her back. A child quickly [4] _____ back

and forth along the water's edge, as the waves break on the shore. Then, with a

[5] _____ of his wrist, he uses a shovel to dig in the wet sand. Some

people stretch out their beach blankets far from others, while some "set up camp"

[6] _____ in the heart of the crowd. It can be fun to watch people at

the beach!

Exercise B *Write a complete sentence to answer each question. For each item, use a word from Word List B to replace each underlined word or group of words without changing its meaning.*

1. What kinds of feelings do you think a <u>winner</u> has after achieving a big <u>triumph</u>?
   _____

2. Why would you and a friend likely be <u>out of breath</u> after pedaling your <u>two-wheelers</u> up a steep hill?
   _____

3. If only one ferry boat <u>leaves</u> the island each day, why is it important to get to the dock on time when you want to go home?
   _____

4. At which activity have you ever <u>intensely</u> tried to succeed?
   _____

Name _____ Date _____

Read the following passage. Pay special attention to the underlined words. Then, read it again, and complete the activities. Use a separate sheet of paper for your written answers.

Roger was studying to be a marine biologist. He remembered the day he had decided to become one. He had been in the seventh grade, and his class trip had been to a nearby city. There the class explored the state's biggest aquarium.

The first tanks were made to look like the South Pole, where penguins live. Many different kinds of penguins stood about on the rocks around the tank. The aquarium guide had told them, "Watch this penguin closely. He <u>plunges</u> into the water from the highest rock when it's feeding time." Roger and his classmates laughed as they saw the penguin do just that. Then he would dive <u>deep</u> into the water to get the fish the guide had tossed there.

Roger was spellbound as he looked at one <u>watery</u> exhibit after another. There were fish of every color and size. They came from all parts of the world. He learned how each type of fish was able to stay alive in its special surroundings. Roger could remember seeing sharks, stingrays that seem to be flying rather than swimming, and a school of fish that <u>darts</u> quickly from place to place to avoid enemies.

In one large tank, Roger watched a baby beluga whale. It liked to come to the edge of the tank and look back at the children. This whitish whale would swim in a twisting fashion and then <u>float</u> on its back.

After exploring the tanks, Roger and his friends entered a theater. There they watched dolphins perform. A worker spoke about these sea mammals. The playful animals caught rings on their noses with a <u>flick</u> of their necks and jumped high in the air through hoops.

Roger would always remember that trip to the aquarium as the day he knew he would like to learn more about the interesting animals that live in the ocean.

1. Underline the words that tell where the penguin <u>plunges</u>. Define *plunges*.

2. Circle the words that tell why the penguin would dive <u>deep</u> into the water. Use *deep* in a sentence.

3. Circle the words that tell what was <u>watery</u> at the aquarium. Define *watery*.

4. Circle the words that tell what <u>darts</u> from place to place. Use *darts* in a sentence.

5. Underline the words that tell which animal Roger saw <u>float</u> on its back. What other things can *float*?

6. Circle the words that tell what the dolphins did with a <u>flick</u> of their necks. What does *flick* mean?

Name _____ Date _____

Poetry Collection: Naomi Shihab Nye, William Jay Smith, and Buson
Reading Warm-up B

Read the following passage. Pay special attention to the underlined words. Then, read it again, and complete the activities. Use a separate sheet of paper for your written answers.

Each July, more than 150 contestants race their bicycles in a competition known as the Tour de France. The Tour is the most popular bike race in the world. It lasts between 25 to 30 days and covers about 2,000 miles.

The course departs from a point in France. It goes over many roads in France and also passes through other European countries, such as Switzerland, Germany, Belgium, and Spain. Each year the course changes, but it always finishes along a famous street in Paris called the Champs-Elysees.

Each racer belongs to a team of nine. The team leader is the cyclist with the best all-around times. The race is divided into stages on most days. Each stage tests a different bicycling skill. For example, sprinting or racing uphill are two such skills. The racers desperately wish to achieve the best time in each event every day. That is because the best combined time is how the leader of the race is determined. This racer gets to wear a yellow shirt. People watching the race can easily spot the biker with the best times by this brightly colored shirt.

The other team members give support to the leader. As the racer drives into the wind, the team members may try to shelter the cyclist. The team offers encouragement to a tired racer who is panting and short of breath while racing up a steep hill.

The Tour de France is very popular among its fans. Some watch it in person, and others see it on television. When the champion wins the race, he or she is given the yellow shirt as a trophy. The racers are professionals, which means they race for a cash prize. The leader shares the prize with the other members of his or her team. After the race, the winner's victory is honored at a special ceremony, which takes place in Paris.

1. Underline the words that tell the name of the race in which the riders of bicycles compete. Use *bicycles* in a sentence.

2. Underline the words that tell from where the course departs. Define *departs*.

3. Circle the words that tell what the racers desperately wish to do. What does *desperately* mean?

4. Underline the words that give a clue about what panting means. When might someone be *panting*?

5. Circle the words that tell what the champion does in order to be given the yellow shirt. What is a *champion*?

6. Circle the words that tell how the victory is honored. Use *victory* in a sentence.

Poetry Collection: Naomi Shihab Nye, William Jay Smith, Buson

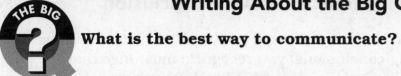

Writing About the Big Question

What is the best way to communicate?

Big Question Vocabulary

communicate	contribute	enrich	entertain	express
inform	learn	listen	media	produce
react	speak	teach	technology	transmit

A. *Use one or more words from the list above to complete each sentence.*

1. Helping others to _____ new skills is a good way to communicate.

2. One way to communicate what you know is to _____ a skill to someone else.

3. When you _____ your knowledge to others, they find out about you as well as your subject.

4. You can use _____ such as computers to communicate your knowledge.

B. *Respond to each item with a complete sentence.*

1. Write down two things you have taught another person. Use at least two of the Big Question vocabulary words.

   _____

   _____

2. Write two sentences explaining how you communicated the knowledge you taught.

   _____

   _____

   _____

C. *In "Poetry Collection 1," three poets use different forms to share their thoughts or observations. Complete these sentences. Then, write a short paragraph connecting the sentences to the Big Question.*

Through poetry, writers **communicate** _____

   _____

I most enjoy reading poems that **express** _____

   _____

Poetry Collection: Naomi Shihab Nye, William Jay Smith, Buson
Reading: Ask Questions to Draw a Conclusion

Drawing conclusions means arriving at an overall judgment or idea by pulling together several details. By drawing conclusions, you recognize meanings that are not directly stated. **Asking questions** can help you identify details and make connections that lead to a conclusion. You might ask yourself questions such as these:

- What details does the writer include and emphasize?
- How are the details related?
- What do the details mean all together?

Consider, for example, this haiku by Buson:

> After the moon sets,
>
> slow through the forest, shadows
>
> drift and disappear

What do the details suggest? The moon has set, so it must be morning. Why, though, do "shadows / drift and disappear"? Is it because it has grown darker or because it has grown lighter, because the sun is rising? The reader might conclude that Buson's haiku vividly evokes the darkness that precedes dawn.

DIRECTIONS: *Complete the following chart. First, ask a question about the poem. Then, record the details that prompted the question. Finally, write a conclusion that you can draw based on the question and the related details.*

Poem	Question	Details Relating to Question	Conclusion
"The Rider"			
"Seal"			
"O foolish ducklings"			
"Deep in a windless wood"			

Poetry Collection: Naomi Shihab Nye, William Jay Smith, Buson
Literary Analysis: Forms of Poetry

There are many different **forms of poetry.** A poet will follow different rules depending on the structure of a poem. These are the three forms represented by the poems in this collection:

- A **lyric poem** expresses the poet's thoughts and feelings about a single image or idea in vivid, musical language.
- In a **concrete poem,** the poet arranges the letters and lines to create a visual image that suggests the poem's subject.
- **Haiku** is a traditional form of Japanese poetry that is often about nature. In a traditional haiku, the first line always has five syllables, the second line always has seven syllables, and the third line always has five syllables.

DIRECTIONS: *Write your responses to the following questions.*

1. If you were to rewrite "The Rider" as a concrete poem, what shape would you use to express the main idea of the poem? Why?

   _____

   _____

2. If you were to rewrite "Seal" as a haiku, what seven-syllable line might you write that contained the phrase "Quicksilver-quick"?

   _____

3. If you were to rewrite one of Buson's haiku as a lyric poem, on what single image would you focus? Why?

   _____

   _____

4. If you were to rewrite "The Rider" as a haiku, what would one of your lines be?

   _____

5. If you were to rewrite "Seal" as a lyric poem, how would you change it? Why?

   _____

   _____

Poetry Collection: Naomi Shihab Nye, William Jay Smith, Buson
Vocabulary Builder

Word List

luminous   minnow   swerve   translates   utter   weasel

A. DIRECTIONS: *Provide an explanation for your answer to each question.*

1. Would you be able to see *luminous* stars in a clear night sky?

   _____

   _____

2. If someone did not *utter* a word, would she be likely to win a debate?

   _____

   _____

3. Would you be likely to see a *weasel* in the Large Mammals section of a zoo?

   _____

   _____

4. Would a driver likely go into a *swerve* to avoid hitting something in the road?

   _____

   _____

5. Would you find a *minnow* in a forest?

   _____

   _____

6. If someone *translates* a poem into English, could you read it?

   _____

   _____

B. WORD STUDY: *The Latin root -lum- means "light." Write a sentence that answers each question, using the italicized word.*

1. If a soccer field is *illuminated*, what time of day is the game probably being played?

   _____

2. What part of the ocean is a *bioluminescent* fish likely to live in?

   _____

3. If someone is a *luminary* in the field of medicine, what do people probably think of the person?

   _____

Poetry Collection: Naomi Shihab Nye, William Jay Smith, Buson

Enrichment: Seals

Seals are members of a group called pinnipeds. Some seals have no visible ear flaps; they are true seals. True seals include the harbor seal, harp seal, and monk seal. Other seals have ears that can be seen. They include the sea lion and fur seal.

DIRECTIONS: *Do some research on one species of seal. Complete the following chart with information that you find in an encyclopedia, in another reference book, or on the Internet.*

Type of seal: _____

Physical Characteristics and Life Span	Social Behavior and Breeding Habits	Habitat and Migration Patterns	Diet	Natural Enemies

Poetry Collection: Naomi Shihab Nye, William Jay Smith, and Buson
Open-Book Test

Short Answer *Write your responses to the questions in this section on the lines provided.*

1. What kind of poem is "The Rider"? Use examples from the poem to explain your answer.

   _____

   _____

2. In "The Rider," Nye describes pink azalea petals as "luminous." Use the definition of *luminous* to explain why that description is appropriate for the poem.

   _____

   _____

   _____

3. In the last stanza of "The Rider," the poet personifies loneliness. What human qualities does she give to the emotion? Use details from the poem to explain your answer.

   _____

   _____

   _____

4. How do you know that "Seal" is a concrete poem? Explain your answer, and tell whether the form of the poem makes sense.

   _____

   _____

   _____

5. What conclusion can you draw about the personality of the seal in "Seal"? Use the graphic organizer below to list details from the poem that convey the seal's character. Then, explain what you conclude about the seal's personality.

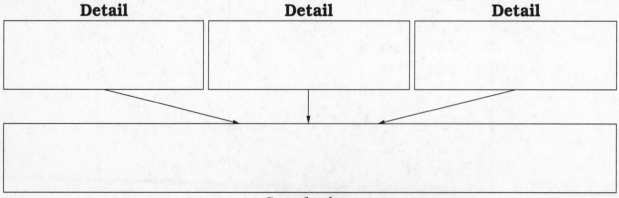

Detail	**Detail**	**Detail**

Conclusion

6. In "Seal," why is the use of the word *swerve* appropriate? Use the definition of *swerve* in your answer.

_____

_____

_____

7. In the first haiku by Buson, what does the poet seem to expect will happen? Use details from the poem to support your answer.

_____

_____

_____

8. The three poems by Buson are haiku. Use specific features of the poems to explain how you know this.

_____

_____

_____

_____

9. Reread the second poem by Buson. What conclusion does the poet draw, and what details does he use to draw it? Use details from the poem to explain your answer.

_____

_____

_____

10. Of the three different haiku by Buson, which conveys the strongest feelings to the reader? Justify your answer with support from each of the three poems.

_____

_____

_____

_____

Essay

Write an extended response to the question of your choice or to the question or questions your teacher assigns you.

11. As a concrete poem, "Seal" suggests much movement and activity on the part of the seal. In a brief essay, describe the journey of the seal as he moves from one activity to another. Explore how he might feel at certain points in his journey.

12. "Seal" by William Jay Smith and the haiku by Buson are about parts of the natural world. In a brief essay, explain which treatment of nature you like more, and why. Use specific examples from the poems to support your ideas.

13. As a lyric poem, "The Rider" explores the speaker's thoughts and feelings about one particular subject. In an essay, discuss the subject and the poet's feelings about it. Use specific examples from the poem.

14. **Thinking About the Big Question: What is the best way to communicate?**
Think about the three forms of poetry you read: the lyric poem "The Rider," the concrete poem "Seal," and the haiku by Buson. Which form do you find to be the best way to communicate through poetry? Write a brief essay that explains your answer. Use examples from the poems.

Oral Response

15. Go back to question 3, 5, or 10 or to the question your teacher assigns you. Take a few minutes to expand your answer and prepare an oral response. Find additional details in the poem or poems that support your points. If necessary, make notes to guide your oral response.

Poetry Collection: Naomi Shihab Nye, William Jay Smith, Buson
Selection Test A

Critical Reading *Identify the letter of the choice that best answers the question.*

____ 1. Why does the roller skater in "The Rider" want to move fast?
   A. to beat the bicycle rider
   B. to escape his loneliness
   C. to win the race
   D. to prove a point

____ 2. Which adjective best describes the speaker in "The Rider"?
   A. afraid
   B. lonely
   C. angry
   D. happy

____ 3. What aspect of "The Rider" tells you that it is a lyric poem?
   A. It contains some long lines and some short lines.
   B. It expresses the poet's thoughts on a single idea.
   C. It consists of only four verses.
   D. It could easily be set to music.

____ 4. According to "Seal," what noise does a seal make?
   A. a hiss
   B. a purr
   C. a click
   D. a bark

____ 5. What is the shape of the poem "Seal"?
   A. It forms a curve.
   B. It forms an L.
   C. It forms a T.
   D. It forms a fish.

____ 6. Which words best describe the seal in "Seal"?
   A. fierce and mean
   B. fearful and shy
   C. slow and lazy
   D. quick and soft

_____ 7. What is the seal doing in "Seal"?
   A. diving for food
   B. escaping from sharks
   C. fighting for its life
   D. performing for an audience

_____ 8. What do the details in "Seal" tell you about seals?
   A. They are quick and friendly.
   B. They have many enemies.
   C. They live only in cold water.
   D. They avoid human company.

_____ 9. What conclusion can you draw about the events surrounding the first haiku by Buson?
   A. The speaker is going to protect the weasel.
   B. The ducklings are going to fly away.
   C. The speaker is going to rescue the ducklings.
   D. The weasel is going to kill the ducklings.

_____ 10. What feeling is created by the second of the three haiku by Buson?
   A. hopelessness
   B. suspense
   C. joy
   D. calmness

_____ 11. Which of your senses helps you imagine the scene described in the third haiku by Buson?
   A. hearing
   B. smell
   C. sight
   D. touch

Vocabulary and Grammar

_____ 12. In which sentence is the word *utter* used correctly?
   A. The seals *utter* past crabs and seaweed.
   B. The seals will not *utter* minnow feed.
   C. The playful seals *utter* cries of delight.
   D. The sting ray and the shark *utter* the seal.

___ 13. Which of the following events, characters, or objects can be said to make a *swerve*?

    A. a snowstorm and a cloudburst

    B. a roller skater and a seal

    C. a rainstorm and a bicyclist

    D. a seal and a dill pickle

___ 14. Which of these sentences contains an infinitive?

    A. The rider wants to escape his loneliness.

    B. The rider speaks to the skateboarder.

    C. The rider pedals faster than his loneliness.

    D. The rider is afraid of his loneliness.

___ 15. Which of these sentences contains an infinitive phrase?

    A. The seal dives and comes back to the surface.

    B. The speaker enjoys watching the seal dive and swim.

    C. The seal is an animal to watch for its grace and swiftness.

    D. The speaker admires the seal's quick turns and leaps.

Essay

16. In your opinion, which poet does the better job of communicating his feelings about nature or his observations of the natural world: William Jay Smith in "Seal" or Buson in his haiku? Discuss your choice in a brief essay. Be sure to tell why one poet is more successful than the other: What does he do that the other poet does not? Support your opinion with references to at least one passage from each poet's work.

17. The author of "The Rider" expresses her thoughts and feelings about a single idea. In an essay, describe the idea on which the poet focuses. Then, describe the images she uses to express that idea.

18. **Thinking About the Big Question: What is the best way to communicate?** Think about the three forms of poetry you read: the lyric poem "The Rider," the concrete poem "Seal," and the haiku by Buson. In an essay, explain which you think is the best way to communicate through poetry. Support your answer with examples from the poems.

Poetry Collection: Naomi Shihab Nye, William Jay Smith, Buson
Selection Test B

Critical Reading *Identify the letter of the choice that best completes the statement or answers the question.*

____ 1. What is the single idea that Naomi Shihab Nye is expressing in "The Rider"?
   A. It is easier to escape loneliness by rollerskating than by riding a bicycle.
   B. Racing to escape from loneliness is a good reason to try to win a race.
   C. Winning a race can help you appreciate the beauty of nature.
   D. Riding a bicycle is a more satisfying activity than rollerskating.

____ 2. Which of your senses can best help you picture this passage from "The Rider"?
   while you float free into a cloud of sudden azaleas /
   luminous pink petals that have / never felt loneliness
   A. sight
   B. taste
   C. hearing
   D. smell

____ 3. Why might Nye have included these lines in "The Rider"?
   What I wonder tonight / pedaling hard down King William Street / is if it translates to bicycles.
   A. to show that she is lonely, too
   B. to show how fast she can ride
   C. to create a sense of joyous speed
   D. to compare bicycles to roller skates

____ 4. The speaker in "The Rider" imagines floating "free into a cloud of sudden azaleas."
   What is she referring to?
   A. falling into a flowerbed
   B. a dream she once had
   C. being free of loneliness
   D. the feeling of riding in a race

____ 5. Which characteristics make "The Rider" a lyric poem?
   A. It uses vivid language and expresses feelings.
   B. It tells a story about a historical event.
   C. It rhymes and has a regular rhythm.
   D. It uses repetition and describes a natural event.

____ 6. A concrete poem, such as "Seal,"
   A. has few or no figures of speech.
   B. is divided into verses.
   C. has a shape that suggests its subject.
   D. expresses the poet's ideas on a subject.

____ 7. In "Seal," the seal ends its swim with
   A. a huge splash.
   B. a mouthful of fish.
   C. a long, slow dive.
   D. an enormous splash.

____ 8. In "Seal," to which sense does the phrase "softer than spray" appeal?
   A. taste
   B. hearing
   C. touch
   D. sight

____ 9. The seal in "Seal" may best be described as
   A. aloof.
   B. angry.
   C. fierce.
   D. friendly.

____ 10. Which statement about the second of Buson's three haiku is accurate?
   A. The woods are described as if they were something else—the universe.
   B. It uses words that imitate the sounds the poet wants the reader to hear.
   C. It appeals to all five senses—sight, touch, taste, smell, and hearing.
   D. The leaf is given human characteristics—it is afraid to move.

____ 11. In the third haiku, what feeling is Buson most likely trying to convey?
   A. mystery
   B. security
   C. warmth
   D. harshness

____ 12. Which characteristics indicate that Buson's poems are haiku?
   A. The letters and lines are arranged to create a visual image of the subject of each poem.
   B. The poet's thoughts about a single image or idea are expressed in vivid language.
   C. The poems are mysterious and leave a great deal to the reader's imagination.
   D. The first line has five syllables, the second has seven, and the third has five.

____ 13. Like most haiku, all three of Buson's haiku concern
   A. the passage of time.
   B. loneliness.
   C. nature.
   D. human behavior.

Vocabulary and Grammar

____ 14. Like the pink petals of the azalea blossoms in "The Rider," something that is *luminous*
   A. can be seen only at night.
   B. cannot be seen at night.
   C. gives off light.
   D. is beautiful.

____ 15. In "Seal," the *swerve* with which the seal swims is best described as
A. a leap.
B. a curve.
C. a dive.
D. a circle.

____ 16. In which sentence is the word *utter* used logically *and* in the same way it is used in "Seal"?
A. In the deepest part of the ocean, there is *utter* darkness.
B. When they dive, seals *utter* past all the other creatures.
C. The lines of "Seal" are arranged to reveal that it is an *utter* poem.
D. The sounds that animals *utter* are rendered differently in different languages.

____ 17. In these lines from "The Rider," which words form an infinitive?
To leave your loneliness / panting behind you on some street corner

A. "To leave"
B. "your loneliness"
C. "panting behind you"
D. "on some street corner"

____ 18. Which words in this sentence form an infinitive phrase?
The poem's speaker, a bicycle rider, says that she plans to pedal fast.

A. "poem's speaker"
B. "The poem's speaker"
C. "to pedal"
D. "to pedal fast"

Essay

19. In an essay, discuss the way in which Naomi Shihab Nye treats loneliness in "The Rider." What does loneliness mean to the speaker in the poem? How does bicycling help her leave her loneliness behind? Cite passages from the poem to support your points.

20. Both "The Rider" and "Seal" deal with motion; in both poems, it is an important image. In an essay, compare Naomi Shihab Nye's and William Jay Smith's use of motion or movement and its role in the poems. Answer these questions: What feeling does motion create in each poem? How or why is motion important to each poem? Cite passages from the poems to support your conclusions.

21. **Thinking About the Big Question: What is the best way to communicate?** Think about the three forms of poetry you read: the lyric poem "The Rider," the concrete poem "Seal," and the haiku by Buson. Which form do you find to be the best way to communicate through poetry? Write a brief essay that explains your answer. Use examples from the poems.

Vocabulary Warm-up Word Lists

Study these words from the poetry of Nikki Giovanni, Mary Ellen Solt, and Bashō . Then, complete the activities that follow.

Word List A

collect [kuh LEKT] *v.* to gather together
  We will <u>collect</u> empty bottles and recycle them.

layers [LAY uhrz] *n.* single thicknesses or folds
  The cake has nine <u>layers</u>.

mountain [MOWN tuhn] *n.* a natural formation of the earth that rises sharply from the surrounding land, larger than a hill
  We were out of breath while climbing up the steep <u>mountain</u>.

oatmeal [OHT meel] *n.* porridge made from rolled oats or oat flakes
  The hot <u>oatmeal</u> made a filling breakfast for us.

remain [ri MAYN] *v.* to stay or to be left behind when the rest has gone away
  Who will <u>remain</u> at home to mind the dog while we go on vacation?

winter [WIN tuhr] *n.* the coldest season of the year
  Joan likes to ice skate on the frozen pond during the <u>winter</u>.

Word List B

blossoms [BLAHS uhmz] *n.* flowers
  The summer garden was full of colorful <u>blossoms</u>.

forsythia [fawr SITH ee uh] *n.* a shrub that has yellow blooms that flower early in spring
  The bright yellow blooms of the <u>forsythia</u> brightened up the landscape.

fragrant [FRAY gruhnt] *adj.* having a pleasant odor
  The freshly cut evergreen boughs were very <u>fragrant</u>.

grow [GROH] *v.* to come into being or be made naturally
  Matt's beard will <u>grow</u> quickly.

preparing [pree PAIR ing] *v.* making ready or suitable for some event
  We always pack a suitcase of clothes when we are <u>preparing</u> to go away.

spring [SPRING] *n.* the season after winter when plants begin to grow and the weather warms
  Martha loved the first few warm days of <u>spring</u>.

Poetry Collection: Nikki Giovanni, Mary Ellen Solt, and Bashō
Vocabulary Warm-up Exercises

Exercise A *Fill in each blank in the paragraph below with an appropriate word from Word List A. Use each word only once.*

Robby loved to go camping during the brisk, cold days of [1] _____. He and his older brother Don would [2] _____ all their gear for the trip, including sleeping bags and a tent. They also brought along plenty of clothes so they could dress in [3] _____ depending on how cold it was. That way, if it warmed up, they could take off some clothes. If it got colder, they could add some. The boys also brought along skis to use on the snowy trails of the [4] _____ where they camped. Each morning Robby would tend the camp fire and make them a breakfast of warm [5] _____. Camping with his brother would always [6] _____ one of Robby's happiest memories.

Exercise B *Revise each sentence so that the underlined vocabulary word is used in a logical way. Be sure to keep the vocabulary word in your revision.*

Example: The bright yellow flowers of the <u>forsythia</u> are seen late in the fall.
The bright yellow flowers of the <u>forsythia</u> are seen early in the spring.

1. The carefully tended rose garden did not have any colorful <u>blossoms</u>.
   _____

2. We disliked smelling the <u>fragrant</u>, freshly baked bread.
   _____

3. Did you ever hear the saying "mighty oaks from tiny acorns do not <u>grow</u>"?
   _____

4. Anna wanted everything to be perfect for the party, so she spent very little time <u>preparing</u> for it.
   _____

5. The cold days of <u>spring</u> are a welcome treat after the long winter.
   _____

Poetry Collection: Nikki Giovanni, Mary Ellen Solt, and Bashō
Reading Warm-up A

Read the following passage. Pay special attention to the underlined words. Then, read it again, and complete the activities. Use a separate sheet of paper for your written answers.

What do you think of when you think of <u>winter</u>? What does this season of the year mean to you? Do you think of riding sleds on cold, snowy afternoons? Do you think of ice skating on a frozen pond? Perhaps winter makes you think of cold mornings and hot breakfasts of <u>oatmeal</u> and cream of wheat.

Winter is the coldest time of the year in the northern part of the world, but what causes this season? Winter happens when the Earth is tilting away from the sun. At this time of year, the countries located in the North receive less daylight than at other times of the year. Usually, every day by four o'clock in the afternoon, very few hours of daylight <u>remain</u> during the winter months. The northern countries also do not receive as much warmth from the sun because of their position in relation to the sun. That is why we experience cold, short days during the winter.

During the winter, many plants lose their leaves. In a way, these plants are "sleeping." They will not wake up until spring draws near. Many animals begin to prepare for winter in the fall. For example, squirrels <u>collect</u> acorns at that time. They bury the acorns to save them for later. They know that food will be hard to find during the coming months. These creatures also grow extra <u>layers</u> of fur as winter approaches. This extra-thick coat will keep them warm on cold winter days. Some animals, such as skunks and bears, sleep or go into a sort of sleep during the winter season. Up on the snowy <u>mountain</u>, a skunk may be sleeping beneath rocks or under the ground. Bears may be snoozing in a cave. On a warmish day, the bear may venture out to find some food. Then it returns and sleeps away the colder days.

The next time you think of all you like to do in the winter, also think of how and why this special season happens!

1. Circle the word that tells what <u>winter</u> is. Which seasons come before and after **winter**?

2. Circle the words that describe what <u>oatmeal</u> is. Use **oatmeal** in a sentence.

3. Underline the words that tell what few things <u>remain</u> on a winter afternoon. Define **remain**.

4. Underline the word that tells what squirrels <u>collect</u> before winter. What does **collect** mean?

5. Circle the words that tell why some animals grow extra <u>layers</u> of fur. Use **layers** in a sentence.

6. Circle the words that tell what animals may be sleeping up on a <u>mountain</u> during winter. What is a **mountain**?

Name _____ Date _____

Read the following passage. Pay special attention to the underlined words. Then, read it again, and complete the activities. Use a separate sheet of paper for your written answers.

Spring is a beautiful time of year. The bitter, cold days of winter have drawn to an end. The northern part of the Earth is beginning to tilt toward the sun at this time. This means the daylight hours are getting longer, and the weather is warmer.

All around us, we can observe new life, as plants begin to grow. Buds for new leaves grow larger on the trees as the days get warmer. Soon they burst into the blooms that bring leaves. The grass turns green, too, and flowers and other plants begin their growing cycle.

As flowers bloom, we enjoy the beauty and colors of their blossoms. The bright yellow flowers of the forsythia are one of the first signs of the spring season. This shrub, which is a member of the olive family, looks like a fountain of color when it blooms. Its green leaves emerge only after the yellow flowers have bloomed. Many of the season's flowers have fragrant blooms. Roses and lilacs are two such flowers, and their lovely perfume makes the air pleasant to smell.

We find such flowers beautiful to see and to smell, but they also have an important part to play in the world of nature. Flowers help in preparing the plant to make new seeds. For seeds to grow, the pollen from one part of the flower must join with the "eggs" for seeds that are in another part of the flower. This process is called *pollination*. The colors of the flower petals and the flower's scent attract bees and hummingbirds. These creatures help pollination when they collect nectar because they carry pollen on their legs. That is how the pollen reaches the eggs so seeds will grow. In this way, the cycle continues, and new plants are able to grow from the seeds.

1. Underline the words that tell what happens in the northern part of the Earth during spring. Define **spring**.

2. Circle the words that tell what begins to grow in spring. What other things can you think of that **grow**?

3. Circle the words that tell what we enjoy about the blossoms. What are **blossoms**?

4. Underline the words that describe the forsythia. Use **forsythia** in a sentence.

5. Circle the two types of fragrant blooms mentioned in the story. What other things are **fragrant**?

6. Underline the words that tell what flowers help in preparing. Define **preparing**.

Name _____ Date _____

Poetry Collection: Nikki Giovanni, Mary Ellen Solt, Matsuo Bashō

Writing About the Big Question

What is the best way to communicate?

Big Question Vocabulary

communicate	contribute	enrich	entertain	express
inform	learn	listen	media	produce
react	speak	teach	technology	transmit

A. *Use one or more words from the list above to complete each sentence.*

1. One of the most direct ways to get to know someone is to _____ with the person in a conversation.

2. When you have a conversation, is it important to _____ to what the other person says.

3. The way you _____ to someone's statements may show in your face or body.

4. You can use facial expressions and body language to _____ your feelings.

B. *Respond to each item with a complete sentence.*

1. Describe a facial expression and what it can communicate to another person. Use a Big Question vocabulary word in your description.

   _____

   _____

2. Describe an example of body language and what it can communicate to another person. Use a Big Question vocabulary word in your description.

   _____

   _____

C. *In "Poetry Collection 2," each poem describes an aspect of nature. Complete this sentence. Then, write a short paragraph connecting the sentences to the Big Question.*

   Descriptive language can **contribute** to _____

   _____

   _____

Name _____ Date _____

Reading: Ask Questions to Draw a Conclusion

Drawing conclusions means arriving at an overall judgment or idea by pulling together several details. By drawing conclusions, you recognize meanings that are not directly stated. **Asking questions** can help you identify details and make connections that lead to a conclusion. You might ask yourself questions such as these:

- What details does the writer include and emphasize?
- How are the details related?
- Taken together, what do all the details mean?

Consider, for example, this haiku by Bashō:

On sweet plum blossoms
The sun rises suddenly.
Look, a mountain path!

What do those details mean? As the sun rises, it shines on a blossoming plum tree. You can conclude that it is a spring morning.

DIRECTIONS: *Complete the following chart. First, ask a question about the poem. Then, record the details that prompted the question. Finally, write a conclusion that you can draw based on the question and the related details.*

Poem	Question	Details Relating to Question	Conclusion
"Winter"			
"Forsythia"			
"Has spring come indeed?"			
"Temple bells die out"			

Name _____ Date _____

Poetry Collection: Nikki Giovanni, Mary Ellen Solt, Bashō
Literary Analysis: Forms of Poetry

There are many different **forms of poetry.** A poet will follow different rules, depending on the structure of a poem. These are the three forms represented by poems in this collection:

- A **lyric poem** expresses the poet's thoughts and feelings about a single image or idea in vivid, musical language.
- In a **concrete poem,** the poet arranges the letters and lines to create a visual image that suggests the poem's subject.
- **Haiku** is a traditional form of Japanese poetry that is often about nature. In a traditional haiku, the first line always has five syllables, the second line always has seven syllables, and the third line always has five syllables.

DIRECTIONS: *Write your answers to the following questions.*

1. If you were to rewrite one of Bashō's haiku as a concrete poem, what shape would you use to express the main idea? Why?

   _____

   _____

   _____

2. If you were to rewrite "Winter" as a haiku, what seven-syllable line might you write that contained the phrase "Bears store fat"?

   _____

3. If you were to rewrite "Forsythia" as a lyric poem, on what single idea would you focus? Why?

   _____

   _____

   _____

4. If you were to rewrite "Forsythia" as a haiku, what would one of your lines be?

   _____

5. If you were to rewrite one of Bashō's haiku as a lyric poem, how would you change it? Why?

   _____

   _____

   _____

Poetry Collection: Nikki Giovanni, Mary Ellen Solt, Bashō
Vocabulary Builder

Word List

burrow   forsythia   fragrant   telegram

A. DIRECTIONS: *Provide an explanation for your answer to each question.*

1. Would you see a *forsythia* flowering in the fall?

   _____

2. Would a *telegram* be likely to include a long description?

   _____

3. Would an animal *burrow* in the sand to escape an enemy?

   _____

4. Would a bouquet of roses smell *fragrant*?

   _____

B. WORD STUDY: *The Greek root -gram- means "write, draw, or record." Write a sentence that answers each question, using the italicized word.*

1. What could an *electrocardiogram* show about your heart?

   _____

2. What does a *grammarian* study?

   _____

3. What might be an *anagram* of the word "bat"?

   _____

Poetry Collection: Nikki Giovanni, Mary Ellen Solt, Bashō
Enrichment: Preparing for Winter

In "Winter," Nikki Giovanni names ways in which animals prepare for winter: Frogs burrow into mud, snails bury themselves, dogs grow thicker coats, bears store fat, and chipmunks gather nuts. Humans, too, prepare for winter weather.

A. DIRECTIONS: *Think about what you or those in your region do to prepare for winter. If you live in an area where winter is mild, imagine living in a place where winters are severe. For each category named below, describe how you or someone else might prepare for winter.*

Clothing: _____

_____

Outdoor sports: _____

_____

Indoor activities: _____

_____

Food: _____

_____

Health: _____

_____

Emergency supplies: _____

_____

B. DIRECTIONS: *On the lines below, write what you like best and least about winter or what you imagine that you would like best and least about it.*

_____

_____

_____

_____

_____

Name _____ Date _____

Integrated Language Skills: Grammar

Infinitives and Infinitive Phrases

An **infinitive** is a verb that acts as a noun, an adjective, or an adverb. An infinitive usually begins with the word *to*.

Some dogs like *to swim*. (infinitive as a noun serving as the object of the verb *like*)

To travel is my objective. (infinitive as a noun serving as the subject of the sentence)

Paris is the city *to visit*. (infinitive as an adjective modifying the noun *city*)

Everyone waited *to hear*. (infinitive as an adverb modifying the verb *waited*)

An **infinitive phrase** is an infinitive plus its own modifiers or complements.

Some dogs like *to swim all year round*. (phrase serving as object of the verb *like*)

To travel in Europe is my objective. (phrase serving as subject of the sentence)

Paris is the city *to visit in the spring*. (phrase modifying the noun *city*)

Everyone waited *to hear the news*. (phrase modifying the verb *waited*)

A. PRACTICE: *Underline the infinitive in each sentence, and circle any infinitive phrases.*

1. In "Winter," the speaker goes outside to air her quilts.
2. To create a poem that looks like a forsythia bush was the aim of Mary Ellen Solt.
3. In "The Rider," the roller skater wants to escape his loneliness.
4. In one of Buson's haiku, "not one leaf dares to move."
5. In "Seal," the seal loves to swim fast.

B. Writing Application: *Review the poems in these collections. Then, write a sentence that captures your reaction to each poem and includes an infinitive or an infinitive phrase.*

1. **"The Rider":** _____

   _____

2. **"Seal":** _____

   _____

3. **One of Buson's haiku:** _____

   _____

4. **"Winter":** _____

   _____

5. **"Forsythia":** _____

   _____

6. **One of Bashō's Haiku:** _____

   _____

Poetry Collections: Naomi Shihab Nye, William Jay Smith, Buson;
Nikki Giovanni, Mary Ellen Solt, Bashō

Integrated Language Skills: Support for Writing a Lyric Poem, Concrete Poem, or Haiku

In the chart below, write details that you might use in your poem.

Subject: _____

Vivid Descriptions	Action Words	Thoughts	Feelings

Now, use the details you have collected to draft a **lyric poem, concrete poem,** or **haiku.**

Poetry Collections: Naomi Shihab Nye, William Jay Smith, Buson;
Nikki Giovanni, Mary Ellen Solt, Bashō

Integrated Language Skills: Support for Extend Your Learning

Listening and Speaking

With the other members of your group, choose a recording of a poet reading his or her lyric poems. Before you listen to the poems, write down the name of the poet and the names of the poems you plan to listen to. Then, as you listen or just after you finish listening, record your opinion of the poems, and list two reasons for your opinion. You might want to listen to the recording several times. Finally, use your notes to deliver a brief **presentation** to your group in which you express your opinion of the reading and cite the reasons for your opinion.

Poet: _____

Poems: _____

_____

My opinion: _____

_____

_____

_____

Reason 1: _____

_____

_____

_____

Reason 2: _____

_____

_____

_____

Name _____ Date _____

Short Answer *Write your responses to the questions in this section on the lines provided.*

1. Which element of "Winter" tells you that it is a lyric poem? Think about how many ideas are introduced and how they connect to one another. Use an example to show where the reader's thoughts are directed by the poet.

   _____

   _____

2. In line 1 of "Winter," frogs "burrow." Why would the coming of winter suggest that frogs should begin to burrow? Use your understanding of the word *burrow* to help you answer.

   _____

   _____

3. In "Winter," how does the word choice in lines 3, 5, and 9 support the musical feel of the poem? Support your answer with details about the rhythm of these lines.

   _____

   _____

4. Suppose you did not know the meaning of the title "Forsythia." What does the poem seem to be about, based on the visual image on the page? Describe the concrete image the poem presents to the reader. Include in your answer a guess as to why the poem might be presented on a colored page.

   _____

   _____

   _____

5. What conclusion can you draw about the overall message of "Forsythia"? Reread the poem and explain what the poet seems to be saying. Use at least two of the poem's words in your explanation.

   _____

   _____

   _____

6. In "Forsythia," the poet chose to write each letter several times (F, O, R, and so on). Each line of letters goes in a different direction. What is a possible reason that the lines go in so many directions? Explain your answer, using the visual image of the poem as support.

   _____

   _____

7. In the first line of the first haiku by Bashō, what feeling does the poet create? Explain your answer, using a word or words from the first line of the poem.

_____

_____

_____

8. Reread the first and third lines in the poems by Bashō. How do these lines help you know the form of each poem? Explain your reasoning, based upon your understanding of this poetic form.

_____

_____

_____

9. What conclusion can you draw about the subject of the three haiku by Bashō? Use the graphic organizer to write details that support your choice of a subject. Then, write a conclusion about how Bashō feels about the subject.

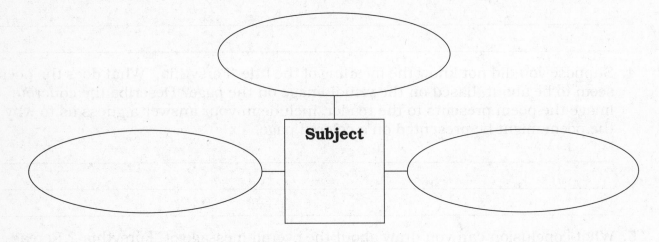

10. How does the punctuation of the three haiku by Bashō support the poet's purpose in each poem? Consider what he wants the reader to feel. Justify your answer with support from each of the three poems.

_____

_____

_____

_____

Essay

Write an extended response to the question of your choice or to the question or questions your teacher assigns you.

11. Each word of "Forsythia" creates an image in the reader's mind. Read each word to yourself, noticing what the word causes you to think of. Then, in a brief essay, explore why the word "telegram" is effective. Support your response by discussing how the meaning of the word "telegram" relates to the subject of the poem.

12. Which of the three haiku by Bashō seems to most intensely celebrate nature? In a brief essay, explore the haiku of your choosing. Support your choice with words and phrases from the haiku. You might use examples from one or both of the other haiku to show a contrast between another view of nature and that of the haiku you chose.

13. In "Winter," what seems to be the poet's overall attitude toward the coming of winter? In an essay, explore the emotional feeling that the poet conveys. Use details to analyze the way in which humans and animals prepare for the change in season. In your answer, explore the particular way in which the poet prepares herself.

14. **Thinking About the Big Question: What is the best way to communicate?** Think about the three poetic forms used by Giovanni, Solt, and Bashō—lyric, concrete, and haiku. Which form did you respond to most? In an essay, choose one of the poetic forms, and describe how you responded to it. In your analysis, explore whether the form you chose communicates more effectively than the other forms.

Oral Response

15. Go back to question 3, 4, or 7 or to the question your teacher assigns you. Take a few minutes to expand your answer and prepare an oral response. Find additional details in the poem or poems that support your points. If necessary, make notes to guide your oral response.

Poetry Collection: Nikki Giovanni, Mary Ellen Solt, Matsuo Bashō
Selection Test A

Critical Reading *Identify the letter of the choice that best answers the question.*

____ 1. When the speaker in "Winter" says, "I collect books / For the coming winter," what is her attitude toward the coming cold weather?
   A. positive
   B. fearful
   C. uninterested
   D. angry

____ 2. In "Winter," what is one thing the speaker does to get ready for winter?
   A. She makes oatmeal.
   B. She airs her quilts.
   C. She takes medicine.
   D. She gathers nuts.

____ 3. What does the speaker in "Winter" collect?
   A. quilts
   B. nuts
   C. snails
   D. books

____ 4. What conclusion can you draw about the details in the three verses of "Winter"?
   A. They all tell about winter storms.
   B. They all tell about the joys of winter.
   C. They all tell about preparing for winter.
   D. They all tell about avoiding winter.

____ 5. What kind of poem is "Forsythia"?
   A. a lyric poem about a single image
   B. a lyric poem about a single idea
   C. a concrete poem
   D. a haiku

____ 6. "Forsythia" contains few details. Which statement most likely explains the sparseness of details?
   A. The poet was not able to finish the poem.
   B. The shape of the poem provides the details.
   C. The poet has nothing to say about forsythia.
   D. There is no word that rhymes with *forsythia*.

_____ 7. Which adjective best describes Mary Ellen Solt's attitude toward forsythia?
   A. disrespectful
   B. enthusiastic
   C. appalled
   D. awestruck

_____ 8. To what method of communication does the speaker of "Forsythia" refer?
   A. a telegram
   B. an e-mail
   C. a letter
   D. a poster

_____ 9. How many syllables does a traditional Japanese haiku contain?
   A. three
   B. five
   C. seven
   D. seventeen

_____ 10. In the first of Bashō's three haiku, what does the speaker point out?
   A. plums
   B. plum blossoms
   C. the sun
   D. a path

_____ 11. In Bashō's haiku, what time of year does the poet seem most concerned with?
   A. early winter
   B. springtime
   C. late summer
   D. fall

_____ 12. In Bashō's three haiku, how is the poet's attitude toward nature best described?
   A. appreciative
   B. uninterested
   C. unobservant
   D. hostile

Vocabulary and Grammar

____ 13. When the frogs in "Winter" *burrow* the mud, what are they doing?
   A. climbing a wall
   B. digging holes
   C. hiding their food
   D. sleeping through the winter

____ 14. Which sentence contains an infinitive?
   A. Winter is approaching, and the speaker talks of how she is going to prepare.
   B. The speaker says that she will air her quilts because winter is approaching.
   C. One can imagine the speaker in "Winter" reading stories to the children.
   D. The speaker in "Winter" compares herself to the bears and the chipmunks.

____ 15. Which of the following sentences contains an infinitive phrase?
   A. Is it true that bears go to caves when they hibernate?
   B. One way of preparing for winter is to collect books.
   C. "Forsythia" can be read as a celebration of spring.
   D. The speaker of Bashō's haiku looks forward to spring.

Essay

16. What do the details in "Winter" suggest about the speaker's attitude toward winter? In an essay, answer that question. Refer to two or three details in the poem that the speaker appears to emphasize. Then, show how the details are related. Finally, explain how those details led you to your conclusion about the speaker's attitude toward winter.

17. The poems in this collection—Giovanni's "Winter," Solt's "Forsythia," and Bashō's three haiku—focus on nature and the natural world. In an essay, discuss the poem in this collection that you think best captures what nature is about. In explaining your choice, cite at least one passage from the poem.

18. **Thinking About the Big Question: What is the best way to communicate?** Think about the three poetic forms used by Giovanni, Solt, and Bashō—lyric, concrete, and haiku. Which form did you respond to most? In an essay, explain why you think this form communicated to you more effectively than the others. Use specific examples from the poems to support your answer.

Poetry Collection: Nikki Giovanni, Mary Ellen Solt, Matsuo Bashō
Selection Test B

Critical Reading *Identify the letter of the choice that best completes the statement or answers the question.*

____ 1. In "Winter," what image does the poet most likely want to convey with the following lines?

I air my quilts / preparing for the cold

A. a woman scrubbing quilts by hand in a large tub
B. a woman snuggling under quilts during a snowstorm
C. a woman hanging up quilts in the fall sun to freshen them
D. a woman watching quilts tumble in the dryer at a laundromat

____ 2. In "Winter," what does the poet most likely mean by the following lines?

little boys and girls / take Father John's Medicine.

A. The medicine helps the children stay warm.
B. The children take the medicine only in the winter.
C. The children are likely to get sick during the winter.
D. The medicine is available only in cold weather.

____ 3. In "Winter," the speaker is

A. taking care of her children.
B. taking care of animals.
C. getting ready for cold weather.
D. reading books and sewing quilts.

____ 4. What is the mood expressed by the speaker in "Winter"?
A. anticipation
B. concern
C. joy
D. anxiety

____ 5. Which question best relates to these details in "Winter"?

Frogs burrow the mud / snails bury themselves

A. What happens to frogs in the winter?
B. How do animals differ from people in the winter?
C. Why do snails bury themselves?
D. How do creatures prepare for winter?

____ 6. Which characteristics of the following lines indicate that "Winter" is a lyric poem?

Frogs burrow the mud / snails bury themselves

A. The lines do not rhyme.
B. The lines tell a story.
C. The lines contribute to a single idea.
D. The lines contains five syllables apiece.

____ 7. The tone of "Forsythia"—the poet's attitude toward her subject—may best be
described as
A. disdainful.
B. academic.
C. excited.
D. bored.

____ 8. In "Forsythia," Solt uses capital letters, dots and dashes, and a concise message.
Based on those details, you can conclude that she most likely wishes the reader to
think of
A. an e-mail.
B. a telegram.
C. a poster.
D. a letter.

____ 9. The shape of "Forsythia" combined with its message suggests that
A. the bush is blooming chaotically.
B. the bush has been trimmed by a gardener.
C. the growing season of the bush is extremely short.
D. the growth of the bush has been disrupted by a sudden frost.

____ 10. Which characteristics make "Forsythia" a concrete poem?
A. It contains precisely seventeen syllables.
B. Its message is expressed as a single image.
C. It expresses the poet's ideas about nature.
D. Its form suggests the subject of the poem.

____ 11. What conclusion can you draw from the details in these lines by Bashō?
The sun rises suddenly. / Look, a mountain path!
A. The speaker is surprised.
B. The speaker is lost.
C. The speaker is angry.
D. The speaker is bewildered.

____ 12. In the second of Bashō's three haiku, what is the speaker's tone—his attitude toward
the subject?
A. sad
B. angry
C. certain
D. doubtful

____ 13. What emotion is most likely felt by the speaker in Bashō's third haiku?
A. excitement
B. anger
C. dissatisfaction
D. contentment

____ 14. What conclusion can you draw based on the relationship between the details in Bashō's first and third haiku?
   A. The poet felt exceedingly lonely.
   B. The poet lived in an urban setting.
   C. The poet appreciated flower blossoms.
   D. The poet's favorite season was spring.

Vocabulary and Grammar

____ 15. In which sentence is *burrow* used correctly *and* in the same way it is used in "Winter"?
   A. The children filled the *burrow* with apples and nuts.
   B. The mice dug a *burrow* that led to the basement.
   C. The *burrow* carried provisions into the canyon.
   D. The moles *burrow* tunnels all through the backyard.

____ 16. Which sentence contains an infinitive?
   A. The hiker scrambled to the summit of the mountain.
   B. The poet read her work to an appreciative audience.
   C. The students prepared to take an English examination.
   D. The researchers came to a conclusion about the study.

____ 17. What is the function of the infinitive in this sentence?
   The forsythia is a beautiful sight to see in the spring.

   A. an adjective modifying *sight*
   B. an adverb modifying *in the spring*
   C. an adverb modifying *beautiful*
   D. an adjective modifying *forsythia*

____ 18. What is the function of the infinitive phrase in this sentence?
   The speaker loves to hear the temple bells ringing.

   A. an adjective modifying *speaker*
   B. an adverb modifying *loves*
   C. a noun serving as the object of the verb *loves*
   D. a noun serving as the subject of the sentence

Essay

19. Consider the poets whose works you have read in this collection—Giovanni, Solt, and Bashō. Choose two of those poets, and in an essay compare the two poets' attitude toward nature. Is one poet's view more practical than the other? Is it more delicate or more joyous? Cite at least two details in each poet's work to support your response.

20. In an essay, compare and contrast the mood of the three haiku by Bashō. What is the speaker's attitude toward the subject in each haiku? In what way is the speaker's attitude the same in each haiku? In what way is it different? Support your points with references to the poems.

21. **Thinking About the Big Question: What is the best way to communicate?** Think about the three poetic forms used by Giovanni, Solt, and Bashō–lyric, concrete, and haiku. Which form did you respond to most? In an essay, choose one of the poetic forms, and describe how you responded to it. In your analysis, explore whether the form you chose communicates more effectively than the other forms.

Vocabulary Warm-up Word Lists

Study these words from the poetry of Naomi Long Madgett, Wendy Rose, and Edna St. Vincent Millay. Then, complete the activities that follow.

Word List A

amuse [uh MYOOZ] *v.* to keep somebody entertained
The kitten's lively antics can <u>amuse</u> us for hours.

infant [IN fuhnt] *n.* a baby
The new mother rocked her <u>infant</u> daughter to sleep.

instead [in STED] *adv.* in place of someone or something
Carlos sold his old car <u>instead</u> of trading it for a new one.

spare [SPAIR] *v.* to conveniently part with or make available to another
Each evening Elise would <u>spare</u> some time to read to her sister.

treasure [TRE zhuhr] *v.* to treat someone or something as very special
Sandy will always <u>treasure</u> the memory of her graduation day.

watch [WAHCH] *n.* a small clock you wear on your wrist or in your pocket
John was late because his <u>watch</u> was 30 minutes slow.

Word List B

ashes [ASH ez] *n.* the soft powder that remains after something has been burned
The wind blew the <u>ashes</u> from the campfire into our eyes.

centuries [SEN chuh reez] *n.* 100-year periods of time
The foundation of our government, the United States Constitution, is more than two <u>centuries</u> old.

fascinated [FAS uh nay ted] *v.* to have captured and held someone's attention
Shelly was <u>fascinated</u> with video games.

shudder [SHUD uhr] *v.* to shake violently
The hurricane's winds made the house <u>shudder</u> on its foundation.

source [SAWRS] *n.* the thing, place, or person from which something comes
Earth's greatest <u>source</u> of light and energy is the sun.

trembling [TREM buhl ing] *v.* shaking, shivering
We left the horror movie still <u>trembling</u> with fright.

Poetry Collection: Naomi Long Madgett, Wendy Rose, and Edna St. Vincent Millay
Vocabulary Warm-up Exercises

Exercise A *Fill in each blank in the paragraph below with an appropriate word from Word List A. Use each word only once.*

Melissa had no idea that caring for a six-month-old [1] _____ was so much work. Throughout the day she has been feeding, rocking, changing diapers, and finally singing the baby to sleep. At least she doesn't have to [2] _____ the baby while it is sleeping. She wants to watch TV, but she puts away the baby's toys and tidies the nursery [3] _____. Melissa checks her [4] _____. It is 8:45. She has a few minutes to [5] _____ before Mr. and Mrs. Cahill return home. She decides not to watch TV and just [6] _____ these few quiet moments at the end of a tiring day.

Exercise B *Write a complete sentence to answer each question. For each item, use a word from Word List B to replace each underlined word or group of words without changing its meaning.*

Example: What will cause the earth to <u>shake</u> violently under your feet?
An earthquake will cause the earth to <u>shudder</u> under my feet.

1. What structure in Egypt is <u>hundreds of years</u> old?
   _____

2. How do you keep from <u>shivering</u> when the temperature drops?
   _____

3. How would you clean out the <u>burnt remains</u> in a fireplace?
   _____

4. Why are people so <u>attracted</u> to the lives of celebrities?
   _____

5. What do you believe is the <u>origin</u> of all happiness?
   _____

Name _____ Date _____

Poetry Collection: Naomi Long Madgett, Wendy Rose, and Edna St. Vincent Millay
Reading Warm-up A

Read the following passage. Pay special attention to the underlined words. Then, read it again, and complete the activities. Use a separate sheet of paper for your written answers.

"What can we do that would entertain you?" Aunt Grace asked her niece she put away the dinner dishes.

Sandy plopped down on the sofa and checked the time on her <u>watch</u>. "Turn on the television, I guess."

Aunt Grace turned to hide her smile. *Kids! They have no idea of how to <u>amuse</u> themselves.*

Sandy moved some books on the coffee table so she could put her stocking-feet up. Thank goodness I'm staying only one night with my aunt, she thought. This place is such a bore. *Blam!* One of the books she had moved fell onto the floor. It was a photo album. Several loose photos slid out onto the carpet.

"Sorry!" Sandy exclaimed as she jumped down to gather up the photos. "Who's this?" she asked, staring at a wedding photo. The groom was dressed in a soldier's uniform.

Aunt Grace knelt down beside her. "That's my parents on their wedding day," she answered. "It's the only picture I have of them together, and I really <u>treasure</u> it. My dad was killed in the Vietnam War, about three months after this picture was taken."

"How sad," Sandy sympathized.

"My mom remarried four years later. Her second husband was your grandfather." Aunt Grace picked up a baby picture. The <u>infant</u> was dressed in a pink bunny suit. "This picture is of me," she said, laughing.

Aunt Grace turned pages in the album while telling family stories. Sandy learned how her grandmother had overcome many hardships to raise her two daughters. "She was a very strong woman," Aunt Grace said as she closed the album. "I admired her greatly and still do." She picked up a loose photo of her mom. "Here's a picture of her that I can <u>spare</u>. Would you like to have it?"

"I would, thank you," Sandy replied. Then she asked, "Do you have another album? I'd rather look at family photos <u>instead</u> of TV. Photographs are so much more interesting!"

1. Circle the word that tells what Sandy checked on her <u>watch</u>. Write a sentence that describes a *watch*.

2. Circle the word that is an antonym for <u>amuse</u>. Write the meaning of *amuse*.

3. Underline the words that tell what Aunt Grace <u>treasures</u>. Write about something you *treasure*.

4. Circle the word that is a synonym for <u>infant</u>. Use *infant* in a sentence.

5. Underline the words that tell what Aunt Grace has to <u>spare</u>. Describe something that you could not part with or *spare*.

6. Underline the words that tell what Sandy wanted to do <u>instead</u> of watching TV. Write about something you like to do *instead* of watching TV.

Poetry Collection: Naomi Long Madgett, Wendy Rose, and Edna St. Vincent Millay
Reading Warm-up B

Read the following passage. Pay special attention to the underlined words. Then, read it again, and complete the activities. Use a separate sheet of paper for your written answers.

On May 18, 1980, Mount St. Helens in Washington put on one of the greatest shows on the planet. The curtain went up in March 1980 when the volcano awoke, <u>trembling</u> from a series of earthquakes and steam explosions. Ten days and 10,000 earthquakes later, a huge bulge had formed on the northern side of the volcano, a sure sign that the mountain was getting ready to blow its top.

People who study volcanoes came from around the world to study the event. News reporters gathered at the site. People glued their attention to TV screens, <u>fascinated</u> by the terrifying force about to reveal itself. Mount St. Helens did not disappoint them.

The <u>source</u> of volcanic activity is steam and gas from the Earth's core that builds inside vents that lead to the Earth's surface. As the pressure mounts, the ground begins to <u>shudder</u> and shake. Sometimes the pressure becomes so great that the steam and gases explode through the vent. That's exactly what happened at Mount St. Helens on May 18, 1980.

At 8:32 A.M., following a major earthquake, the volcano's bulge and snow-covered summit slid away, causing the biggest landslide in recorded history. This triggered explosions that blasted volcanic gas and steam upward and outward at the speed of 300 miles per hour. Volcanic <u>ashes</u> and steam rose more than 15 miles into the atmosphere. Ash, pumice, and gas poured out of the new crater at temperatures of about 1,300° F (700° C). More than 520 million tons of black ash filled the sky, causing complete darkness for 250 miles downwind. Rocks and melted ice formed mudflows that stripped the mountainside, ripping up enough trees to build 300,000 two-bedroom homes. Fifty-seven people and countless wild animals died before it was all over.

Today, Mount St. Helens still rumbles, though it may be <u>centuries</u> before she puts on another explosive performance like the one in 1980.

1. Circle the word that tells what was <u>trembling</u>. Rewrite the sentence, using a synonym for *trembling*.

2. Underline the phrase that tells what <u>fascinated</u> TV viewers. Write a sentence, telling about a recent event that *fascinated* you.

3. Underline the phrase that describes the <u>source</u> of volcanic activity. What is a synonym for *source*?

4. Circle the phrase that tells what causes the mountain to <u>shudder</u>. Write a sentence using the word *shudder*.

5. Circle the word that tells what kind of <u>ashes</u> rose into the atmosphere. Write a sentence that describes where other kinds of *ashes* may be found.

6. What does the writer suggest may happen <u>centuries</u> from now? How many years into the future would that be?

Poetry Collection: Naomi Long Madgett, Wendy Rose, and Edna St. Vincent Millay

Writing About the Big Question

What is the best way to communicate?

Big Question Vocabulary

communicate	contribute	enrich	entertain	express
inform	learn	listen	media	produce
react	speak	teach	technology	transmit

A. *Use one or more words from the list above to complete each sentence.*

1. The _____, such as newspapers and television, is a useful way to communicate.

2. News articles can _____ you about important events and issues.

3. Stories about other cultures can _____ your understanding about how others live.

4. Reading and listening to the news can _____ a greater understanding of the world.

B. *Respond to each item with a complete sentence.*

1. Write two things you have learned about other cultures from newspapers or television. Use two Big Question vocabulary words in your response.

   _____

   _____

   _____

2. Explain how your knowledge of other cultures has helped you understand the world more fully. Use two Big Question vocabulary words in your response.

   _____

   _____

   _____

C. *In Poetry Collection 1, each poem includes one or more comparisons between objects or ideas. Complete this sentence:*

When you make connections between unrelated things, you **enrich**

_____

_____ and **learn** _____.

_____

Poetry Collection: Naomi Long Madgett, Wendy Rose, Edna St. Vincent Millay
Reading: Connect the Details to Draw a Conclusion

A **conclusion** is a decision or an opinion that you reach after considering the details in a literary work. **Connecting the details** can help you draw conclusions as you read. For example, if the speaker in a poem uses the words *spits, growls, snarls, trembling, shudder, unravel,* and *dislodge,* you might conclude that he or she is expressing dissatisfaction, anger, or some aspect of violence. As you read, identify important details. Then, look at the details together and draw a conclusion about the poem or the speaker.

DIRECTIONS: *In the first column of the chart below are details from the poems in this collection. Consider each set of details, and use them to draw a conclusion about the poem. Write your conclusion in the second column.*

Details	Conclusion
"Life": • The speaker says that life is a toy. • The toy ticks for a while, amusing an infant. • The toy, a watch, stops running.	
"Loo-Wit": • The old woman is "bound" by cedar. • Huckleberry "ropes" lie around her neck. • Machinery operates on her skin.	
"The Courage That My Mother Had": • The speaker's mother had courage. • The speaker has a brooch her mother wore. • The speaker wants her mother's courage.	

Poetry Collection: Naomi Long Madgett, Wendy Rose, Edna St. Vincent Millay

Literary Analysis: Figurative Language

Figurative language is language that is not meant to be taken literally. Writers use figures of speech to express ideas in vivid and imaginative ways. Common figures of speech include the following:

- A **simile** compares two unlike things using a word such as *like* or *as*.
- A **metaphor** compares two unlike things by stating that one thing is another thing. In an **extended metaphor,** several related comparisons extend over a number of lines.
- **Personification** gives human characteristics to a nonhuman subject.
- A **symbol** is an object, a person, an animal, a place, or an image that represents something else.

Look at this line from "Life." What figure of speech does the speaker use?

Life is but a toy that swings on a bright gold chain.

The speaker uses a metaphor to compare life to a toy, one "that swings on a bright gold chain."

DIRECTIONS: *As you read the poems in this collection, record the similes, metaphors, extended metaphors, personification, and symbols.*

Poem	Passage	Figurative Language
"Life"		
"Loo-Wit"		
"The Courage That My Mother Had"		

Poetry Collection: Naomi Long Madgett, Wendy Rose, Edna St. Vincent Millay
Vocabulary Builder

Word List

crouches   dislodge   fascinated   granite   prickly   unravel

A. DIRECTIONS: *Read each sentence, paying attention to the italicized word. Then, explain whether the sentence makes sense. If it does not make sense, rewrite the sentence or write a new sentence, using the italicized word correctly.*

1. The angry woman *crouches* as she stretches herself on her bumpy bed.

   Explanation: _____

   New sentence: _____

2. If you *dislodge* the stones, they may start an avalanche.

   Explanation: _____

   New sentence: _____

3. Anita was so *fascinated* by the movie that she fell asleep.

   Explanation: _____

   New Sentence: _____

4. The sweater was so well made that it began to *unravel.*

   Explanation: _____

   New sentence: _____

5. The rough wool sweater felt *prickly* and uncomfortable.

   Explanation: _____

   New Sentence: _____

6. The piece of *granite* dissolved in the hard rain.

   Explanation: _____

   New Sentence: _____

B. WORD STUDY: *The Latin suffix -ly means "like; in the manner of." Answer each question, using the italicized word with the suffix added.*

1. How can you tell if someone is *brave?*

   _____

2. What might a person who is *ambitious* do at work?

   _____

3. Why is it important to be *careful* when you are hiking?

   _____

Poetry Collection: Naomi Long Madgett, Wendy Rose, Edna St. Vincent Millay
Enrichment: Animated Film

One poem in this collection, "Loo-Wit," presents an inanimate object, a volcano, as a living creature—an angry woman. Another poem, "Life," presents human life as if it were a toy watch. Figurative language allows you to imagine how the woman looks and acts and how the watch might look and work.

Imagine Loo-Wit or the watch starring in an animated movie. Think of animated movies you have seen and how the inanimate objects were brought to life. Might the watch in "Life" have a personality? Might Loo-Wit have a deep, loud voice?

A. DIRECTIONS: *You have been assigned the job of translating "Loo-Wit" and "Life" into animated films. On the lines below, write details about the physical appearance and personality of each "character."*

1. *The watch in "Life":* _____

   _____

2. *Loo-Wit:* _____

   _____

B. DIRECTIONS: *Create your own animated character. You will need at least eight pieces of paper, all the same size and shape (not larger than about 3 inches by 4 inches), plus something to draw with and a stapler.*

- Choose one of the characters you described above, and draw it on one of the pieces of paper. Give it human characteristics, such as a face, arms, legs, hairstyle, and/or clothing. You may choose to draw a stick figure.
- Draw that same character again on each of the remaining pieces of paper. Try to capture the same details in each drawing and position the figure in the same place on the page. Each time you draw the figure, however, make a slight alteration. For example, you can close one eye in one drawing, raise an eyebrow in the next, and close both eyes in the one after that. If you are drawing a stick figure, change the position of its arms, legs, or body each time.
- Staple the pages together. Then, fan the pages quickly and watch your character come to life.

Poetry Collection: Naomi Long Madgett, Edna St. Vincent Millay, Wendy Rose

Open-Book Test

Short Answer *Write your responses to the questions in this section on the lines provided.*

1. In "Life," the poet uses a metaphor to compare two unlike things. Explain what two things she is comparing and why you think she has chosen this metaphor.

   _____

   _____

   _____

2. Reread lines 3 and 4 of "Life." What makes the "keeper" change his opinion about the toy? Use details from the poem to support your answer.

   _____

   _____

   _____

3. Using "Life," what conclusion can you draw about what happens to people at the end of their lives? Support your answer with details from line 6.

   _____

   _____

   _____

4. In the first stanza of "The Courage That My Mother Had," the poet uses a metaphor to compare two unlike things. Explain what two things she is comparing and why she might have chosen that metaphor.

   _____

   _____

   _____

5. What conclusion can you draw about how the speaker feels about her mother's brooch in "The Courage That My Mother Had"? Use details from lines 7 and 8 in your explanation.

   _____

   _____

   _____

6. Look at the third stanza of "The Courage That My Mother Had." What does the speaker seem to be feeling in lines 9 through 12? Explain your answer, using words or phrases from the lines to support your response.

   _____

   _____

   _____

7. The poet uses personification in several lines of "Loo-Wit." Use the graphic organizer to cite specific examples and show where in the poem they occur. Then, explain how the personification in the poem creates an effective image.

Line number	Example of Personification

_____

_____

8. In "Loo-Wit," the poet suggests that the eruption of the volcano was caused by something. Use details from the poem to explain why the volcano erupted.

_____

_____

_____

9. As the old woman in "Loo-Wit" "crouches," other events begin to happen. Is the thing the woman represents actually crouching? Use the definition of *crouch* in your answer.

_____

_____

_____

10. After the old woman in "Loo-Wit" moves, stones "dislodge." What will happen as more and more stones continue to dislodge? Include in your answer a description of what happens in the natural world when stones *dislodge*.

_____

_____

Essay

Write an extended response to the question of your choice or to the question or questions your teacher assigns you.

11. What impression of an old woman does the poet create in "Loo-Wit"? In a brief essay, analyze the type of old woman that is described by the poet. Use details from the poem as support. Include in your answer an opinion about whether you would be comfortable being in the company of this woman.

12. Why did the poet of "Life" choose to make the poem so short? In a brief essay, express an opinion about the length of the poem. Include in your answer an explanation about how the length of the poem serves the poet's purpose.

13. What are the speaker's feelings toward her mother in "The Courage That My Mother Had"? In an essay, explore the emotions of the speaker. Use examples from the poem to support your statements.

14. **Thinking About the Big Question: What is the best way to communicate?** Think about the figurative language used in the three poems by Madgett, Millay, and Rose. Which use of figurative language—simile and metaphor, personification, or symbolism—did you find most effective in communicating the message of a specific poet? In an essay, choose one of the poems, and analyze the power of the figurative language.

Oral Response

15. Go back to question 1, 5, or 7 or to the question your teacher assigns you. Take a few minutes to expand your answer and prepare an oral response. Find additional details in the poem or poems that support your points. If necessary, make notes to guide your oral response.

Poetry Collection: Naomi Long Madgett, Wendy Rose, Edna St. Vincent Millay
Selection Test A

Critical Reading *Identify the letter of the choice that best answers the question.*

_____ 1. In the poem "Life," to what is life compared?
   A. a running race
   B. a summer carnival
   C. a ticking watch
   D. a small child

_____ 2. In "Life," what happens when the old man grows tired of the game?
   A. He takes a long nap.
   B. He does not rewind the watch.
   C. He forgets where he is.
   D. He winds the watch too far.

_____ 3. In "Life," what does the winding down of the watch represent?
   A. the renewal of life
   B. the approach of death
   C. a long sleep
   D. an unexplained fear

_____ 4. Which kind of figurative language is used when Loo-Wit is called "this old woman"?
   A. personification
   B. simile
   C. metaphor
   D. symbolism

_____ 5. Which of your senses can best help you picture this passage from "Loo-Wit"?
   Around her / machinery growls, snarls and plows / great patches / of her skin.
   A. sight and hearing
   B. sight and smell
   C. hearing and smell
   D. hearing and taste

_____ 6. By connecting the details in "Loo-Wit," what can you conclude is going on in the poem?
   A. A rainstorm is approaching.
   B. A tidal wave is hitting land.
   C. A volcano is erupting.
   D. A woman is becoming angry.

_____ 7. How might the following lines from "The Courage That My Mother Had" best be described?

> Oh, if instead she'd left to me / The thing she took into the grave!—

A. as a question

B. as a demand

C. as a wish

D. as a suggestion

_____ 8. The reader of "The Courage That My Mother Had" can conclude that the speaker's mother has died. Which details point to that conclusion?

A. She had great courage.

B. She wore a golden brooch.

C. She is now in a granite hill.

D. She is compared to granite.

_____ 9. Which statement best captures the meaning of the following lines about the golden brooch in "The Courage That My Mother Had"?

> I have no thing I treasure more: / Yet, it is something I could spare.

A. There are many things that I treasure more than the brooch.

B. I treasure the brooch, but it is not my most valued possession.

C. Courage is important, but it cannot match the value of the brooch.

D. I do not value the brooch highly, so I could easily live without it.

_____ 10. Which trait does granite symbolize in these lines from "The Courage That My Mother Had"?

> Rock from New England quarried; / Now granite in a granite hill.

A. courage

B. stubbornness

C. will

D. love

Vocabulary and Grammar

_____ 11. Which activity is an animal that *crouches* most likely engaged in?

A. stretching after a sound sleep

B. preparing to pounce on its prey

C. climbing a tree

D. chasing its prey

___ **12.** Which of the following things is most likely to *unravel*?

    A. an apple pie

    B. a knit scarf

    C. a crouching animal

    D. a homework assignment

___ **13.** Which of these sentences contains an appositive?

    A. A symbol is an object, person, animal, place, or image that stands for something else.

    B. One type of figurative language, personification, gives human traits to non-human things.

    C. A simile is figurative language that compares unlike things using a word such as *like* or *as*.

    D. Another type of figurative language, called metaphor, also compares unlike things.

Essay

14. Both "Life" and "Loo-Wit" focus on natural events. Which poem do you prefer? In an essay, state your opinion. Then, explain why you like one poem better than the other. Cite at least one passage from the poem to support your argument.

15. "The Courage That My Mother Had" uses a metaphor to characterize the speaker's mother. In an essay, describe the comparison the speaker makes, citing details in the poem to illustrate your point. Then, explain what the comparison tells you about the kind of person the speaker's mother was.

16. **Thinking About the Big Question: What is the best way to communicate?**
Think about the figurative language used in the three poems by Madgett, Rose, and Millay. Which kind of figurative language—simile and metaphor, personification, or symbolism—communicated most effectively for you? Explain your response in an essay supported by specific examples from the text.

Poetry Collection: Naomi Long Madgett, Wendy Rose, Edna St. Vincent Millay
Selection Test B

Critical Reading *Identify the letter of the choice that best completes the statement or answers the question.*

___ 1. Which kind of figurative language is represented by this line from "Life"?
Life is but a toy that swings on a bright gold chain
   A. personification
   B. metaphor
   C. symbolism
   D. simile

___ 2. What conclusion can you draw from the details in these lines from "Life"?
Life is but a toy that swings on a bright gold chain / Ticking but for a little while
   A. The speaker thinks that life is a toy.
   B. The speaker thinks that life is short.
   C. The speaker is a toymaker.
   D. The speaker has a watch that ticks.

___ 3. In "Life," the line "And lets the watch run down" indicates that
   A. time stands still.
   B. life ends.
   C. the infant grows up.
   D. the toy is broken.

___ 4. In "Life," to what is life compared?
   A. a very old man
   B. a boring game
   C. a toy watch
   D. a young child

___ 5. What happens to Loo-Wit while she is sleeping?
   A. The world forgets about her.
   B. Other volcanoes erupt.
   C. She loses the power to erupt.
   D. Cedar trees grow on her.

___ 6. How long has it been since "Loo-Wit" last erupted?
   A. one night
   B. a woman's lifetime
   C. hundreds of years
   D. several days

___ 7. What conclusion can you draw about the following details in "Loo-Wit"?
Around her machinery growls, / snarls and plows / great patches / of her skin.
   A. Road crews are struggling with outdated equipment.
   B. Forestry equipment is cutting away swatches of woodland.
   C. A farmer is imagining that his fields are a woman's skin.
   D. A woman is dreaming that she is undergoing surgery.

____ 8. What figure of speech is used in these lines from "Loo-Wit"?
shaking the sky / like a blanket about her

    A. simile
    B. metaphor
    C. symbol
    D. personification

____ 9. What is the speaker saying in these lines from "The Courage That My Mother Had"?
The courage that my mother had / Went with her, and is with her still

    A. The speaker's mother has gone away.
    B. The speaker misses her mother greatly.
    C. The speaker's mother lost her courage when she went away.
    D. The speaker's mother took her courage with her to the grave.

____ 10. In "The Courage That My Mother Had," why is the speaker willing to give up the gold brooch?
    A. It makes her sad by reminding her of her mother.
    B. It makes her angry because it is all her mother left her.
    C. She believes gold is not worth as much as granite.
    D. She would rather have her mother's courage.

____ 11. What two symbols does the speaker use to represent her mother in "The Courage That My Mother Had"?
    A. gold and silver
    B. a rock and a hill
    C. a grave and a quarry
    D. granite and a brooch

____ 12. Which statement best expresses the meaning of these lines from "The Courage That My Mother Had"?
That courage like a rock, which she / Has no more need of, and I have.

    A. The speaker equates her mother's courage with a rock.
    B. The speaker needs the kind of courage her mother showed.
    C. The speaker realizes her mother no longer needs courage.
    D. The speaker realizes her mother found courage in rocks.

Vocabulary and Grammar

____ 13. In which sentence is *dislodge* used correctly?
    A. The noisy guests were asked to *dislodge* from their hotel room.
    B. Construction workers used a bulldozer to *dislodge* the boulder.
    C. If you *dislodge* a book in the library, it may be missing for ages.
    D. You should not *dislodge* from a train before it stops moving.

____ 14. Which item is likely to be *prickly*?
    A. silk
    B. rose stems
    C. courage
    D. time

____ 15. What is someone who *crouches* likely to be doing?
    A. making a blind guess
    B. preparing to sprint
    C. voicing a complaint
    D. reaching to the ceiling

____ 16. What is the appositive in this sentence?
    The woman, Loo-Wit, spit tobacco as she lay in bed.
    A. "woman"
    B. "Loo-Wit"
    C. "she"
    D. "bed"

____ 17. What is the appositive phrase in this sentence?
    Granite, a hard stone, is quarried in New England.
    A. "Granite"
    B. "a hard stone"
    C. "is quarried"
    D. "in New England"

____ 18. What is the appositive phrase in this sentence?
    Volcanoes, vents in the crust of the earth, may spew out rock, lava, or steam.
    A. "Volcanoes, vents"
    B. "vents in the crust"
    C. "vents in the crust of the earth"
    D. "rock, lava, or steam"

Essay

19. In an essay, identify the four basic types of figurative language that are considered in this collection of poetry. Define each type, and cite an example of it from "Life," "Loo-Wit," or "The Courage That My Mother Had."

20. Both "Life" and "The Courage That My Mother Had" deal with life and death. In an essay, explain how each poem portrays life and death. How do the speakers' attitudes toward life and death differ? Are they similar in any way? Support your conclusions by citing details from the poems.

21. **Thinking About the Big Question: What is the best way to communicate?** Think about the figurative language used in the three poems by Madgett, Rose, and Millay. Which use of figurative language—simile and metaphor, personification, or symbolism—did you find most effective in communicating the message of a specific poet? In an essay, choose one of the poems, and analyze the power of the figurative language.

Vocabulary Warm-up Word Lists

Study these words from the poetry of Langston Hughes, Henry Wadsworth Longfellow, and Carl Sandburg. Then, complete the activities that follow.

Word List A

crystal [KRIS tuhl] *n.* a sparkling glass of fine quality
   The bowl of <u>crystal</u> glittered in the firelight.

deed [DEED] *n.* something that is done or accomplished
   Jim knew he had done a good <u>deed</u> when he returned the lost wallet.

fog [FAHG] *n.* cloudy air near the ground that is difficult to see through
   Max could hardly see the road through the thick <u>fog</u>.

harbor [HAHR buhr] *n.* an area of water near land where ships can safely stay
   The captain steered his ship into the <u>harbor</u> to unload his cargo of fish.

rejoice [ri JOYS] *v.* to celebrate or show that you are very happy
   Thanksgiving Day is a time to <u>rejoice</u> and be grateful.

task [TASK] *n.* a job or particular piece of work that needs to be done
   We were given the <u>task</u> of counting votes after the election.

Word List B

anvil [AN vil] *n.* a heavy iron block on which pieces of metal are shaped using a hammer
   The blacksmith placed hot iron on the <u>anvil</u> and beat it with a hammer.

brow [BROW] *n.* forehead
   Jamie's hair fell over his <u>brow</u> and into his eyes.

forge [FORJ] *n.* a fireplace in a blacksmith's shop
   The <u>forge</u> filled the blacksmith's shop with heat and light.

fortunes [FOR chuhnz] *n.* people's destinies; what people become or accomplish during their lives
   Some say our <u>fortunes</u> are born of our dreams.

onward [ON werd] *adv.* forward
   The explorers pushed <u>onward</u> over the frozen tundra.

toiling [TOYL ing] *v.* working very hard
   The farmer spent his day <u>toiling</u> in the fields.

Poetry Collection: Langston Hughes, Henry Wadsworth Longfellow, and Carl Sandburg
Vocabulary Warm-up Exercises

Exercise A *Fill in each blank in the paragraph below with an appropriate word from Word List A. Use each word only once.*

Sarah, the captain's wife, would [1] _____ each time she saw her

husband's ship sail into the [2] _____. Even through a thick

[3] _____, Sarah could distinguish the ship among all others. Her hus-

band, John Cooley, captained a merchant ship that traveled to Europe and Asia. His

[4] _____ was to bring back fine porcelain, [5] _____

glassware, silver plates and other rich goods for the ship's owner who sold the merchan-

dise. Sometimes her neighbors did her a good [6] _____ by alerting her

that Captain Cooley's ship was in, but she usually knew before they did.

Exercise B *Answer the questions with complete explanations.*

Example: If you spent the day <u>toiling</u>, are you likely to feel rested at night? Why or
why not?
   It is not likely I will feel rested after <u>toiling</u> all day because I have been working hard.

1. If we wish to create our own <u>fortunes</u>, is it only necessary to make a lot of money?
   Why or why not?
   _____

2. If your <u>brow</u> is shaded from the sun, is it likely you are wearing a hat?
   _____

3. If soldiers are moving <u>onward</u>, is it likely they are in retreat? Why or why not?
   _____

4. If your job is to repair tires, is it likely you would use an <u>anvil</u>? Why or why not?
   _____

5. If the <u>forge</u> is cold, is it likely the blacksmith is doing work? Why or why not?
   _____

Poetry Collection: Langston Hughes, Henry Wadsworth Longfellow, and Carl Sandburg

Reading Warm-up A

Read the following passage. Pay special attention to the underlined words. Then, read it again, and complete the activities. Use a separate sheet of paper for your written answers.

The fog rolled in from the sea, a misty cloud, turning the town into a ghostly landscape. Brandon stared over the harbor where fishermen moored their boats. It was on a day such as this that he and his mother had been stranded at sea.

They had gone out in a boat to a protected cove where sea lions came to raise their babies. His mother's task had been to count the number of young sea lions for the Marine Institute. It was a part of her job she loved. She thought her seven-year-old son would enjoy it too, so he had gone with her.

They were returning to land when a heavy fog rolled in, stranding them in the open water. His mother cut the motor and lowered anchor. "Better to stay put," she said. "If we drift farther out we might collide with another boat."

To pass the time, his mother had talked about her father who had died at sea when Brandon was still a baby. "He was such a generous man," she said. "He tried to do a good deed a day; at least one act of kindness everyday. I hope you will make me proud by following his example."

"Do you miss him?" asked the young Brandon. "Do you feel sad?"

"Every person has a share of sorrow," his mother had replied, "especially when someone we love dies. For a while the sadness swallows us up, like this fog, but then it lifts and we sail on. I miss my dad, but I have you and your father. For that I rejoice. I celebrate every moment we share."

Remembering that day so long ago, Brandon hoped his life had made his mother proud. Suddenly, the fog lifted and the breaking sun turned the sea into bowl of sparkling crystal. It was as if his mother had answered his thoughts.

1. Underline the words that describe the fog. Write a sentence, telling why you do or do not like *fog*.

2. Circle the word that tells what was in the harbor. Write the meaning of the word *harbor*.

3. Underline the words that describe the mother's task. Write a sentence describing a *task* you need to do.

4. Circle the phrase that means almost the same as "a good deed." Then, write about something that you consider a good *deed*.

5. Circle the word that is a synonym for rejoice. Write about something for which you *rejoice*.

6. Circle the word that describes crystal. Tell what *crystal* means.

Poetry Collection: Langston Hughes, Henry Wadsworth Longfellow, and Carl Sandburg

Reading Warm-up B

Read the following passage. Pay special attention to the underlined words. Then, read it again, and complete the activities. Use a separate sheet of paper for your written answers.

We don't see many blacksmiths today, but to those who watch old cowboy movies the blacksmith is a familiar sight. He was a muscular man covered in soot from his <u>brow</u> to his boots. <u>Toiling</u> from sunup to sundown, the early blacksmith was an imposing figure, indeed. His job was to make and repair metal objects that included pots and pans, farm implements, building tools, fences, weather vanes, anchors, horseshoes, and nails. It was a heavy labor.

The blacksmith usually worked in a one-room shop. The shop was kept dark so he could read the temperature of the red-hot metal he heated in the <u>forge</u>. In the center of the room stood a large chunk of metal on which the blacksmith pounded the hot iron into shape with an enormous hammer. This was his <u>anvil</u>. Next to the anvil stood a bucket of water. Near that, a collection of tongs, punches and wrenches. A large bellows, for air supply, hung above the fireplace.

The blacksmith heated iron in the flaming forge until it turned soft. Then he dipped it into the bucket of water to cool it before pounding the metal into its desired form. When the iron became too cool, he returned it to the forge to reheat. He was always careful to keep the temperature within a certain range. If the iron grew too hot it became too soft to shape. If it grew too cold it would break.

From colonial days until the early 1900s, the clang of the blacksmith's hammer was a familiar sound in most towns and villages. It was the sound of industry and strength. Then time moved <u>onward</u> and left the blacksmith behind. Today the village blacksmith is no longer a central figure in our society, but he still earns our respect. In a time when people's <u>fortunes</u> were shaped by the honesty of their labor, the village blacksmith stood tall.

1. Rewrite the second sentence of the passage. Use your own words to replace the phrase "from his <u>brow</u> to his boots." Then tell what *brow* means.

2. Underline the words that hint at the meaning of <u>toiling</u>. Write a sentence, using the word *toiling*.

3. Underline the words that tell what the blacksmith heated in the <u>forge</u>. Write a synonym for *forge*.

4. Underline the words that describe the <u>anvil</u>. Write a sentence using the word *anvil*.

5. Circle the word that tells what moved <u>onward</u>. Write the antonym for *onward*.

6. Underline the words that tell what shaped people's <u>fortunes</u>. Write about what you think will help shape your *fortunes*, using a synonym for the word.

Name _____ Date _____

Poetry Collection: Langston Hughes, Henry Wadsworth Longfellow, and Carl Sandburg

Writing About the Big Question

What is the best way to communicate?

Big Question Vocabulary

communicate	contribute	enrich	entertain	express
inform	learn	listen	media	produce
react	speak	teach	technology	transmit

A. *Use one or more words from the list above to complete each sentence.*

1. Some people like to _____ others through music, dance, or acting.

2. The arts are a good way to _____ your thoughts and feelings.

3. When you _____ to a musician or actor, you can hear the feelings of both the performer and the composer or playwright.

4. A performer can _____ thoughts and feelings in the audience, too.

B. *Answer each question with a complete sentence.*

1. Describe two times when you have listened to a musical or dramatic piece that moved you.

   _____

   _____

2. Explain how you reacted to one of the preceding experiences. Tell what feelings or thoughts it produced in you.

   _____

   _____

C. *In Poetry Collection 4, the poets use evocative language to make their poems memorable. Complete this sentence: Then, write a short paragraph connecting the sentences to the Big Question.*

   Words that **express** strong emotions _____.

   _____

   _____

   _____

   _____

Name _____ Date _____

Reading: Connect the Details to Draw a Conclusion

A **conclusion** is a decision or an opinion that you reach after considering the details in a literary work. **Connecting the details** can help you draw conclusions as you read. For example, if the speaker in a poem uses the words *tacks, splinters, boards, bare,* and *dark,* you might conclude that he or she wishes to create an image of hardship. As you read, identify important details. Then, look at the details together and draw a conclusion about the poem or the speaker.

DIRECTIONS: *In the first column of the chart below are details from the poems in this collection. Consider each set of details, and use them to draw a conclusion about the poem. Write your conclusion in the second column.*

Details	Conclusion
"Mother to Son": • The speaker describes the staircase she has climbed: it had tacks, splinters, bare boards, and places with no light. • The speaker is still climbing.	_____ _____ _____ _____ _____ _____
"The Village Blacksmith": • On the blacksmith's brow is "honest sweat." • The blacksmith "owes not any man." • The blacksmith works long and hard.	_____ _____ _____ _____ _____ _____
"Fog": • The fog arrives "on little cat feet." • The fog sits "on silent haunches." • The fog looks "over harbor and city / . . . and then moves on."	_____ _____ _____ _____ _____ _____

Name _____ Date _____

Poetry Collection: Langston Hughes, Henry Wadsworth Longfellow, Carl Sandburg
Literary Analysis: Figurative Language

Figurative language is language that is not meant to be taken literally. Writers use figures of speech to express ideas in vivid and imaginative ways. Common figures of speech include the following:

- A **simile** compares two unlike things using a word such as *like* or *as*.
- A **metaphor** compares two unlike things by stating that one thing is another thing. In an **extended metaphor,** several related comparisons extend over a number of lines.
- **Personification** gives human characteristics to a nonhuman subject.
- A **symbol** is an object, a person, an animal, a place, or an image that represents something else.

Look at this line from "The Village Blacksmith." What figure of speech does the speaker use?

　　And the muscles of his brawny arms

　　Are strong as iron bands.

The speaker uses a simile to compare the blacksmith's muscles to iron bands.

DIRECTIONS: *As you read the poems in this collection, record the similes, metaphors, extended metaphors, personification, and symbols you find in the poems.*

Poem	Passage	Figurative Language
"Mother to Son"		
"The Village Blacksmith"		
"Fog"		

Poetry Collection: Langston Hughes, Henry Wadsworth Longfellow, Carl Sandburg

Vocabulary Builder

Word List

brawny   crystal   haunches   parson   sinewy   wrought

A. DIRECTIONS: *Read each sentence, paying attention to the italicized word. Then, explain whether the sentence makes sense. If it does not make sense, rewrite the sentence or write a new sentence, using the italicized word correctly.*

1. The cheetah sprang from its *haunches* to bring down the fleeing antelope.

   Explanation: _____

   New sentence: _____

2. Because the blacksmith was *brawny*, he easily lifted the heavy sledgehammer.

   Explanation: _____

   New sentence: _____

3. The *sinewy* construction worker could carry only the lightest loads.

   Explanation: _____

   New sentence: _____

4. The *crystal* vase shattered when it hit the ground.

   Explanation: _____

   New Sentence: _____

5. The *parson* had always been too shy to speak in public.

   Explanation: _____

   New Sentence: _____

6. The bracelet was *wrought* from white gold.

   Explanation: _____

   New Sentence: _____

B. WORD STUDY: *The Latin suffix -y means "marked by, having." Answer each question, using the italicized word with the suffix added.*

1. How does a person who feels *anger* behave?

   _____

2. How would someone who learns with *ease* probably do in school?

   _____

3. Why is it important not to make a *mess* on a test paper?

   _____

Name _____ Date _____

Enrichment: Inspiring People

Two of the poems in this collection, "Mother to Son" and "The Village Blacksmith," focus on individuals who are meant to serve as an inspiration: The mother hopes to inspire her son; the blacksmith has obviously inspired the speaker of Longfellow's poem.

A. DIRECTIONS: *Think about someone who has inspired you in some way. It might be a teacher, a family member, a neighbor, or someone you know of from current events or history. On the lines below, jot down details about that person. Then, translate those details into figurative language.*

Name: _____

Activities the person often does or did: _____

_____

Figurative language describing those activities: _____

_____

Something the person says or said: _____

_____

Figurative language describing the thing said: _____

_____

Outstanding traits: _____

_____

Figurative language describing those traits: _____

_____

Ways in which the person has inspired me: _____

_____

Figurative language describing inspiration: _____

_____

B. DIRECTIONS: *Use the details you have jotted down to write a biographical sketch of your subject.*

_____

_____

_____

_____

_____

Poetry Collections: Naomi Long Madgett, Wendy Rose, Edna St. Vincent Millay;
Langston Hughes, Henry Wadsworth Longfellow, Carl Sandburg

Integrated Language Skills: Grammar

Appositives and Appositive Phrases

An **appositive** is a noun or pronoun that is placed after another noun or pronoun to
identify, rename, or explain it. In the following sentence, the appositive is underlined:

In "Fog," the poet compares an animal, a <u>cat</u>, to fog.

An **appositive phrase** is a noun or pronoun, along with any modifiers, that is placed
after another noun or pronoun to identify, rename, or explain it. In the following
sentence, the appositive is underlined; the words that make up the appositive phrase
are in italics:

Longfellow made the village blacksmith, *an honest and reliable <u>man</u>*, into a hero.

A. PRACTICE: *In each sentence, underline the appositive phrase. Then, circle the noun
that the appositive phrase identifies or explains.*

1. Loo-Wit, a volcano, is about to erupt.

2. Death, an old man, lets the watch run down.

3. The speaker in "The Courage That My Mother Had" mentions New England, a
   region in the northeast.

4. The speaker in "The Courage That My Mother Had" compares her mother's courage
   to granite, a hard rock.

5. The village blacksmith weeps when he hears the voice of his daughter, a singer in
   the choir.

6. In "Mother to Son," a poem by Langston Hughes, a mother gives advice to her son.

B. Writing Application: *Use each phrase in brackets as an appositive phrase in the
sentence that follows it. Set off each phrase with commas or dashes.*

1. [a beautiful golden pin] In "The Courage That My Mother Had," the speaker's
   mother has given the speaker a brooch.

   _____

   _____

2. [a blanket of white mist] In "Fog," fog covers a harbor.

   _____

3. [a symbol of an easy life] The mother in "Mother to Son" speaks of the crystal stair.

   _____

   _____

Name _____ Date _____

Integrated Language Skills: Support for Writing an Extended Metaphor

Use the word web below to collect ideas for an **extended metaphor** about a quality or an idea, such as love, loyalty, life, or death. Decide on the quality or idea, and then decide what you will compare it to. It may be an object, an animal, or an idea. Write your ideas in the center of the web. Then, complete the web by writing down ideas that relate to your central idea. Use vivid images and descriptive language. Your extended metaphor may include similes, metaphors, personification, and symbols.

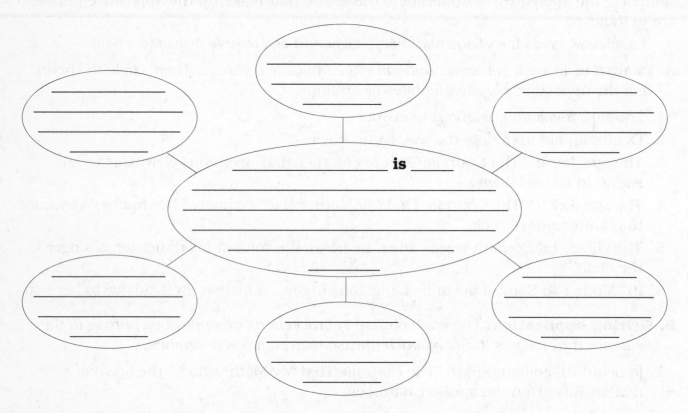

Now, use your notes to write an extended metaphor about a quality or an idea. Be sure to use vivid images and descriptive language.

Poetry Collections: Naomi Long Madgett, Wendy Rose, Edna St. Vincent Millay;
Langston Hughes, Henry Wadsworth Longfellow, Carl Sandburg

Integrated Language Skills: Support for Extend Your Learning

Poetry Collection: Naomi Long Madgett, Wendy Rose, Edna St. Vincent Millay

Research and Technology

With two classmates, decide on topics to research in preparation for your presentation of a **scientific explanation** of volcanic eruptions. Come up with three topics, one for each of you to work on. You might research how volcanoes form, the warning signs of an eruption, where and why volcanoes erupt, famous eruptions, or topics of your own choosing. On the following graphic organizer, note the topic that you will research, and record the information that you gather. Make notes about diagrams, illustrations, photographs, maps, and other visual aids that you can use in the presentation.

Topic	Notes	Visual Aids

Poetry Collection: Langston Hughes, Henry Wadsworth Longfellow, Carl Sandburg

Research and Technology

With a partner, decide how you will divide up the research you need to do to find out the differences between fog and smog. Then, use this chart to record your findings. Make notes about Venn diagrams, comparison charts, photographs, and/or diagrams you might use in your presentation of the **scientific explanation** of fog and smog.

Topic	Fog	Smog	Visual Aids
Definition			
Similarities			
Differences			
Types			

Name _____ Date _____

Short Answer *Write your responses to the questions in this section on the lines provided.*

1. In "Mother to Son," the speaker says she has not had an easy life. What symbol does the poet use to represent the mother's hard life? Use details from the poem.

   _____

   _____

2. Reread lines 8–13 of "Mother to Son." The poet continues the use of a metaphor comparing life to a staircase. What do these lines tell about?

   _____

   _____

   _____

3. What conclusions can you draw about the mother in "Mother to Son"? Support your answer with details from the poem.

   _____

   _____

   _____

4. Why might the poet have chosen a crystal stair to represent an easy life in "Mother to Son"? Use details from the poem to support your answer.

   _____

   _____

   _____

5. "The Village Blacksmith" is described as having sinewy hands. How do sinewy hands help him do his job more effectively? Explain your answer, using your understanding of the poem as support.

   _____

   _____

   _____

6. What conclusions can you draw about the village blacksmith? Offer an opinion about his character, using details from the poem in your explanation.

   _____

   _____

   _____

   _____

7. Look at the final stanza of "The Village Blacksmith." What metaphor is used to describe life? Explain why the poet chose this metaphor, using words or phrases from the lines to support your response.

_____

_____

8. In "Fog," the fog sits on its haunches. What kind of image does the poet offer by using the word *haunches* to suggest the position of the fog? Use your understanding of the poem to explain your answer.

_____

_____

9. In "Fog," a metaphor is used to compare fog to something. Use the organizer below to list details that support the metaphor. Then, explain what the metaphor is and why it is effective.

Line number	Example of Metaphor

_____

_____

10. "Fog" is one of Sandburg's most famous poems. Why do you think people find the poem so appealing?

_____

_____

Essay

Write an extended response to the question of your choice or to the question or questions your teacher assigns you.

11. How does the shortness of the poem "Fog" contribute to its effectiveness? In a brief essay, explain how the length of the poem adds to the image the poet is trying to convey. Include in your answer an opinion about how well this image works. Use details from the poem.

12. What lesson about life is offered in "The Village Blacksmith"? In a brief essay, analyze the poet's purpose in writing this poem. Include in your answer an opinion about why the speaker thanks the blacksmith in the final stanza. Use details from the poem for support.

13. Why do you think the poet chose to use dialect for the speaker's voice in "Mother to Son"? In an essay, explore the poet's purpose in making this choice. Use examples from the poem to support your analysis.

14. Thinking About the Big Question: What is the best way to communicate?
Think about the images conveyed in "Mother to Son," "The Village Blacksmith," and "Fog." Two of the poems portray people, and the other poem portrays an act of nature. Which image did you find most effective in communicating the message of the poet? In an essay, choose one of the poems, and offer an opinion about the strength of the image's ability to communicate the poet's message.

Oral Response

15. Go back to question 1, 4, or 6 or to the question your teacher assigns you. Take a few minutes to expand your answer and prepare an oral response. Find additional details in the poem or poems that support your points. If necessary, make notes to guide your oral response.

Poetry Collection: Langston Hughes, Henry Wadsworth Longfellow, Carl Sandburg

Selection Test A

Critical Reading *Identify the letter of the choice that best answers the question.*

_____ 1. Which word best summarizes the content of "Mother to Son"?
   A. celebration
   B. description
   C. entertainment
   D. advice

_____ 2. Who is "honey" in the following line from "Mother to Son"?
   For I'se still goin', honey
   A. the landlord
   B. the employer
   C. the mother
   D. the son

_____ 3. Which details in "Mother to Son" point to the conclusion that the mother has had a hard life?
   A. She declares that she has been "a-climbin' on."
   B. She says that life has had "tacks in it, / And splinters."
   C. She warns, "Don't you set down on the steps."
   D. She has been "reachin' landin's, / And turnin' corners."

_____ 4. What is the speaker's message in "Mother to Son"?
   A. Sit and rest once in a while.
   B. Strive to climb crystal stairs.
   C. Keep trying no matter what.
   D. Walk on carpeted floors.

_____ 5. Which of your senses can best help you picture this passage from "The Village Blacksmith"?
   Under a spreading chestnut tree / The village smithy stands; / The smith, a mighty man is he, / With large and sinewy hands.
   A. sight
   B. hearing
   C. taste
   D. touch

____ 6. Which kind of figurative language is represented by these lines from "The Village Blacksmith"?

> You can hear him swing his heavy sledge, . . . / Like a sexton ringing the village bell.

    A. simile

    B. metaphor

    C. symbolism

    D. personification

____ 7. Why does the blacksmith in "The Village Blacksmith" weep when his daughter sings?

    A. She has a beautiful voice.

    B. He loves music.

    C. She has overcome hardships.

    D. He is reminded of her mother.

____ 8. Which details in "The Village Blacksmith" lead you to conclude that the black-smith is a good man?

    I.   He works hard.

    II. He is dependable.

    III. He sits in church with his sons.

    IV. He rejoices when he hears his daughter sing.

    A. I

    B. I and II

    C. III and IV

    D. I, II, III, and IV

____ 9. Which statement best expresses the main point of "The Village Blacksmith"?

    A. A strong man is capable of loving his wife and children.

    B. Although he appears to be strong, the blacksmith is weak.

    C. Honesty, love, and hard word help us get through life.

    D. A blacksmith is likely to be the most honest man in town.

____ 10. To which animal is the fog compared in "Fog"?

    A. a lion

    B. a tiger

    C. a cat

    D. a dog

_____ 11. Which word best describes the fog in the poem "Fog"?

A. noisy

B. silent

C. spooky

D. transparent

_____ 12. Which kind of figurative language is used in "Fog"?

A. simile

B. symbol

C. extended metaphor

D. personification

Vocabulary and Grammar

_____ 13. Who is most likely to be described as *brawny*?

A. a doctor

B. an athlete

C. a baby

D. a teacher

_____ 14. What part of the body is most likely to be described as *sinewy*?

A. the teeth

B. the shoulders

C. the eyes

D. the blood

_____ 15. Which sentence contains an appositive phrase?

A. The mother talks to her son about her attitude toward life.

B. The mother, the speaker in the poem, wants to help her son.

C. The mother tells her son about her life, which has been hard.

D. The mother, who is the speaker in the poem, talks to her son.

Essay

16. In an essay, discuss the use of figurative language in "Fog." First, identify the type of figurative language that characterizes the poem, and then explain how that language is represented in the poem. Include a definition of the kind of figurative language that you discuss.

17. The mother in "Mother to Son" and the blacksmith in "The Village Blacksmith" serve as models. In an essay, write about one of those poems. Explain the lesson about life that the mother or the blacksmith teaches, and explain why that lesson is important. Cite at least three details from the poem that support the conclusions you draw.

18. **Thinking About the Big Question: What is the best way to communicate?** Think about the images featured in "Mother to Son," "The Village Blacksmith," and "Fog." Two of the poems feature people, and the other poem features an act of nature. Which image communicated the poem's message to you most effectively? Explain your response in an essay supported by specific examples from the text.

Poetry Collection: Langston Hughes, Henry Wadsworth Longfellow, Carl Sandburg
Selection Test B

Critical Reading *Identify the letter of the choice that best completes the statement or answers the question.*

____ 1. In "Mother to Son," what does the "crystal stair" represent?
   A. an easy life
   B. a hard life
   C. a satisfactory life
   D. a transparent life

____ 2. What is the mother referring to in the following lines from "Mother to Son"?
   It's had tacks in it, / And splinters, / And boards torn up.

   A. repairs to be made
   B. successes of the past
   C. hopes for the future
   D. difficulties in life

____ 3. What lesson does the mother in "Mother to Son" try to impart to her son?
   A. Rest when you grow weary.
   B. Strive to become wealthy.
   C. Keep going no matter what.
   D. Stay physically active.

____ 4. Which phrase best captures the symbolic meaning of this line from "Mother to Son"?
   places with no carpet on the floor— / Bare.

   A. bare elegance
   B. lack of luxury
   C. street life
   D. easy comfort

____ 5. What conclusion about the mother can you draw from the details in these lines from "Mother to Son"?
   For I'se still goin', honey, / I'se still climbin'.

   A. She is full of despair.
   B. She has not given up.
   C. She is becoming exhausted.
   D. She knows she will die soon.

____ 6. What is Longfellow's attitude toward the blacksmith in "The Village Blacksmith"?
   A. deep admiration
   B. mild puzzlement
   C. slight annoyance
   D. lighthearted criticism

_____ 7. What conclusion can you draw about the blacksmith from the details in these lines
from "The Village Blacksmith"?

Week in, week out, from morn till night, / You can hear his bellows blow.

A. He likes to work at night.
B. He ignores his family.
C. He works hard.
D. He gets up early.

_____ 8. To which of your senses does this line from "The Village Blacksmith" appeal?

[He] swing[s] his heavy sledge / With measured beat and slow.

A. taste and touch
B. sight and hearing
C. smell and touch
D. sight and smell

_____ 9. Who is "my worthy friend" in the following lines from "The Village Blacksmith"?

Thanks, thanks, to thee, my worthy friend, / For the lesson thou hast taught!

A. the blacksmith's mother
B. the blacksmith's daughter
C. the blacksmith
D. the speaker in the poem

_____ 10. Which of the following lines from "The Village Blacksmith" contains a simile?
A. "Week in, week out, from morn till night / You can hear his bellows blow."
B. "And catch the burning sparks that fly / Like chaff from a threshing floor."
C. "He hears his daughter's voice, . . . / And it makes his heart rejoice."
D. "Thus at the flaming forge of life / Our fortunes must be wrought."

_____ 11. What is the meaning of these lines from "The Village Blacksmith"?

He . . . looks the whole world in the face, / For he owes not any man.

A. He is poor.
B. He is not in debt.
C. He has few possessions.
D. He earns a great deal of money.

_____ 12. The figure of speech most prominent in "Fog" is
A. a simile.
B. a symbol.
C. a metaphor.
D. an extended metaphor.

_____ 13. To what is the fog compared in "Fog"?
A. a woman
B. a cat
C. a harbor
D. a city

____ 14. In "Fog," how does the fog move?
- A. silently
- B. cautiously
- C. awkwardly
- D. sleekly

Vocabulary and Grammar

____ 15. In which sentence is *haunches* used correctly?
- A. Doing a headstand, the acrobat carried her weight on her *haunches*.
- B. As it prepared to pounce on its prey, the tiger crouched on its *haunches*.
- C. Jumping off the washing machine, the cat landed feet first, on its *haunches*.
- D. Lifting weights with his hands, the athlete developed powerful *haunches*.

____ 16. Where would you most likely see a *brawny* person?
- A. on a football team
- B. on a debating team
- C. in law school
- D. in an orchestra

____ 17. Who would most likely be *sinewy*?
- A. a construction worker
- B. a train conductor
- C. a physicist
- D. a truck driver

____ 18. What is the appositive phrase in this sentence?

The village blacksmith, a mighty man, is loved by his neighbors.

- A. "The village blacksmith"
- B. "a mighty man"
- C. "is loved by"
- D. "his neighbors"

____ 19. What is the appositive phrase in this sentence?

Wanting to help her son, the mother in "Mother to Son," the speaker in the poem, gives him advice.

- A. "Wanting to help her son"
- B. "the mother in 'Mother to Son'"
- C. "the speaker in the poem"
- D. "gives him advice"

Essay

20. Carl Sandburg's poem "Fog" hints at a scene at a specific moment in time but provides few details. In an essay, name and describe the scene and the moment, and explain the change that occurs. Then, describe the scene more fully, adding details that provide a fuller picture.

21. In an essay, cite an example of a simile and of an extended metaphor in "Mother to Son," "The Village Blacksmith," or "Fog." Then, explain what makes each comparison a simile or an extended metaphor.

22. **Thinking About the Big Question: What is the best way to communicate?** Think about the images conveyed in "Mother to Son," "The Village Blacksmith," and "Fog." Two of the poems portray people, and the other poem portrays an act of nature. Which image did you find most effective in communicating the message of the poet? In an essay, choose one of the poems, and offer an opinion about the strength of the image's ability to communicate the poet's message.

Study these words from the poems. Then, complete the activities that follow.

Word List A

clattered [KLAT uhrd] *v.* rattled noisily
The window shutters <u>clattered</u> during the storm.

clutching [KLUTCH ing] *v.* holding tightly
<u>Clutching</u> a flashlight, Liz entered the dark basement.

dazed [DAYZD] *adj.* stunned or bewildered
<u>Dazed</u> from a blow to his head, Sam stumbled, unable to walk straight.

gusty [GUS tee] *adj.* windy, especially in bursts
The <u>gusty</u> weather made it difficult for the captain to steer the ship.

notions [NOH shuhnz] *n.* general ideas or impressions
Myra's <u>notions</u> about Italy changed after she visited Venice.

shattered [SHAT uhrd] *v.* broke into pieces
The ceramic vase <u>shattered</u> as it hit the cement floor.

Word List B

arc [AHRK] *n.* a part of a curve, especially of a circle
The <u>arc</u> of the thrown ball was high and wide.

bar [BAHR] *v.* to block as if with bars; prevent
Nick's injury will <u>bar</u> him from playing in the football game.

cascade [kas KAYD] *n.* a waterfall or similar fall of material
A <u>cascade</u> of water rushed forth when the dam gave way.

desperation [des puh RAY shuhn] *n.* a state of hopelessness that causes reckless behavior
In <u>desperation</u>, Sally sold her Persian carpet so she could buy food.

dusk [DUSK] *n.* the darkest part of twilight, just before night falls
The baseball game continued past <u>dusk</u> and into the night.

tawny [TAW nee] *adj.* light brown or brownish-orange in color
The big cat's <u>tawny</u> fur helped it blend in with the dry grass.

Name _____ Date _____

Poetry by Alfred Noyes and Gregory Djanikian
Vocabulary Warm-up Exercises

Exercise A *Fill in each blank in the paragraph below with an appropriate word from Word List A. Use each word only once.*

Carla had some interesting [1] _____ about roller coasters. She feared that on a [2] _____ day, the wind could blow a car right off the track. To have Carla face her fear, her friends decided to bring her to the amusement park. That day, they convinced her to ride the roller coaster. Carla stood nervously while the empty coaster [3] _____ up the track and pulled alongside her. She climbed in and, [4] _____ the safety bar, she waited. Her eyes were closed. The coaster took off, zipped around, and came to a stop. The ride was over before Carla knew it. She left the car with a [5] _____ expression on her face. "My fears have been [6] _____!" Carla exclaimed. "Let's get in line again!"

Exercise B *Answer the questions with complete sentences or explanations.*

1. Describe the <u>arc</u> a ball might take if the batter hit a home run.

   _____

2. What might someone use to <u>bar</u> entrance to a room?

   _____

3. What would you call a constant, naturally flowing <u>cascade</u> of water?

   _____

4. If driven by <u>desperation</u>, what might a basketball team do at the last minute?

   _____

5. If you were in a car at <u>dusk</u>, would you expect the driver to turn on the headlights?

   _____

6. Would you describe someone with black hair as having <u>tawny</u> hair?

   _____

   _____

Name _____ Date _____

Poetry by Alfred Noyes and Gregory Djanikian
Reading Warm-up A

Read the following passage. Pay special attention to the underlined words. Use a separate sheet of paper for your written answers.

The year was 1896. It was a bright August day. An American named George Washington Carmack was crouching down at the bank of an ice-cold creek, sifting sand. Suddenly he let out a loud yell that <u>shattered</u> the silence. This alerted his two companions to what he had found. <u>Clutching</u> one another with joy, he and his two friends embraced and began to dance. Finally, the men fell to the ground and lay <u>dazed</u> by their discovery.

What made them act like this? They had discovered gold. Their dreams of instant wealth suddenly seemed within reach. Seldom in American history have economic conditions been as bad as they were then. The Depression of the 1890s pushed people to desperate things. The discovery of gold in the Yukon would start a stampede of tens of thousands of prospectors—men and women.

Eighty percent of the prospectors were Americans. Most who ventured north thought they were headed for Alaska. Instead, they were going to an area of northwest Canada, near the Arctic Circle. Cold, <u>gusty</u> weather marked the region.

Some inexperienced prospectors had strange <u>notions</u> about the area. They thought they could buy food along the trail. How wrong they were! After some of these people starved to death, the Canadian government stepped in. It required that everyone entering the Klondike carry in enough supplies for a year. Imagine the noise the prospectors made as they <u>clattered</u> across the hostile landscape hauling all that equipment.

The Klondike gold rush lasted until early 1900. Then gold was discovered in Nome, Alaska, and another rush was on.

1. Circle the words that tell what <u>shattered</u> the silence. What does *shattered* mean in this passage?

2. Circle the word that is close in meaning to <u>clutching</u>. Write a sentence using the word *clutching*.

3. Rewrite the sentence with <u>dazed</u>, using a synonym for the word. Then, use *dazed* in a sentence of your own.

4. Circle the word that tells what was <u>gusty</u>. Define *gusty*.

5. Underline the sentence that explains one of the strange <u>notions</u> the prospectors had. Give a synonym for *notions*.

6. Underline the words that help you understand <u>clattered</u>. Write a sentence using the word *clattered*.

Name _____ Date _____

Poetry by Alfred Noyes and Gregory Djanikian
Reading Warm-up B

Read the following passage. Pay special attention to the underlined words. Use a separate sheet of paper for your written answers.

The sun was low in the sky and the baseball game had already been going on for three hours. The score was tied at the bottom of the twelfth, and none of the Sharks wanted the game to go another extra inning. As <u>dusk</u> approached and the sky grew darker, Billy, the youngest member of the Sharks, was tired, worried, and nervous. He was fighting off, as best he could, the feeling of <u>desperation</u> that kept trying to intrude on his mind. Losing this game would end the Sharks' season. Even worse, a loss would <u>bar</u> them from the playoffs, and Billy wasn't sure he could handle the disappointment.

His best chum, Anthony, was sitting on the bench as Billy warmed up for his next at-bat. Anthony gave Billy a thumbs-up sign, as if to say Billy could save the day.

As Billy took his place at bat the catcher crouched behind him, signaling to the pitcher. The catcher thought he knew all about Billy—his strengths and weaknesses. For the first five pitches, it seemed as if the catcher had been right. After three balls and two strikes, Billy knew this was the moment. He took a swing and connected hard. The ball sailed in a high <u>arc</u> toward the bleachers.

As the other team howled in disappointment, Billy ran the bases. In the bleachers, his grandfather stood up, held out his hand, and laughed in glee as the ball dropped into his old, <u>tawny</u> leather baseball mitt. "That's my grandson," he said proudly to the people sitting near him.

By the time Billy reached home plate, Anthony was standing with a bucket, ready to shower his friend in a <u>cascade</u> of water. He poured the bucket over Billy's head as if offering him a crown. The soaking hero was then carried on his team members' shoulders in a victory celebration on the field.

1. Underline the words that describe what happened as <u>dusk</u> approached. What is a typical activity you might be doing at *dusk*?

2. Underline the nearby sentence that tells the cause of Billy's feeling of <u>desperation</u>. Then, use *desperation* in a sentence.

3. Circle the word that tells what a loss would <u>bar</u> the Sharks from. Write a synonym for *bar*.

4. Circle the word that tells what sailed in an <u>arc</u>. Write a sentence, describing something else that might sail or fly in an *arc*.

5. Circle the two words that tell what was <u>tawny</u>. What else might be described as *tawny*?

6. Circle the three nearby words that give clues to the meaning of <u>cascade</u>. Where might you see a *cascade* of water?

Name _____ Date _____

Poetry by Alfred Noyes and Gregory Djanikian
Writing About the Big Question

What is the best way to communicate?

Big Question Vocabulary

communicate	contribute	enrich	entertain	express
inform	learn	listen	media	produce
react	speak	teach	technology	transmit

A. *Use one or more words from the list above to complete each sentence.*

1. Words are a great way to _____ with other people.

2. You can _____ yourself to others through the words you choose.

3. When you _____, what you say tells others about yourself.

4. Your choice of words can _____ to others' understanding of you.

B. *Respond to each item with a complete sentence.*

1. Write the words you might speak to introduce yourself to someone new.

   _____

   _____

   _____

2. Explain what you would like to communicate about yourself to someone you have just met. Use two Big Question vocabulary words in your response.

   _____

   _____

   _____

C. *In each of these narrative poems, people communicate in an unconventional way. Complete this sentence. Then, write a short paragraph connecting the sentences to the Big Question.*

_____

can be more expressive than words.

Name _____ Date _____

Poetry by Alfred Noyes and Gregory Djanikian
Literary Analysis: Comparing Narrative Poems

Narrative poetry combines elements of fiction and poetry to tell a story. Like short stories, narrative poetry usually includes characters, setting, plot, conflict, and point of view. Like other poems, narrative poetry uses sound devices, such as rhythm and rhyme, to bring out the musical qualities of the language. It also uses figurative language to create memorable images, or word pictures.

Narrative poetry is well suited to a wide range of stories. For example, narrative poems may tell romantic tales about knights and ladies, heroic deeds, amazing events, or larger-than-life characters. In contrast, the form may be used to relate everyday stories about ordinary people.

The poems presented in this collection blend elements of fiction and poetry in a memorable way. As you read these poems, look for ways in which each one blends the elements of narration and poetry.

DIRECTIONS: *Complete this chart about the narrative poems in this collection. In the second column, briefly describe the poem's plot and conflict. In the third column, describe the sound devices and/or figurative language in the poem.*

Poem	Plot and Conflict	Poetic Devices
"The Highwayman"		
"How I Learned English"		

Name _____ Date _____

Poetry by Alfred Noyes and Gregory Djanikian
Vocabulary Builder

Word List

bound   strive   torrent   transfixed   whimper   writhing

A. DIRECTIONS: *Pay attention to the way the italicized vocabulary word is used in each sentence. Decide whether each statement is true or false. Write* T *or* F. *Then, explain your answer.*

1. If a dog were *bound* to a tree, it would be free to roam.

   T / F: _____ **Explanation:** _____

2. Someone *writhing* in pain is lying still.

   T / F: _____ **Explanation:** _____

3. A *torrent* of rain is likely to cause a river to overflow its banks.

   T / F: _____ **Explanation:** _____

4. If children *whimper*, they are probably content.

   T / F: _____ **Explanation:** _____

5. Someone *transfixed* by fear is running to escape danger.

   T / F: _____ **Explanation:** _____

6. People who *strive* are usually very lazy.

   T / F: _____ **Explanation:** _____

B. WORD STUDY: *Change each underlined word into another form from its word family. Answer the question using the new word.*

1. What can cause a small waterfall to become a *torrent*?

   _____

2. Why are people often *transfixed* when they watch a scary movie?

   _____

3. Why should a wound be *bound*?

   _____

Name _____ Date _____

Poetry by Alfred Noyes and Gregory Djanikian
Integrated Language Skills: Support for Writing to Compare Literary Works

Use this chart to take notes for an essay comparing and contrasting the stories that are told in the narrative poems in this collection.

Point of Comparison	"The Highwayman"	"How I Learned English"
Who narrates the poem? Is it a character in the poem or someone outside the poem?		
Is there any suspense? If so, when does it occur, and why?		
How do the poetic elements increase my interest in or my appreciation of the story?		

Now, use your notes to write an essay comparing and contrasting the poems' stories.

Poetry by Alfred Noyes and Gregory Djanikian
Open-Book Test

Short Answer *Write your responses to the questions in this section on the lines provided.*

1. Think about what the word *highwayman* means. What is the highwayman preparing to do when he tells Bess to wait for him? Use details from the poem to support your answer.

   _____

   _____

   _____

2. In "The Highwayman," Bess is bound to the foot of her bed. Because she is bound, what is she prevented from doing? Explain.

   _____

   _____

   _____

3. Why does the highwayman rush back to the inn after hearing how Bess died? Use details from the poem to support your answer.

   _____

   _____

   _____

4. In "How I Learned English," the speaker is transfixed as the ball approaches. Why would it be a mistake for a deer to be transfixed by the headlights of a car? Explain.

   _____

   _____

   _____

5. In "How I Learned English," the narrator laughs at his situation and then Joe Barone helps him up. Explain why both of these events are important in the narrator's eyes.

   _____

   _____

   _____

6. In "How I Learned English," in what way is the narrator "doing all right" by the end of the poem? Use details from the poem to support your answer.

   _____

   _____

   _____

7. Rhyme is the repetition of sounds at the end of words. Which poem rhymes, "The Highwayman" or "How I Learned English"? Give an example from the first two lines of the poem.

   _____

   _____

   _____

8. Explain what makes "The Highwayman" and "How I Learned English" narrative poems.

   _____

   _____

9. Complete the chart by listing the point of view of the narrator of each poem. Then, on the lines, explain how the point of view of "The Highwayman" differs from that of "How I Learned English."

	Narrator
"The Highwayman"	
"How I Learned English"	

   _____

   _____

10. Compare how suspense is created in the "The Highwayman" with how it is created in "How I Learned English." Include details from the poems in your answer.

   _____

   _____

   _____

   _____

Essay

Write an extended response to the question of your choice or to the question or questions your teacher assigns you.

11. The setting is where and when a story takes place. Like short stories, narrative poems include a setting that is important to the overall effect. In an essay, compare the settings of "The Highwayman" and "How I Learned English." Describe the setting of each poem and explain why it is important to the poem. Then, tell in which poem you think the setting could more easily change without affecting the story. Support your opinion with examples from the poem of your choice.

12. Narrative poems tell a story, so like a short story they include a conflict. In an essay, compare the conflicts in "The Highwayman" and "How I Learned English." Describe the conflict in each poem and tell how it is resolved. Then, discuss which poem's conflict is more realistic, and why. Use examples from the poems to support your ideas.

13. The plot of "The Highwayman" could easily and effectively be told in prose. In an essay, explain why you think the poetic version of the story has remained popular. Give examples from the poem to support your ideas. Conclude the essay by telling what the story would lose or gain if it were written in prose.

14. **Thinking About the Big Question: What is the best way to communicate?** Think about the communication that takes place in both "The Highwayman" and "How I Learned English." In an essay, explain what each poem suggests is the best way to communicate. Use details from the poems to support your ideas.

Oral Response

15. Go back to question 1, 6, 8, or 10 or to the question your teacher assigns you. Take a few minutes to expand your answer and prepare an oral response. Find additional details in "The Highwayman" and "How I Learned English" that will support your points. If necessary, make notes to guide your response.

Name _____ Date _____

Poetry by Alfred Noyes and Gregory Djanikian
Selection Test A

Critical Reading *Identify the letter of the choice that best answers the question.*

_____ 1. Who overhears the conversation between the highwayman and Bess?
   A. Tim the ostler
   B. the landlord
   C. the redcoats
   D. the narrator

_____ 2. What is the highwayman planning to do when he asks Bess to wait for him?
   A. take part in a riding contest
   B. commit a robbery
   C. exchange some possessions for gold
   D. fight the redcoats

_____ 3. What is suspenseful about "The Highwayman"?
   A. knowing that the redcoats are waiting to capture the highwayman
   B. knowing that Bess does not realize that Tim the ostler loves her
   C. knowing that Bess has plaited a red love knot into her long hair
   D. knowing that the redcoats have not said anything to the landlord

_____ 4. The opening of "The Highwayman" states, "The moon was a ghostly galleon tossed upon cloudy skies." What does that statement suggest about the atmosphere, or mood, of the poem?
   A. It will be humorous.
   B. It will be sad.
   C. It will be dramatic.
   D. It will be jolly.

_____ 5. In what way is the setting of "How I Learned English" important to the subject of the poem?
   A. The all-American setting contrasts with the narrator's foreignness.
   B. The ballpark setting helps create great tension.
   C. The Pennsylvania setting emphasizes the theme of liberty.
   D. The schoolyard setting suggests that the narrator has a lot to learn.

_____ 6. Where does "How I Learned English" take place?
   A. in an empty lot
   B. in a city park
   C. in a stadium
   D. in a backyard

____ 7. Why does the narrator of "How I Learned English" call his head his shin?

A. He is confused because he has been hit in the head.

B. He is trying to get the other boys to laugh.

C. *Shin* means "head" in his native language.

D. He does not know much English.

____ 8. In what way is "How I Learned English" different from "The Highwayman"?

A. It does not rhyme.

B. It is not funny.

C. There is no conflict.

D. The characters are not named.

____ 9. Which two kinds of literature are narrative poems like?

A. biographies and essays

B. narrative essays and stories

C. other poems and lyrics

D. short stories and other poems

Vocabulary

____ 10. Why might a *torrent* be dangerous?

A. People could starve because of it.

B. People could drown because of it.

C. People could be electrocuted by it.

D. People could be burned by it.

____ 11. What is most likely true of people who *strive*?

A. They get what they want.

B. They are exceedingly lazy.

C. They have a lot of friends.

D. They are exceedingly poor.

____ 12. What is a *transfixed* deer doing?

A. waiting

B. looking around

C. listening

D. standing still

Essay

13. Both "The Highwayman" and "How I Learned English" describe memorable characters. In an essay, compare Bess in "The Highwayman" with the narrator of "How I Learned English." Answer these questions: What does each character do that is important? Which character is more memorable? Support your opinion with at least two details from the relevant poem.

14. Like short stories, narrative poems include a setting that contributes to the overall effect. In an essay, compare the settings of the poems in this collection: "The Highwayman" and "How I Learned English." Answer these questions about the two poems: What is the setting of each poem? Why is the setting important to the poem? Which setting do you find more interesting? Why? Support your opinion with at least two details from the poem whose setting you find more interesting.

15. **Thinking About the Big Question: What is the best way to communicate?** Think about the communication that takes place in both "The Highwayman" and "How I Learned English." In "The Highwayman," there is communication between two lovers. In "How I Learned English," there is communication between young boys in a playground. In an essay, explain what each poem suggests is the best way to communicate. Use details from the poems to support your ideas.

Poetry by Alfred Noyes and Gregory Djanikian
Selection Test B

Critical Reading *Identify the letter of the choice that best completes the statement or answers the question.*

____ 1. Which of these lines from "The Highwayman" best contributes to a feeling of suspense?
   A. "And he rode with a jeweled twinkle"
   B. "Bess, the landlord's daughter"
   C. "Plaiting a dark red love knot into her long black hair"
   D. "Nearer he came and nearer. Her face was like a light."

____ 2. How do the redcoats know that the highwayman will come to see Bess?
   A. It is common knowledge in the town.
   B. Tim the ostler has told them.
   C. They had spies follow him many times.
   D. Bess's father has told them.

____ 3. Which of these details is most closely related to the central conflict in "The Highwayman"?
   A. Bess plaits a "dark red love knot into her long black hair."
   B. The highwayman's horse makes a *tlot-tlot* sound as it gallops.
   C. Bess hears the highwayman coming before the redcoats do.
   D. The highwayman hears the news that Bess has died.

____ 4. Why does the highwayman hurry back to the inn after he hears that Bess has died?
   A. He wants to attend her funeral.
   B. He wants to comfort her father.
   C. He wants to view her body.
   D. He wants to take revenge.

____ 5. Which group of words best summarizes the themes of "The Highwayman"?
   A. love, betrayal, honor, death
   B. riding, whistling, waiting, dying
   C. secrecy, passion, theft, fear
   D. trouble, escape, return, sorrow

____ 6. At the end of "The Highwayman," what effect do the phrases "blood-red" and "wine-red" have?
   A. They show that the highwayman pays close attention to his clothing.
   B. They emphasize the bloodshed that has already occurred and will soon occur.
   C. They hint that the highwayman is smeared with Bess's blood.
   D. They show that the highwayman has not yet fought with the soldiers.

____ 7. How is the setting of "The Highwayman" important to the poem's mood?
   A. It creates a mood of joy and anticipation.
   B. It creates a mood of terror.
   C. It creates a dramatic tense mood.
   D. It creates a mood of humor and silliness.

____ 8. What makes "How I Learned English" a narrative poem?
   A. It uses regular rhythm and rhyme.
   B. The speaker is a character in the poem.
   C. It contains a surprise ending.
   D. It is a poem that tells a story.

____ 9. In "How I Learned English," why do the other boys laugh at the narrator when he gets hit in the head with a baseball?
   A. He has missed the ball repeatedly.
   B. He has tripped over his own feet.
   C. He has a foreign accent.
   D. He calls his head his shin.

____ 10. In "How I Learned English," why is it important that Joe Barone helps the narrator up and dusts him off?
   A. It shows that the boys accept the narrator.
   B. It shows that the narrator is a good sport.
   C. It shows the narrator that the boys are insincere.
   D. It shows that the boys feel pity for the narrator.

____ 11. Who is telling the story of "How I Learned English"?
   A. a character outside the poem
   B. the speaker in the poem
   C. Joe Barone
   D. Bill Corson

____ 12. In which way is "How I Learned English" different from "The Highwayman"?
   A. It contains no rhyme or rhythm.
   B. Its narrator is a character in the poem.
   C. It is not set in the Arctic.
   D. It contains a conflict.

____ 13. In which way is the narrator of "The Highwayman" different from the narrator of "How I Learned English"?
   A. The narrator is a man.
   B. The narrator is a woman.
   C. The narrator is a character in the poem.
   D. The narrator is not a character in the poem.

____ 14. What makes "The Highwayman" and "How I Learned English" narrative poems?
   A. They use figurative language creatively.
   B. They use sound devices, like rhyme and rhythm.
   C. They combine elements of fiction and poetry to tell a story.
   D. They tell stories of heroic deeds performed by larger-than-life characters.

Vocabulary

_____ 15. In which sentence does the word *torrent* make sense?

A. A *torrent* of rain flooded the highway.

B. The highwayman was not *torrent* of the red coats.

C. The redcoats might *torrent* poor Bess.

D. The sky was tipped with *torrent* clouds.

_____ 16. In which sentence does *strive* make sense?

A. The highwayman had to *strive* on his horse.

B. The moon would soon *strive* across the clouds.

C. Gregory Djanikian would *strive* to play baseball well.

D. The ballplayers had to *strive* when the ball hit the new boy.

_____ 17. What would a *transfixed* person be doing?

A. crossing a road

B. making a change

C. receiving help

D. standing still

_____ 18. A *writhing* person is most likely

A. in pain.

B. angry.

C. in trouble.

D. happy.

Essay

19. Both "The Highwayman" and "How I Learned English" describe memorable characters. In an essay, compare the highwayman and the narrator of "How I Learned English." Answer these questions: What does each character do that is memorable? Is either character inclined to take risks? Does either character do anything extraordinary or heroic? Explain your answers, citing details from the poems to support your points.

20. The setting plays a large part in both "The Highwayman" and "How I Learned English." In an essay, compare the influence of each poem's setting on its characters, plot, and conflict. Answer these questions: How does the setting of "The Highwayman" affect the tone of the poem? How does the setting of "How I Learned English" affect the speaker in that poem? What does the setting—Williamsport, Pennsylvania—contribute to the story?

21. Narrative poems tell a story, and like a short story or a novel, include a conflict. In an essay, compare the conflicts in the selections in this collection: "The Highwayman" and "How I Learned English." Tell what the conflict is in each poem. Then, answer these questions: Do the conflicts create suspense? How are they resolved? Which poem's conflict is more realistic? Which conflict makes the poem more enjoyable to read?

22. **Thinking About the Big Question: What is the best way to communicate?** Think about the communication that takes place in both "The Highwayman" and "How I Learned English." In an essay, explain what each poem suggests is the best way to communicate. Use details from the poems to support your ideas.

Name _____   Date _____

Exposition: Problem-and-Solution Essay

Prewriting: Finding a Topic

Complete the following chart to help you brainstrom for problems to solve.

Problems to solve in neighborhood, community, or city:
1._____
2._____
3._____

Problems to solve in school:
1._____
2._____
3._____

Problems to solve in nation
1._____
2._____
3._____

Prewriting: Brainstorming for Solutions

Choose one of the problems you listed in the chart above. Then use this chart to help you brainstorm several solutions to that problem, and list their strengths and weaknesses (if any).

Solution 1: _____

Strengths: _____
_____
Weakness: _____
_____

Problem: _____

Solution 2: _____

Strengths: _____
_____
Weakness: _____
_____

Solution 3: _____

Strengths: _____
_____
Weakness: _____
_____

Writing Workshop—Unit 4, Part 1
Writing for Assessment: Integrating Grammar Skills

Revising Sentences by Adding Verbals

A **verbal** is a verb form used as another part of speech. **Participles** are one type of verbal. **Present participles** end in -*ing*. **Past participles** usually end in -*ed*. The past participles of some verbs are irregular, formed with endings other than -*ed*. For example, *broken* is the past participle of *break*. A **participial phrase** consists of a present or past participle and its modifiers or complements. The entire phrase acts as an adjective, modifying a noun or a pronoun.

One way to eliminate choppy sentences is to combine them using participles and participial phrases.

Choppy:	The water boiled. It sent steam into the air.
Combined:	The *boiling* water sent steam into the air.
Choppy:	Leah boiled the potatoes. She added salt and pepper.
Combined:	*Boiling the potatoes*, Leah added salt and pepper.

Identifying Participles or Participial Phrases

A. DIRECTIONS: *Underline the single participle or participial phrase in each sentence, and circle the noun or pronoun it modifies.*

1. A talented poet visited our school.
2. Standing in front of the students, she read her poetry aloud.
3. Her stirring voice carried to all corners of the room.
4. The students, fascinated by her performance, listened in silence.

Fixing Choppy Sentences by Using Verbals

B. DIRECTIONS: *For each item, combine the two choppy sentences into one sentence that uses a single participle or a participial phrase. Write your new sentence on the line provided.*

1. A speaker visited. She told us all about Robert Frost.

   _____

2. Frost was born in San Francisco. He grew up in New England.

   _____

3. He traveled to England. He published his first book of poetry there.

   _____

4. The poet became very famous. He was very talented.

   _____

Unit 4: Poetry
Benchmark Test 7

MULTIPLE CHOICE

Reading Skill: Drawing Conclusions

1. Which of these steps is most important when drawing conclusions?
   A. focusing on the main ideas
   B. pulling together several details
   C. separating fact from opinion
   D. restating in simpler words

2. Why is asking questions important when you are drawing conclusions?
   A. to gather people's opinions
   B. to check facts for accuracy
   C. to identify details and make connections
   D. to understand background information

3. What do the images in the following poem lead you to conclude?

   Young birds seesaw on their first flights.
   Melting snows churn and gurgle in woodland streams.
   Early crocuses splatter purple, yellow, and white on people's lawns.

   A. It is spring.
   B. It is summer.
   C. It is autumn.
   D. It is winter.

4. After reading the following poem, what conclusion can be drawn about the speaker?

   The memory of cannon fire fades like evening mists.
   Footsteps echo softly on the grass above me.
   My bride kneels at a stone.

   A. The speaker is a soldier in his first battle, fearful of what is to come.
   B. The speaker is a soldier killed in war who left a wife behind.
   C. The speaker is a soldier who feels bad about those he killed in war.
   D. The speaker is a soldier returning home from war.

Read this selection from a poem by Lewis Carroll. Then, answer the questions about it.

> The sun was shining on the sea,
>   Shining with all his might:
> He did his very best to make
>   The billows smooth and bright—
> And this was odd, because it was
>   The middle of the night.
>
> The moon was shining sulkily
>   Because she thought the sun
> Had got no business to be there
>   After the day was done—
> "It's very rude of him," she said,
>   "To come and spoil the fun!"
>
> —from "The Walrus and the Carpenter" by Lewis Carroll

5. Which conclusions can be drawn about Lewis Carroll's poem?

    A. It is realistic and gritty.   C. It is horrible and scary.

    B. It is elegant and sophisticated.   D. It is whimsical and fantastic.

6. What is the relationship between the sun and moon in Lewis Carroll's poem?

    A. They are friends.   C. They are brother and sister.

    B. They are rivals.   D. They are complete strangers.

7. Which of these details helps you conclude that Lewis Carroll's purpose was humor?

    A. The sun is shining on the sea.   C. The moon is shining on the sea.

    B. The sun is shining brightly.   D. The moon is shining sulkily.

Reading Skill: Follow Technical Directions

The following selection is part of a manual on how to use a digital camera. Read the selection. Then, answer the questions that follow.

Taking Pictures in Auto Mode

In this mode, all you have to do is press the shutter button and let the camera do everything else.

1. Check that the camera is in *Shooting* mode.

2. Turn the shooting mode dial to *Auto*.

3. Aim the camera at the subject you wish to shoot.

4. Use the zoom lever to achieve the desired composition (relative subject size in the viewfinder).

5. Press the shutter button halfway. This automatically sets the exposure and focus.

  • Two beeps will sound when the camera has finished metering, and the upper indicator will light green or orange (flash on).

  • The lower indicator will blink yellow, and the beep will sound one time if the subject is difficult to focus on.

6. Press the shutter button all the way, fully releasing the shutter.

  • You will hear the shutter sound when the shot is complete.

  • The upper indicator blinks green when data is recorded onto the memory card.

  • The picture appears for about three seconds on the LCD monitor.

---

8. If you want to take a picture in the auto mode, which of the following should you do first?

    A. aim the camera   C. use the zoom lever

    B. press the shutter button halfway   D. turn the shooting mode dial to *Auto*

9. According to the passage, when could you see a yellow light?

    A. after pressing the shutter button half-way   C. while aiming the camera at the subject

    B. when turning the shooting mode dial   D. after pressing the shutter button all the way

10. What should you do if you want the subject to appear larger in the picture?
   A. fully release the shutter
   B. adjust the zoom lever
   C. turn the shooting mode dial
   D. press the shutter button halfway

Literary Analysis

11. Which of the following statements applies to a typical lyric poem?
   A. It is short and musical.
   B. It is long and complex.
   C. It tells a story.
   D. It sounds like spoken English.

12. Which of the following lines is most likely to begin a lyric poem?
   A. Once upon a time
   B. I wandered lonely as a cloud
   C. 'Twas the night before Christmas
   D. You are old, Father William

13. What is a concrete poem?
   A. a poem that provides concrete images as opposed to abstract ideas
   B. a poem that uses a strict pattern of rhyme and rhythm
   C. a poem arranged in a visual image that suggests its meaning
   D. a poem that states its theme instead of merely hinting at it

14. Where did the haiku originate?
   A. China
   B. Japan
   C. Korea
   D. India

15. Which statement describes the traditional form of a haiku poem?
   A. a three-line poem with seven syllables in the first and third lines and five syllables in the middle line
   B. a nine-line poem with five syllables in odd-numbered lines and seven syllables in even-numbered lines
   C. a poem of varying length in which all of the lines have at least five syllables and every other line ends in a rhyme
   D. a three-line poem with five syllables in the first and third lines and seven syllables in the middle line

16. What is the most common subject of traditional haiku poetry?
   A. nature
   B. love
   C. faith
   D. death

17. Which of the following is an example of figurative language?
   A. It's raining heavily today.
   B. It's raining so hard that the roof is beginning to shake.
   C. It's raining cats and dogs.
   D. The sound of the pounding rain echoes in the night.

18. Which of the following choices contains a simile?
   A. You look like a million dollars.
   B. I'll be there as long as you need me.
   C. I like to see it lap the miles.
   D. Try as he might, he still could not fly.

19. How is a metaphor different from a simile?
   A. It uses *like* instead of *as*.
   B. It compares more than two things.
   C. It states that one thing is another.
   D. It is not meant to be taken literally.

20. Which of the following is an example of personification?
    A. The dog barked louder than a thunderstorm.
    B. The thunder roared like a lion in a rage.
    C. The bus driver turned the corner abruptly.
    D. The clouds cried in sorrow.

21. What is the specific term for an object, a person, an animal, or a place that represents something other than itself?
    A. a simile
    B. a metaphor
    C. a symbol
    D. a figure of speech

22. What is the main purpose of a narrative poem?
    A. to describe a setting
    B. to convey character
    C. to express feelings
    D. to tell a story

23. A narrative poem blends elements of two main types of literature. What are they?
    A. poetry and essays
    B. drama and essays
    C. drama and nonfiction
    D. poetry and fiction

Vocabulary: Roots and Suffixes

24. Using your knowledge of the root -lum-, what does the word *luminous* mean in the following sentence?

    The sky was luminous with stars.
    A. shining
    B. speckled
    C. beautiful
    D. crowded

25. How does the meaning of the word *illuminate* reflect the meaning of the root -lum-?
    A. When you illuminate something, you show it to others.
    B. When you illuminate something, you are being helpful.
    C. When you illuminate something, you shed light on it.
    D. When you illuminate something, you conceal it.

26. How does the meaning of the word *diagram* reflect the meaning of the root -gram-?
    A. A diagram breaks up the text.
    B. A diagram is something you see.
    C. A diagram explains something.
    D. A diagram is something that is drawn.

27. What is the meaning of the word formed by adding the suffix -ly to the end of the word *proud*?
    A. showing a lack of pride
    B. in the manner of being proud
    C. acting in a way to make others proud
    D. hiding one's pride from others

28. To which word could you successfully add the suffix -y meaning "having"?
    A. hair
    B. arm
    C. foot
    D. wrist

29. Using your knowledge of the suffix -*y*, what does *sinewy* mean in the following sentence?

The athlete had sinewy arms.

A. enormous   C. powerful

B. capable   D. graceful

Grammar

30. Which of the following sentences contains an infinitive phrase?

A. Jake went to the library.   C. He likes to read poetry.

B. He is borrowing several books.   D. Reading poetry is fun.

31. What is the function of the infinitive phrase in the following sentence?

We lacked the strength to resist the advertiser's persuasive words.

A. noun   C. adjective

B. verb   D. adverb

32. What part of speech is an appositive?

A. noun or pronoun   C. adjective or adverb

B. noun or verb   D. noun, adjective, or adverb

33. Identify the appositive in the following sentence.

British mathematician Charles Lutwidge Dodgson used the pen name Lewis Carroll.

A. British mathematician   C. pen name

B. Charles Lutwidge Dodgson   D. Lewis Carroll

34. What type of participle is used in the following sentence?

The watered lawn looked refreshed.

A. present participle   C. future participle

B. past participle   D. participial phrase

35. Which of the following is the best definition of a participial phrase?

A. a phrase that is used as an adverb
   that modifies other adverbs

B. a phrase that usually ends in -*ed*, but
   may have irregular endings, and acts
   as a noun

C. a phrase that is often used as an adjective, modifying a noun or pronoun and
   can stand alone

D. a phrase that consists of a present or
   past participle and its modifiers, and
   acts as an adjective

ESSAY

36. Imagine that you are writing for assessment and are given the following writing prompt. As part of your prewriting, you are now gathering details for your response. On your paper or on a separate sheet, jot down key elements of your answer that you gather as part of the prewriting stage.

   Computers have many good points, but they also have some problems as well. Write a short essay about some of the benefits and drawbacks of computers. Consider their effects on lifestyle, productivity, and health.

37. Think about the types of poems you have read—lyric poems, concrete poems, and haikus. Choose a topic that interests you and write a poem using one of the types of poems above.

38. Write a short, creative paragraph that includes figurative language. You may write about the topic of your choice. Be sure to include several examples of similes and metaphors. Below your paragraph, explain what effect your use of figurative language has on your writing.

Unit 4: Poetry Skills Concept Map—2
What is the best way to communicate?

Literary Analysis:
Poetry

| A poem | has | sound devices | and | rhythm |

(demonstrated in this selection)
Selection name:

(demonstrated in this selection)
Selection name:

Basic Elements of Poetry
- Figurative Language
- Sound Devices
- Stanzas

Forms of Poetry
- Narrative
- Haiku
- Free Verse
- Lyric
- Ballads

Reading Skills and Strategies:
Paraphrasing

You can paraphrase a poem   by   reading aloud according to punctuation   and by   rereading the parts that are difficult

Informational Text:
Magazine Article

(demonstrated in this selection)
Selection name:

You can paraphrase, or restate in your own words, a magazine article   to   determine the main idea

Comparing Literary Works:
Imagery

(demonstrated in these selections)
Selection names:
1.
2.

Imagery   describes how subjects   taste, smell

look, sound, feel

Words you can use to discuss the Big Question

_____
_____
_____
_____
_____

Student Log

Complete this chart to track your assignments.

Writing	Extend Your Learning	Writing Workshop	Other Assignments

Vocabulary Warm-up Word Lists

Study these words from the poetry of Shel Silverstein, Eve Merriam, and James Berry. Then, complete the activities that follow.

Word List A

expectancy [ek SPEK tuhn see] *n.* a waiting for something to happen, an expectation
The dog's <u>expectancy</u> is that she will be fed at 6 P.M. each night.

mimic [MIM ik] *v.* to copy or imitate
The comedian humorously will <u>mimic</u> the way the politician speaks.

multiplied [MUHL tuh plyd] *v.* caused something to be an increased number, extent, or amount
The images of her face were <u>multiplied</u> many times in the collage.

remember [ri MEM buhr] *v.* to recall, to have something come to mind again
Dee could not <u>remember</u> where she put her keys.

simply [SIM plee] *adv.* absolutely or completely
The school <u>simply</u> would not allow the use of cell phones during classes.

wait [WAYT] *v.* to stay in a place or remain in readiness for something to happen
Barry will <u>wait</u> for his friends to meet him at the corner.

Word List B

dry [DRY] *adj.* having no moisture
The bread was stale and <u>dry</u>.

puddle [PUHD l] *n.* a small pool of water or rain
The little girl liked to put on her boots and splash in each <u>puddle</u>.

rumble [RUHM buhl] *n.* a deep, heavy, rolling sound
The <u>rumble</u> of the big drum could be heard far away.

soggy [SAHG ee] *adj.* soaked with water or another liquid
Emily squeezed the soapy water out of the <u>soggy</u> sponge.

splatter [SPLAT uhr] *n.* a splash or spatter
The butter will <u>splatter</u> when it is heated in the frying pan.

windowpane [WIN doh payn] *n.* a piece of glass in a window
Frosty designs formed on the <u>windowpane</u> during winter.

Poetry Collection: Shel Silverstein, Eve Merriam, and James Berry
Vocabulary Warm-up Exercises

Exercise A *Fill in each blank in the paragraph below with an appropriate word from Word List A. Use each word only once.*

Daniel's little sister Lucy [1] _____ could not [2] _____
for her pet hamster to have babies. Every day she checked the cage over and over again,
each time with great [3] _____, hoping to find the new babies. Sometimes she would [4] _____ the sound of an ambulance siren before she
checked the cage, pretending to be a doctor rushing to the scene to help the babies to be
born. Daniel would always [5] _____ the special day when the big event
finally happened. Lucy had cried out in great excitement for him to come and see. Sure
enough, the hamster family had [6] _____, and there were now several
tiny hamsters cuddled around their mother.

Exercise B *Decide whether each statement below is true or false. Explain your answers.*

1. The baseball broke the *windowpane* when Mike hit a homerun.
   T / F _____

2. The delicious chocolate pudding was extremely *dry*.
   T / F _____

3. The *rumble* of thunder is usually too soft to hear.
   T / F _____

4. If the potato chips are *soggy*, they are probably not very fresh.
   T / F _____

5. If you mix the pancake batter too vigorously, it is likely to *splatter*.
   T / F _____

6. If there is a *puddle* on the floor, you should be careful not to step in it.
   T / F _____

Poetry Collection: Shel Silverstein, Eve Merriam, and James Berry
Reading Warm-up A

Read the following passage. Pay special attention to the underlined words. Then, read it again, and complete the activities. Use a separate sheet of paper for your written answers.

Marc was busy practicing guitar one afternoon when he heard a knock at the door. He looked outside and saw it was a group of his new friends. They looked at him with a certain <u>expectancy</u>, motioning for him to join them. Marc and his family had recently moved into town, and Marc was very eager to fit in with the kids he had met at school.

"<u>Wait</u> a minute," he called to them from the window. Even though he had wanted to finish practicing his music, he quickly set his guitar down. His friends liked playing basketball, and although it wasn't Marc's favorite thing to do, he hurried out to join them. "Want to shoot some hoops?" asked Peter. More than shooting hoops, Marc <u>simply</u> wanted the others to like him, so he decided to <u>mimic</u> their love of the game. "Sure," he answered, thinking to himself that he would practice later.

After they finished playing, Marc invited his friends back to his house for a snack. The boys were talking about school and the project they had to do for history. It involved acting out a scene from early American history or singing songs or reciting poetry from that time period. The boys could not come up with an idea. Then Peter noticed Marc's guitar. "Hey, can you play that thing?" he asked. Marc nodded. Hesitantly, he agreed to play something for them. When he finished, they applauded. "How can you <u>remember</u> how to play all those notes?" asked another of the boys. They were really impressed.

Suddenly, Marc had an idea. "Maybe we can research some songs for our project," he suggested. "Then I can play them on the guitar, and we can sing them together."

"That would be great!" exclaimed Peter.

Marc thought so, too, and he realized that he had just discovered something important. He had <u>multiplied</u> the number of friends he had by taking a chance on being himself. It felt good.

1. Circle the words that give a clue to what <u>expectancy</u> his friends had of Marc when he looked out at them. Define *expectancy*.

2. Underline the words that tell what Marc did while he told his friends to <u>wait</u> a minute. What might you want to finish doing if you asked someone to *wait* for you?

3. Underline the words that tell what Marc <u>simply</u> wanted. What does *simply* mean?

4. Underline the words that tell what Marc decided to <u>mimic</u>. In the story, what does that mean?

5. Circle the words that tell what Marc was able to <u>remember</u>. Use *remember* in a sentence.

6. Circle the words that tell what Marc had <u>multiplied</u> by taking a chance on being himself. Give an antonym for *multiplied*.

Poetry Collection: Shel Silverstein, Eve Merriam, and James Berry
Reading Warm-up B

Read the following passage. Pay special attention to the underlined words. Then, read it again, and complete the activities. Use a separate sheet of paper for your written answers.

Listen to the rain as it gently hits the <u>windowpane</u>. Look at each droplet cling to the glass and then run down the smooth surface, like a tiny river. Sometimes the rain falls gently. Other times it falls heavily. It hits the ground with a <u>splatter</u> and drenches the Earth.

Did you know that each droplet of rainwater is actually the same water that has fallen as rain throughout time? This process is called the *water cycle*. Nearly all Earth's water has passed through the water cycle over and over again. This means the amount of water that has been created or lost during the past billion years is very small.

Here is how the water cycle works. After a rainfall, have you ever noticed a <u>puddle</u> of water on the ground? If the sun comes out, the heat from its rays hits the Earth. Sometimes this helps to change the air from moist and <u>soggy</u> to <u>dry</u>. When this happens, the water in the puddle *evaporates*, which means it dries up and turns into a gas called water vapor.

Next the water vapor rises into the air. The coolness of the higher air causes the water vapor to *condense*, and it turns back into water droplets. The droplets collect into clouds, which then drop the water back to Earth during the next rainstorm. When a flash of lightning lights the sky, and the <u>rumble</u> of thunder sounds, the same water that was in the puddle will begin to fall to Earth. Then the water cycle is ready to begin again.

Earth's water is sometimes stored underground or collects in huge amounts in our oceans and rivers. Some of it remains frozen for a long time in glaciers and in the polar ice caps. Whether it is falling as rain, evaporating, collecting in the clouds, or being stored on Earth, the miracle of water and its cycle is all around us.

1. Underline the words that describe a <u>windowpane</u>. Use *windowpane* in a sentence.

2. Circle the words that tell what happens when the rain falls with a <u>splatter</u>. Define *splatter*.

3. Circle the words that tell when you might see a <u>puddle</u> on the ground. What other things could form a *puddle*?

4. Underline the word that is a synonym for <u>soggy</u>. Define *soggy*.

5. Circle the sentence that tells what happens when the air becomes <u>dry</u>. What else might lose moisture and dry out when the air is *dry*?

6. Underline the words that tell when you might hear a <u>rumble</u> of thunder. Define *rumble*.

Unit 4 Resources: Poetry
130

Poetry Collection: Shell Silverstein, James Berry, Eve Merriam
Writing About the Big Question

What is the best way to communicate?

Big Question Vocabulary

communicate	contribute	enrich	entertain	express
inform	learn	listen	media	produce
react	speak	teach	technology	transmit

A. *Use one or more words from the list above to complete each sentence.*

1. _____ has made it much faster and easier for people to communicate.

2. It is possible to _____ messages almost instantly.

3. One problem with this form of communication is that people don't see or _____ directly with one another.

4. They cannot see how others _____ to what they say.

B. *Respond to each item with a complete sentence.*

1. Think of a time when you sent a message using technology, such as instant messaging or text messaging, that caused a problem. Describe how the other person reacted to the message.

_____

_____

2. Explain how the other person would have reacted differently if you had spoken directly with him or her.

_____

_____

C. *In "Poetry Collection 5," the poems have a pleasing musical quality. Complete this sentence. Then, write a short paragraph connecting the sentences to the Big Question.*

The use of musical language can **produce** _____

_____

_____

_____

_____

Poetry Collection: Shel Silverstein, Eve Merriam, James Berry

Reading: Read Aloud According to Punctuation in Order to Paraphrase

When you **paraphrase,** you restate something in your own words. To paraphrase a poem, you must first understand it. **Reading aloud according to punctuation** can help you identify complete thoughts in a poem and therefore grasp its meaning. Because poets do not always complete a sentence at the end of a line, pausing simply because a line ends can interfere with your understanding of the meaning. Follow these rules when you read aloud:

- Keep reading when a line has no end punctuation.
- Pause at commas, dashes, and semicolons.
- Stop at end marks, such as periods, question marks, or exclamation points.

As you read poetry, allow the punctuation to help you paraphrase the poet's ideas.

DIRECTIONS: *The following items are from "Sarah Cynthia Sylvia Stout Would Not Take the Garbage Out," "Weather," or "One." Read each item aloud, following the rules above. Then, paraphrase the lines. That is, restate them in your own words.*

1. Dot a dot dot dot a dot dot
   Spotting the windowpane.

   _____

   _____

2. Nobody can get into my clothes for me
   or feel my fall for me, or do my running.
   Nobody hears my music for me, either.

   _____

   _____

   _____

3. Poor Sarah met an awful fate,
   That I cannot right now relate
   Because the hour is much too late.
   But children, remember Sarah Stout
   And always take the garbage out!

   _____

   _____

   _____

   _____

   _____

   _____

Name _____   Date _____

Poetry Collection: Shel Silverstein, Eve Merriam, James Berry
Literary Analysis: Sound Devices

Sound devices create musical effects that appeal to the ear. Here are some common sound devices used in poetry:

- **Onomatopoeia** is the use of words whose sounds suggest their meaning:

  The explosion made a thunderous <u>boom</u>. The snake uttered a <u>hiss</u>.

- **Alliteration** is the repetition of sounds at the beginnings of words:

  <u>She</u> <u>s</u>ells <u>s</u>ea <u>sh</u>ells by the <u>s</u>ea <u>sh</u>ore.

- **Repetition** is the repeated use of words, phrases, and/or rhythms:

  I said, "Come," / I said, "Sit," / My dog would have none of it.

In the last example, there is repetition of both the words (*I said*) and the rhythm. In poetry, a line may contain more than one sound device.

DIRECTIONS: *The following items are from "Sarah Cynthia Sylvia Stout Would Not Take the Garbage Out," "Weather," or "One." Read each item, and decide which sound devices the lines contain. Then, identify the sound devices in each line by writing* Onomatopoeia, Alliteration, *and/or* Repetition. *An item may contain more than one sound device.*

1. Prune pits, peach pits, orange peel

   _____

2. Crusts of black burned buttered toast

   _____

3. A spatter a scatter a wet cat a clatter
   A splatter a rumble outside.

   _____

4. And mirrors can show me multiplied
   Many times

   _____

5. Umbrella umbrella umbrella umbrella
   Bumbershoot barrel of rain.

   _____

6. Sarah Cynthia Sylvia Stout
   Would not take the garbage out!

   _____

7. Slosh a galosh slosh a galosh
   Slither and slather and glide

   _____

Poetry Collection: Shel Silverstein, Eve Merriam, James Berry
Vocabulary Builder

Word List

curdled   expectancy   rancid   slather   stutter   withered

A. DIRECTIONS: *Read each item, and think about the meaning of the italicized word from the Word List. Then, answer the question, and explain your answer.*

1. The *withered* flowers had been in the vase for a week. Were the flowers brightly colored?

   _____

2. The hungry twins found *rancid* cheese in the refrigerator. Would they have thrown it out or eaten it?

   _____

3. The suspect began to *stutter* when he was questioned. Was he nervous? How can you tell?

   _____

4. The milk has *curdled* in the bottle. Would you drink it?

   _____

5. The girl stared out the window with *expectancy*. Why was she probably looking out?

   _____

6. At the beach, Nora was careful to *slather* on sunscreen. Was this a good idea?

   _____

B. WORD STUDY: *The Latin suffix -ancy mean "the state of being." Decide whether each statement is true or false. Write T or F. Then, explain your answer.*

1. The baby was still in its *infancy*.

   T / F: _____ **Explanation:** _____

2. Someone who shows *hesitancy* is sure of himself or herself.

   T / F: _____ **Explanation:** _____

3. A diamond is likely to shine with great *brilliancy*.

   T / F: _____ **Explanation:** _____

Poetry Collection: Shel Silverstein, Eve Merriam, James Berry

Enrichment: Alliteration

Alliteration in poetry is the repetition of sounds at the beginnings of words. It is found in all three of the poems in this collection. Alliteration contributes to the sound and flow of a poem and helps the reader experience the poem. Look at this example from "Sarah Cynthia Sylvia Stout Would Not Take the Garbage Out":

Prune pits, peach pits, orange peel, / Gloppy glumps of cold oatmeal.

In the first line, the repeated *p* sound might make a reader think of the sound someone makes when spitting out a seed or a pit. In the second line, the *gl* sound communicates the disagreeable look and feel of cold oatmeal.

DIRECTIONS: *The following items are from "Sarah Cynthia Sylvia Stout . . . ," "Weather," or "One." Read each item aloud or to yourself. Then, circle the sound or sounds that are repeated, and briefly explain how the alliteration contributes to the poem's effect.*

1. Crusts of black burned buttered toast,
   Gristly bits of beefy roasts . . .

   _____

   _____

2. Moldy melons, dried up mustard,
   Eggshells mixed with lemon custard

   _____

   _____

3. Spack a spack speck flick a flack fleck
   Freckling the windowpane.

   _____

   _____

4. Slosh a galosh slosh a galosh
   Slither and slather and glide

   _____

   _____

5. And mirrors can show me multiplied
   many times

   _____

   _____

Poetry Collection: Shel Silverstein, Eve Merriam, James Berry
Open-Book Test

Short Answer *Write your responses to the questions in this section on the lines provided.*

1. In "Sarah Cynthia . . . ," the poet uses the sound devices of alliteration and repetition. Look at lines 1–6. Give one example of alliteration (repetition of sounds at the beginning of words) and one example of repetition (the repeated use of words, phrases, or rhythms) from these lines.

   _____

   _____

   _____

2. In line 31 of "Sarah Cynthia . . . ," the reader learns that the meat has become *rancid*. Given the context of the poem, does it make sense that the meat has become rancid? Use the definition of *rancid* in your answer.

   _____

   _____

   _____

3. In "Sarah Cynthia . . . ," what seems to be the speaker's attitude at the end of the poem? Reread lines 43–47, and describe how the speaker feels about what happens to Sarah Stout. Use these lines from the poem to support your response.

   _____

   _____

   _____

4. "Weather" contains several examples of sound devices. Use the graphic organizer to list at least two examples from the poem. Identify each as alliteration, repetition, or onomatopoeia. Then, on the lines below, explain how you identified the sound devices.

Line Number	Example	Sound Device

_____

_____

5. Think about what you are able to picture after reading lines 1–4 of "Weather." How do the words help you understand what is going on? Use details from lines 1–4 to explain your answer.

_____

_____

_____

6. Reread lines 9–14 of "Weather." Paraphrase this stanza in two or three sentences.

_____

_____

7. Look at lines 4–6 of "One." Which sound device is being used by the poet, and why? Support your answer with details from lines 4–6.

_____

_____

8. In lines 7 and 8 of "One," why does the speaker describe ways in which he could be imitated? Use details from the lines that suggest how he would feel if someone did imitate those things.

_____

_____

_____

9. Lines 12–17 of "One" offer a powerful statement from the speaker about how he feels about himself. Paraphrase the lines.

_____

_____

_____

10. In line 18 of "One," the speaker says he will "stutter in a rage." Why would being angry cause him to stutter? Explain your answer, using your understanding of the word's meaning.

_____

_____

Essay

11. The visual images created in the reader's mind by "Sarah Cynthia . . . " are especially strong. In a brief essay, choose at least three or four of the poem's images. Describe how the images helped you respond to the poem.

12. Who might most enjoy hearing or reading the poem "Weather"? In a brief essay, use your understanding of the poem to explore which audience might enjoy the poem, and explain why. Include in your answer at least three words or phrases from the poem.

13. The poet in "One" goes back and forth between what "nobody" can do and what "anybody" can do. In an essay, explain why the poet might have used this technique. Use your understanding of the poem to support your answer, and tell whether you found the technique to be effective.

14. **Thinking About the Big Question: What is the best way to communicate?**
Think about how you felt when you read "Sarah Cynthia . . . ," "Weather," and "One." Is there one poem that communicated its message to you in an especially powerful way? In an essay, choose one of the poems, and describe why and how that poem communicated to you. Use details from the poem to support your answer.

Oral Response

15. Go back to question 1, 5, or 9 or to the question your teacher assigns you. Take a few minutes to expand your answer and prepare an oral response. Find additional details in the poem or poems that support your points. If necessary, make notes to guide your oral response.

Poetry Collection: Shel Silverstein, Eve Merriam, James Berry
Selection Test A

Critical Reading *Identify the letter of the choice that best answers the question.*

____ 1. Which line from "Sarah Cynthia Sylvia Stout Would Not Take the Garbage Out" contains alliteration?
   A. "Prune pits, peach pits, orange peel"
   B. "Candy the yams and spice the hams"
   C. "Eggshells mixed with lemon custard"
   D. "And all the neighbors moved away"

____ 2. What is the best paraphrase of this line from "Sarah Cynthia Sylvia Stout Would Not Take the Garbage Out"?
   And though her daddy would scream and shout,
   She simply would not take the garbage out.

   A. Sarah was sure to get into some kind of trouble because she refused to take out the trash.
   B. Although her daddy would scream and shout, she simply would not take the garbage out.
   C. Even though Sarah's father yelled at her about it, Sarah refused to take out the trash.
   D. Sarah was an extremely headstrong girl who would not do anything she was told to do.

____ 3. What happens to Sarah Stout because she refuses to take the garbage out?
   A. She loses all her friends.
   B. She is buried up to her neck in garbage.
   C. Her father takes the garbage out himself.
   D. The reader never learns what her fate is.

____ 4. What conclusion can you draw from these lines from "Sarah Cynthia Sylvia Stout Would Not Take the Garbage Out"?
   She'd scour the pots and scrape the pans, / Candy the yams and spice the hams
   A. Sarah was willing to wash the dishes and cook.
   B. Sarah liked candied yams and spiced hams.
   C. Sarah was forced to do unpleasant chores.
   D. Sarah was praised for her excellent cooking.

___ 5. Which of these lines from "Weather" contains onomatopoeia?

    A. "Spotting the windowpane"

    B. "Umbrella umbrella umbrella umbrella"

    C. "A spatter a scatter a wet cat a clatter"

    D. "A puddle a jump a puddle a jump"

___ 6. What is the poem "Weather" about?

    A. a cat caught in a rainstorm

    B. sounds you might hear during a rainstorm

    C. a person unable to close a window during a rainstorm

    D. people trying to avoid puddles as they run through the rain

___ 7. What idea does the use of alliteration in this line from "Weather" convey?

    Dot a dot dot dot a dot dot

    A. the way a row of periods looks on paper

    B. the way raindrops sound as they hit a window

    C. the way a message sent in Morse code might sound

    D. the way a painter puts dabs of paint on a canvas

___ 8. Which of the following passages from "One" contains repetition?

    A. "Nobody has the fingerprints I have."

    B. "Anybody can howl how I sing out of tune. / And mirrors can show me multiplied"

    C. "Nobody hears my music for me, either."

    D. "But anybody can act how I stutter in a rage. / Anybody can copy echoes I make."

___ 9. What is meant by this passage from "One"?

    But anybody can mimic my dance with my dog. / Anybody can howl how I sing out of tune. / And mirrors can show me multiplied / many times

    A. People can act like me, and mirrors can reflect my image.

    B. I can dance with my dog and sing out of tune.

    C. I sound like a howling dog when I sing.

    D. I have many mirrors in my house.

Vocabulary and Grammar

___ 10. In which sentence is the word *withered* used correctly?

    A. The grass looked *withered* after the cool rain.

    B. The *withered* plums were fresh and delicious.

    C. The *withered* leaves were evidence of the drought.

    D. The florist shop was full of bright, *withered* flowers.

_____ **11.** In which sentence is the word *rancid* used correctly?

    A. Everyone loved the *rancid* asparagus soup.

    B. The restaurant's specials include *rancid* burgers.

    C. The chef prepared a delicious *rancid* casserole.

    D. We threw out the leftovers when they became *rancid*.

_____ **12.** In which sentence is the independent clause underlined?

    A. <u>While Sarah refused to take it out</u>, the garbage piled up.

    B. Sarah agreed to take the garbage out <u>after she lost her friends</u>.

    C. Even though her father shouted at her, <u>Sarah refused to take the garbage out</u>.

    D. <u>Since there was so much of it</u>, the garbage finally reached the ceiling.

Essay

13. Alliteration is the repetition of sounds at the beginnings of words, as in "across the *l*og *l*ay the *l*ion." In an essay, cite two examples of alliteration in "Sarah Cynthia Sylvia Stout Would Not Take the Garbage Out." Then, tell which sound or sounds are repeated in each example. Finally, tell how the alliteration helps communicate the humor of the poem.

14. In "Weather," Eve Merriam uses onomatopoeia—words that sound like what they mean (such as *spatter* and *clatter*)—to describe a rainfall. In an essay, cite two examples of onomatopoeia in the poem, and tell how they contribute to the feeling of experiencing a rainfall. You might answer these questions: What does the onomatopoeia tell you about how hard it is raining? What does it tell you about what it is like to be outside in the rain?

15. Thinking About the Big Question: What is the best way to communicate? Each of the poems in this section communicates important feelings in a different way. Think about how you felt when you read "Sarah Cynthia . . . ," "Weather," and "One." In an essay, choose one of the poems, and describe why and how that poem communicated to you. Use details from the poem to support your answer.

Poetry Collection: Shel Silverstein, Eve Merriam, James Berry

Selection Test B

Critical Reading *Identify the letter of the choice that best completes the statement or answers the question.*

____ 1. Which line from "Sarah Cynthia Sylvia Stout Would Not Take the Garbage Out" contains alliteration?
A. "And so it piled up to the ceilings"
B. "It cracked the window and blocked the door"
C. "Crusts of black burned buttered toast"
D. "At last the garbage reached so high"

____ 2. Which of these lines from "Sarah Cynthia Sylvia Stout Would Not Take the Garbage Out" uses exaggeration for humorous effect?
A. "Brown bananas, rotten peas, / Chunks of sour cottage cheese"
B. "Cellophane from green baloney, / Rubbery blubbery macaroni"
C. "Cold french fries and rancid meat, / Yellow lumps of Cream of Wheat"
D. "At last the garbage reached so high / That finally it touched the sky."

____ 3. What is the best paraphrase of this passage from "Sarah Cynthia Sylvia Stout Would Not Take the Garbage Out"?
And all the neighbors moved away, / And none of her friends would come to play. / And finally Sarah Cynthia Stout said, / "OK, I'll take the garbage out!"
A. All the neighbors moved away, and none of her friends would come to play when Sarah finally said, "OK, I'll take the garbage out!"
B. In order to keep her neighbors and friends, Sarah agreed to take the trash out.
C. When the garbage had piled up very high, Sarah's friends refused to play with her.
D. Sarah's neighbors had moved and her friends had stopped playing with her by the time Sarah agreed to take out the trash.

____ 4. What does Shel Silverstein show by ending the poem with these lines?
But children, remember Sarah Stout / And always take the garbage out!
A. The poem is a threat.
B. The poem is a humorous warning.
C. The poem is a guide to right living.
D. The poem is pure fun.

____ 5. What is the main trait of Sarah Cynthia Sylvia Stout?
A. her skill as a cook
B. her stubbornness
C. her friendliness
D. her willingness to wash dishes

___ 6. Which statement best explains why the speaker in "Sarah Cynthia Sylvia Stout Would Not Take the Garbage Out" does not reveal Sarah's fate?
   A. He does not know what happened to her.
   B. He does not want to embarrass her.
   C. He wants readers to imagine her fate.
   D. He thinks it is time for readers to be in bed.

___ 7. What is the best interpretation of this line from "Weather"?
   A spatter a scatter a wet cat a clatter

   A. A cat is hiding under a car during a rainstorm.
   B. The sound the rain makes is like the sound of a cat.
   C. Several cats run in different directions to get out of the rain.
   D. A cat running to get out of the rain knocks something over.

___ 8. What is most likely happening in these lines from "Weather"?
   A puddle a jump a puddle a jump / A puddle a jump puddle splosh

   A. The rain is making puddles of water on a sidewalk.
   B. The rain is causing something to jump out of puddles.
   C. Someone jumps over three puddles and lands in a fourth.
   D. Someone is jumping from puddle to puddle during a storm.

___ 9. Which of these lines from "Weather" contains both onomatopoeia and repetition?
   A. "Spotting the windowpane"
   B. "A splatter a rumble outside"
   C. "Slosh a galosh slosh a galosh"
   D. "A puddle a jump a puddle a jump"

___ 10. If you were reading "One" aloud, where would you pause?
   And mirrors can show me multiplied / many times, say, dressed up in red / or dressed up in grey.

   A. after "multiplied" and after "red"
   B. after "times" and after "say"
   C. after "say" and after "red"
   D. after "say" and after "or"

___ 11. What is the best paraphrase of this passage from "One"?
   I am just this one. / Nobody else makes the words / I shape with sound, when I talk.

   A. I am the only one who knows what to say.
   B. I am an individual, and no one else sounds like me.
   C. I am only one person, but I can say all there is to say.
   D. No one else can talk when I am talking.

___ 12. Which of these lines from "One" contains alliteration?
   A. "Nobody has the fingerprints I have."
   B. "And mirrors can show me multiplied / many times"
   C. "Nobody can get into my clothes for me."
   D. "But anybody can act how I stutter in a rage."

Vocabulary and Grammar

____ 13. Which sentence uses the word *rancid* correctly?

    A. The *rancid* butter tasted delicious on the fresh bread.

    B. The diners became ill from eating *rancid* meat.

    C. The *rancid* food pleased the hungry diners.

    D. The chef's specialty was *rancid* leg of lamb.

____ 14. In which sentence is the word *stutter* used *incorrectly*?

    A. The speaker will *stutter* so that everyone can understand him.

    B. Often a speaker will *stutter* when he or she feels nervous.

    C. Many people who *stutter* as children speak smoothly as adults.

    D. Speakers who are unsure of themselves are likely to *stutter*.

____ 15. Which of the following is a subordinate clause?

    A. What happened to Sarah Cynthia Sylvia Stout?

    B. The fate of Sarah Cynthia Sylvia Stout is unknown.

    C. Which we find out at the end of the poem.

    D. The alliteration in Silverstein's poem is funny.

____ 16. In which sentence is the independent clause underlined?

    A. Sarah would not take the garbage out <u>until it was too late</u>.

    B. Once Sarah agreed to take the garbage out, <u>it was too late</u>.

    C. <u>Even when her father shouted</u>, Sarah refused to take the garbage out.

    D. <u>Since it is not revealed</u>, Sarah's fate is unknown.

Essay

17. "Sarah Cynthia Sylvia Stout Would Not Take the Garbage Out" contains a number of exaggerations. In an essay, examine one example of exaggeration. Tell what the exaggeration adds to the poem.

18. Choose two of the poems in this collection—"Sarah Cynthia Sylvia Stout Would Not Take the Garbage Out," "Weather," and/or "One." In an essay, compare and contrast the poets' purpose. For example, is the poet teaching, entertaining, informing, or persuading? Is he or she simply expressing feelings? Does he or she have a different purpose altogether? Does he or she have a combination of purposes? State each poet's purpose, and show how the two poets' purposes are alike and/or how they are different. Support your comparison with two examples from each poem.

19. **Thinking About the Big Question: What is the best way to communicate?** Think about how you felt when you read "Sarah Cynthia. . . ," "Weather," and "One." Is there one poem that communicated its message to you in an especially powerful way? In an essay, choose one of the poems, and describe why and how that poem communicated to you. Use details from the poem to support your answer.

Vocabulary Warm-up Word Lists

Study these words from the poetry of William Shakespeare, Eve Merriam, and Louise Bogan. Then, complete the activities that follow.

Word List A

clearing [KLEER ing] *n.* an area of land that is cleared of trees
We liked to walk the dog in the <u>clearing</u> by the park.

distance [DIS tuhns] *n.* the condition of being removed in space or time or the space between two things
The <u>distance</u> from Bill's house to the store was very short.

hear [HEER] *v.* to listen or to perceive sound with the ears
The sleeping girl did not <u>hear</u> her alarm clock ring.

hours [OURZ] *n.* the twenty-four divisions of time in the day, each of which is sixty minutes
It had been many <u>hours</u> from the time Bev began studying.

plains [PLAYNZ] *n.* flat, open areas of land
The tall grass growing on the <u>plains</u> rippled in the breeze.

rushes [RUHSH iz] *v.* to move or go swiftly
Marty <u>rushes</u> down the street to catch the bus in the morning.

Word List B

below [bee LOH] *adv.* in or to a lower place; under
Look <u>below</u> the sink for the extra pans.

clear [KLEER] *adj.* transparent or free from cloudiness
The glass in the window was clean and <u>clear</u>.

coral [KAWR uhl] *n.* the hard skeleton of certain marine polyps, which, when many are gathered together, form a reef under the ocean
The eel hid in the hole in the <u>coral</u>.

sea [SEE] *adj.* having to do with the ocean
Does the <u>sea</u> creature known as the Loch Ness monster really exist?

splashes [SPLASH iz] *v.* splatters, causes a liquid to scatter and fly about
The waterfall <u>splashes</u> when the water hits the rocks.

strange [STRAYNJ] *adj.* different, unusual, or of another place
To Laura's ears, the foreign language sounded very <u>strange</u>.

Poetry Collection: William Shakespeare, Eve Merriam, and Louise Bogan
Vocabulary Warm-up Exercises

Exercise A *Fill in each blank in the paragraph below with an appropriate word from Word List A. Use each word only once.*

Brenda is training to run in a 5K marathon. Most mornings, she eagerly gets

up, puts on her jogging clothes, and [1] _____ across the

[2] _____ by the high school to the track where she begins her

workout. Each day, she runs for a set amount of time. Then she checks the

[3] _____ she has run, to see if her time improves with each run. Over

the months she is in training, Brenda will put in a great many [4] _____

of exercise. On certain days, she does not use the track. Instead, she runs off track

across the open, grassy [5] _____ where the race will be held. Brenda

knows it will be a lot of hard work, but she is looking forward to the moment after the

race when she can [6] _____ herself say, "I did it!"

Exercise B *Answer the questions with complete explanations.*

1. Would you be likely to find a piece of *coral* in the woods?

   _____

2. If someone drives a car through a mud puddle, and it *splashes* on the windshield,
   would he or she have *clear* vision through the window?

   _____

3. If you usually sleep in the same bedroom each night, might it seem *strange* to sleep
   downstairs in another room?

   _____

4. If Jean lives on the top floor of a building, is it likely that people live *below* her?

   _____

5. If you sail a boat on a mountain pond, does a *sea* breeze propel the boat?

   _____

Poetry Collection: William Shakespeare, Eve Merriam, and Louise Bogan

Reading Warm-up A

Read the following passage. Pay special attention to the underlined words. Then, read it again, and complete the activities. Use a separate sheet of paper for your written answers.

In 1849, the Gold Rush began in California. Hoping to strike it rich by mining for gold, huge numbers of people moved to the West coast. This development brought about the need to join the eastern and western states. Theodore Judah was a builder who designed railways. He proposed the construction of one long railroad covering the <u>distance</u> between the two coasts. This project was named the Transcontinental Railroad.

Judah picked a route from the West coast. It led through the mountains. The Central Pacific Railroad did the job, backed by private investors and money from Congress. Workers spent countless <u>hours</u> building over 690 miles of track heading eastward. Chinese workers did the dangerous job of blasting their way through the granite cliffs of the mountains. The crews worked in extreme cold and heat building tunnels and bridges.

From the east, the Union Pacific Railroad built the track leading west from Omaha, Nebraska. This crew was made up of many Irish workers. Their job was to lay track across the wide, open <u>plains</u> and the desert. They also needed to make a <u>clearing</u> if trees stood in their path.

Put yourself back in time. Imagine the excitement people felt as the project neared an end. Think of being in the town of Promontory Summit, Utah, as each train <u>rushes</u> to meet the other. In the distance, you can <u>hear</u> the whistles of two trains riding the new rails. At last, the trains meet. It is an important moment, as the end of six long years of hard work is done!

The linking of the coasts by railroad had a big effect on the nation. It helped to bring about the settling of the West. It damaged Native American culture, as tribes were forced onto reservations. In addition, ranching became a big business, for cattle could be shipped more easily to the coasts.

1. Circle the words that give a clue that the <u>distance</u> between the coasts was big. Use **distance** in a sentence.

2. Underline the word that tells how many <u>hours</u> were spent by the workers. What other units of time can you think of?

3. Underline the words that describe the <u>plains</u>. Define **plains**.

4. Underline the words that tell why a <u>clearing</u> might have needed to be made. What is a **clearing**?

5. Circle the words in the story that tell what <u>rushes</u> along the track. Use **rushes** in a sentence.

6. Circle the words in the story that tell what you might <u>hear</u>. What are some things you **hear** every day?

Name _____ Date _____

Reading Warm-up B

Read the following passage. Pay special attention to the underlined words. Then, read it again, and complete the activities. Use a separate sheet of paper for your written answers.

<u>Below</u> the waves in the tropical parts of the ocean, there is a <u>strange</u> and wonderful world. It is the world of the coral reef.

Living polyps of <u>coral</u> make up the outer layer of the reef. This outer layer grows upon the layers of skeleton of previously living corals. The reef builds up layer by layer. As each generation of coral lives and then dies, it forms a new layer of skeletal remains. The layers form rocklike structures because the calcium in the skeletons is hard. The reefs can grow from about a half an inch to almost eight inches per year. The coral grows in beautiful shapes and colors, and it makes a special habitat for many <u>sea</u> creatures.

Coral reefs need warm water in which to form. These warm, tropical waters are often very <u>clear</u>. The sparkling water makes it easy to see the sea life of the coral reef. You can scuba dive or snorkel around the formations and see all kinds of creatures. Moray eels and sharks hide among the crevices and holes of the coral. Crabs scurry along in the sand, catching food. Colorful fish, such as butterfly fish, swim about. They like to eat the algae that is found in the coral reef.

There are three kinds of coral reefs. They are called a fringing reef, a barrier reef, and an atoll. Fringing reefs form and are attached directly to the shore. Barrier reefs are found apart from the shore, with water in between. Atolls are islands made of coral. You may see many a fish as it jumps and <u>splashes</u> in the water around the atoll. Such a fish is busy catching food.

Pollution and certain fishing practices have damaged some of the world's coral reefs. Many concerned people are working together to preserve these special habitats, for they are truly one of nature's wonders.

1. Underline the words that describe what is found <u>below</u> the waves. What is an antonym for *below*?

2. Circle the words that tell what the <u>strange</u> and wonderful world in the story is. Define *strange*.

3. Circle the words that tell what the living <u>coral</u> makes up. Use *coral* in a sentence.

4. Circle the word that <u>sea</u> describes. What is a synonym for *sea*?

5. Underline the words that further describe how the <u>clear</u> water looks. What else might look *clear*?

6. Underline the words that tell where you might see a fish as it <u>splashes</u>. Use *splashes* in a sentence.

Name _____ Date _____

Writing About the Big Question

What is the best way to communicate?

Big Question Vocabulary

communicate	contribute	enrich	entertain	express
inform	learn	listen	media	produce
react	speak	teach	technology	transmit

A. *Use one or more words from the list above to complete each sentence.*

1. When you have a problem with a friend, you can _____ your opinion by talking it over.

2. It is important to _____ to your friend's opinions, too.

3. Listening well and speaking honestly can _____ a friendship.

B. *Respond to each item with a complete sentence.*

1. Describe two occasions when you have expressed an opinion to a friend. Use two of the Big Question vocabulary words.

   _____

   _____

2. Choose one of the discussions above. Explain how the discussion helped enrich your friendship.

   _____

   _____

C. *In "Poetry Collection 6," each poem uses sound to create an image or to bring about a certain mood. Complete this sentence. Then, write a short paragraph connecting the sentences to the Big Question.*

When you really **listen**, you can _____

_____

_____

Poetry Collection: William Shakespeare, Eve Merriam, Louise Bogan

Reading: Read Aloud According to Punctuation in Order to Paraphrase

When you **paraphrase,** you restate something in your own words. To paraphrase a poem, you must first understand it. **Reading aloud according to punctuation** can help you identify complete thoughts in a poem and therefore grasp its meaning. Because poets do not always complete a sentence at the end of a line, pausing simply because a line ends can interfere with your understanding of the meaning. Follow these rules when you read aloud:

- Keep reading when a line has no end punctuation.
- Pause at commas, dashes, and semicolons.
- Stop at end marks, such as periods, question marks, or exclamation points.

As you read poetry, allow the punctuation to help you paraphrase the poet's ideas.

DIRECTIONS: *The following items are from "Full Fathom Five," "Onomatopoeia," or "Train Tune." Read each item aloud, following the rules above. Then, paraphrase the lines. That is, restate them in your own words.*

1. spurts,
   finally stops sputtering
   and plash!
   gushes rushes splashes
   clear water dashes.

   _____

   _____

2. Back through lightning
   Back through cities
   Back through stars
   Back through hours

   _____

   _____

3. Sea nymphs hourly ring his knell;
   Ding-dong.
   Hark! Now I hear them ding-dong bell.

   _____

   _____

   _____

Poetry Collection: William Shakespeare, Eve Merriam, Louise Bogan
Literary Analysis: Sound Devices

Sound devices create musical effects that appeal to the ear. Here are some common sound devices used in poetry:

- **Onomatopoeia** is the use of words whose sounds suggest their meaning:

The saw cut through the tree with a <u>buzz</u>. The librarian <u>murmured</u> her answer.

- **Alliteration** is the repetition of sounds at the beginnings of words:

<u>P</u>eter <u>P</u>iper <u>p</u>icked a <u>p</u>eck of <u>p</u>ickled <u>p</u>eppers.

- **Repetition** is the repeated use of words, phrases, and/or rhythms:

<u>The leaves blew</u> up, / <u>The leaves blew</u> down, / <u>The leaves blew</u> all around the town.

In the last example, there is repetition of both the words (*The leaves blew*) and the rhythm. In poetry, a line may contain more than one sound device.

DIRECTIONS: *The following items are from "Full Fathom Five," "Onomatopoeia," or "Train Tune." Read each item, and decide which sound devices the lines contain. Then, identify the sound devices in each line by writing* Onomatopoeia, Alliteration, *and/or* Repetition. *An item may contain more than one sound device.*

1. Full fathom five thy father lies

   _____

2. The rusty spigot
   sputters,
   utters
   a splutter

   _____

3. Back through clouds
   Back through clearing
   Back through distance
   Back through silence

   _____

4. finally stops sputtering
   and plash!
   gushes rushes splashes
   clear water dashes

   _____

5. Nothing of him that doth fade
   But doth suffer a sea change
   Into something rich and strange.

   _____

Poetry Collection: William Shakespeare, Eve Merriam, Louise Bogan
Vocabulary Builder

Word List

fathoms   garlands   groves   smattering   spigot   sputters

A. DIRECTIONS: *Read each item, and think about the meaning of the italicized word from the Word List. Then, answer the question, and explain your answer.*

1. If a plumber says you need a new *spigot*, should you purchase a device to keep water from running down the drain?

   _____

2. If a person *sputters* as she speaks, is she likely to be calm?

   _____

3. If there are orange *groves* on your property, are there trees on your property?

   _____

4. If you are measuring the depths of a lake, would you measure in *fathoms*?

   _____

5. If you were hit by a *smattering* of raindrops, would you need to change your clothes?

   _____

6. If someone decorates her house with *garlands*, would it probably smell good?

   _____

B. WORD STUDY: *The Latin suffix* -less *means "without." Decide whether each statement is true or false. Write T or F. Then, explain your answer.*

1. You could trust someone who is *careless* with your most prized possession.

   T / F: _____ **Explanation:** _____

2. A movie that seems *endless* is very long or very dull.

   T / F: _____ **Explanation:** _____

3. A *joyless* person is almost always happy.

   T / F: _____ **Explanation:** _____

Name _____ Date _____

Enrichment: Onomatopoeia

Onomatopoeia is the use of words that imitate the sound or action they describe. You encountered several *onomatopoeic* words in "Full Fathom Five" and "Onomatopoeia." In "Onomatopoeia," those words mimic the sounds of running water: *sputters, splutter, spatters, splatters, spurts, plash.* In "Full Fathom Five," they mimic the sound of a ringing bell: *ding-dong.*

A. DIRECTIONS: *Look at these lists of onomatopoeic words. At the end of each group, add your own examples. Then, come up with one or more categories of your own, and in the last column write some onomatopoeic words that fit into those categories.*

Water Sounds	Animal Sounds	Loud Sounds	Other Sounds
spatter	moo	crash	
splatter	baa	bam	
sputter	tweet	thump	
gush	hiss	smash	
drip	hee-haw	crunch	
spurt	neigh	pow	
splash	meow	crack	

B. DIRECTIONS: *Write a short poem about an animal, the weather, a musical instrument, or any other subject that makes you think of sounds. Use words from the list in your poem.*

_____

_____

_____

_____

_____

_____

_____

_____

Poetry Collections: Shel Silverstein, Eve Merriam, James Berry;
William Shakespeare, Eve Merriam, Louise Bogan

Integrated Language Skills: Grammar

Independent and Subordinate Clauses

A **clause** is a group of words with its own subject and verb. There are two types of clauses: independent clauses and subordinate clauses. An **independent clause** expresses a complete thought and can stand alone as a sentence.

A **subordinate clause** (also called a **dependent clause**) has a subject and a verb, but it does not express a complete thought. Therefore, it cannot stand alone as a sentence. The following sentence contains both an independent clause and a subordinate clause. The subject in each clause is underlined once, and the verb is underlined twice. The subordinate clause appears in italics:

> Shel Silverstein was a cartoonist and a writer, *though he also composed songs.*

A subordinate clause may appear either before or after the independent clause:

> *Though he also composed songs,* Shel Silverstein was a cartoonist and a writer.

A. DIRECTIONS: *In each sentence, underline the independent clause once and the subordinate clause twice.*

1. Eve Merriam's lifelong love was poetry even though she wrote fiction, nonfiction, and drama.
2. Because language and its sound gave Eve Merriam great joy, she tried to communicate her enjoyment by writing poetry for children.
3. Berry moved to the United States when he was seventeen.
4. If Berry had not lost his job as a telegraph operator, he might not have become a writer.
5. Because he did not play ball or dance when he was young, Shel Silverstein began to draw and write.
6. Silverstein began to draw cartoons after he served in the military.

B. Writing Application: *Rewrite each sentence by adding a subordinate clause.*

1. Sarah Stout was a stubborn young woman.

   _____

2. The rain spotted the windowpane.

   _____

3. Anyone can dance like me.

   _____

4. The drowned man's bones had turned to coral.

   _____

Name _____   Date _____

Integrated Language Skills: Support for Writing a Poem Called "Alliteration"

Use this chart as you draft a **poem** called "Alliteration."

"Alliteration": A Poem
Alliteration, defined by the textbook: "Alliteration is the repetition of sounds at the beginning of words."
Alliteration, defined in my own words: _____   _____   _____
Example of alliteration: <u>P</u>eter <u>P</u>iper <u>p</u>icked a <u>p</u>eck of <u>p</u>ickled <u>p</u>eppers.
My own example of alliteration: _____   _____   _____   _____   _____   _____
My poem, combining my definition of alliteration with my examples of alliteration: _____   _____   _____   _____   _____   _____   _____   _____   _____

Look over your poem to be sure your examples work. Do they contain words that begin with the same sound? Then, check your definition. Does it correctly define alliteration? Revise your poem before creating your final draft.

Poetry Collections: Shel Silverstein, Eve Merriam, James Berry;
William Shakespeare, Eve Merriam, Louise Bogan

Integrated Language Skills: Support for Extend Your Learning

Poetry Collection: Shel Silverstein, Eve Merriam, James Berry
Listening and Speaking

Choose a poem from this collection to present in a **poetry reading.**

Title of poem: _____

Is the tone of the poem serious, humorous, or playful? _____

How might the tone affect the speed at which I read the poem and my tone of voice?

_____

Now, read these guidelines, and decide how they apply to the poem you will read.

- Read the poem aloud. Pause only at commas, dashes, and semicolons. Come to a full stop after periods, question marks, and exclamation points. If there is no punctuation mark at the end of a line, *do not pause.*
- If you are unsure of the meaning of a line, paraphrase it.
- Vary your reading rate.
- Use expression in your voice that is appropriate to the meaning of the lines.
- Practice reading the poem loudly and clearly. Make eye contact with your audience.

Poetry Collection: William Shakespeare, Eve Merriam, Louise Bogan
Listening and Speaking

Choose a poem from this collection to present in a **poetry reading.**

Title of poem: _____

Is the tone of the poem serious or playful? _____

How might the tone affect the speed at which I read the poem and my tone of voice?

_____

Now, read these guidelines, and decide how they apply to the poem you will read.

- Read the poem aloud. Pause only at commas, dashes, and semicolons. Come to a full stop after periods, question marks, and exclamation points. If there is no punctuation mark at the end of a line, *do not pause.*
- If you are unsure of the meaning of a line, paraphrase it.
- Vary your reading rate.
- Use expression in your voice that is appropriate to the meaning of the lines.
- Practice reading the poem loudly and clearly. Make eye contact with your audience.

Poetry Collection: William Shakespeare, Eve Merriam, Louise Bogan
Open-Book Test

Short Answer *Write your responses to the questions in this section on the lines provided.*

1. In "Full Fathom Five," how do you know where the listener's father is? Reread the title of the poem, and look at other poem details that show a location. Use the details to help you answer.

   _____

   _____

2. Look at line 2 of "Full Fathom Five." In one or two sentences, paraphrase this line. Use your understanding of line 1 to help you in your response.

   _____

   _____

3. In "Full Fathom Five," which two sound devices does the poet use? Support your answer with details from the beginning and end of the poem.

   _____

   _____

4. Reread lines 4–7 of "Full Fathom Five." Is sadness the only emotion the speaker feels about what has happened? Give your impressions of the speaker's attitude toward the event. Use details from the lines to support your response.

   _____

   _____

   _____

5. The title of "Onomatopoeia" tells you that at least one sound device is used in this poem. In addition, there is a second sound device—identify it on the line. Then, use the graphic organizer to list at least two examples of onomatopoeia and two of the other sound device. On the lines below, explain how these sound devices support the poem's meaning.

Onomatopoeia	**Other Sound Device:**_____

   _____

   _____

6. In "Onomatopoeia," the spigot *sputters* at first. Why might a faucet *sputter* before it releases water? Use your understanding of the poem to help you answer.

_____

_____

_____

7. In "Onomatopoeia," the poet uses several different words to describe how the water emerges from the faucet. Although the sound of these words is interesting, why else would the poet make this choice? Explain your answer, citing specific examples from the poem to support your response.

_____

_____

_____

_____

8. The three sound devices used in this collection are alliteration, onomatopoeia, and repetition. Which two of these are used in lines 1 and 2 of "Train Tune"? In your answer, give specific words and the sound devices they represent.

_____

_____

9. The train in "Train Tune" travels through groves. Do you think the train is traveling through a big city or the countryside? Use the meaning of *groves* in your response.

_____

_____

10. There is no punctuation in "Train Tune." How does this lack of punctuation contribute to your understanding of the poet's message? Include in your answer an opinion about how the poem might be different if the poet had used punctuation.

_____

_____

_____

_____

Essay

Write an extended response to the question of your choice or to the question or questions your teacher assigns you.

11. How does the sound of a bell emphasize the meaning of "Full Fathom Five"? Reread lines 7–9. In a brief essay, discuss the poet's use of a bell to communicate the poem's message.

12. The poem "Onomatopoeia" is expressed using a few well-chosen words. If you were to paraphrase this poem, how would you write a similar description in prose? In a brief essay, paraphrase the poem. Then, explain whether you think your version or the poem is more effective in describing the action of the spigot.

13. In "Train Tune," the poet repeats the word *back* over and over again. How is this word choice unusual in a poem about a train? In an essay, explore the poet's use of this word. Explain why you think the poet might have used it and whether you find it effective.

14. **Thinking About the Big Question: What is the best way to communicate?**
    Think about the rhythm of the sound devices used in "Full Fathom Five," "Onomatopoeia," and "Train Tune." In an essay, compare the rhythm in at least two of the poems. In your answer, explain which rhythm you found most effective, and why.

Oral Response

15. Go back to question 1, 4, or 5 or to the question your teacher assigns you. Take a few minutes to expand your answer and prepare an oral response. Find additional details in the poem or poems that support your points. If necessary, make notes to guide your oral response.

Name _____ Date _____

Critical Reading *Identify the letter of the choice that best answers the question.*

_____ 1. What is the best paraphrase of the line "Full fathom five thy father lies"?
  A. Your father is five fathoms tall.
  B. Your father has lied about his height.
  C. Your father lies five fathoms under the sea.
  D. Your father has been diving to a depth of five fathoms.

_____ 2. Which of these lines from "Full Fathom Five" makes use of alliteration?
  A. "Full fathom five thy father lies"
  B. "Of his bones are coral made"
  C. "Nothing of him that doth fade"
  D. "Sea nymphs hourly ring his knell"

_____ 3. What sound is imitated by some of the words in these lines from "Full Fathom Five"?

  Sea nymphs hourly ring his knell; / Ding-dong. / Hark! Now I hear them—
  ding-dong bell.

  A. a whistle
  B. a bell
  C. the waves
  D. a buoy

_____ 4. What seems to have happened to the father in "Full Fathom Five"?
  A. He has lost his family.
  B. He has turned into a sea nymph.
  C. He has been diving for coral.
  D. He has drowned.

_____ 5. Which of these words from "Onomatopoeia" is an example of onomatopoeia?
  A. rusty
  B. wider
  C. splatters
  D. stops

_____ 6. In "Onomatopoeia," what does the speaker mean to convey with the following lines?

    slash, / splatters, / scatters, / spurts

    A. The water is not running.

    B. The water is running regularly.

    C. The water is running slowly.

    D. The water is running irregularly.

_____ 7. What is "Onomatopoeia" about?

    A. a leaky sink

    B. a broken pipe

    C. a broken sprinkler

    D. a rusty faucet

_____ 8. What is the repetition of the word *back* in "Train Tune" meant to suggest?

    A. the train arriving in a station

    B. the rhythm of the train on the tracks

    C. the progress of the train through time

    D. the passengers' memories

_____ 9. When you read "Train Tune" aloud, what do you do at the end of each line in a verse such as this one?

    Back through clouds / Back through clearing / Back through distance / Back through silence

    A. pause

    B. speed up

    C. keep reading

    D. slow down

_____ 10. What does the absence of punctuation mean in lines such as these from "Train Tune"?

    Back through plains / Back through flowers / Back through birds / Back through rain

    A. The train does not pause on its journey.

    B. The train pauses only to avoid hitting birds.

    C. The train goes faster through the open country.

    D. The train pauses for people to look at the flowers.

Vocabulary and Grammar

____ **11.** In which sentence is the word *sputters* used correctly?

    A. The engine *sputters* when it is started in the cold.

    B. The dog *sputters* when it barks at intruders.

    C. That tree *sputters* when it drops its leaves.

    D. The wave *sputters* as it breaks over the beach.

____ **12.** In which sentence is the independent clause underlined?

    A. Our school has not won a championship yet, <u>though we hope to win tonight</u>.

    B. Because you like astronomy so much, <u>will you be watching the eclipse tonight</u>?

    C. We have always liked our neighbors <u>because they are kind and humorous</u>.

    D. <u>Unless you can be here by six</u>, you will miss having dinner with Margaret.

____ **13.** In which sentence is the subordinate clause underlined?

    A. <u>There is a sale of CDs on Saturday</u>, so I will go shopping.

    B. When you get to the park, <u>meet us at the war monument</u>.

    C. After you study for the test, <u>I will quiz you on the Civil War</u>.

    D. <u>Until the baby has finished eating</u>, be sure to keep her bib on.

Essay

14. In an essay, analyze the use of onomatopoeia in Eve Merriam's poem "Onomatopoeia." Select two examples of the sound device, and describe the sounds that each one makes you think of.

15. In the poems in this collection—"Full Fathom Five," "Onomatopoeia," and "Train Tune"—the poet creates a vivid picture of an action or a setting. Which of these poems did you like best? In an essay, identify your favorite poem. Then, support your choice by referring to at least two words or phrases from the poem.

16. Thinking About the Big Question: What is the best way to communicate? Think about the rhythm of the sound devices used in "Full Fathom Five," "Onomatopoeia," and "Train Tune." In an essay, compare the rhythm in at least two of the poems. In your answer, explain which rhythm you found most effective, and why.

Poetry Collection: William Shakespeare, Eve Merriam, Louise Bogan
Selection Test B

Critical Reading *Identify the letter of the choice that best completes the statement or answers the question.*

____ 1. What is the best paraphrase of these lines from "Full Fathom Five"?

Full fathom five thy father lies; / Those are pearls that were his eyes

   A. Your father lies thirty feet under the sea, having drowned while diving for pearls.
   B. Your father lies thirty feet under the sea, and his eyes have become pearls.
   C. I do not fully understand the five lies your father told, about eyes turning to pearls.
   D. I fully understand where your father lies, and I know that his eyes have become pearls.

____ 2. The speaker in "Full Fathom Five" is describing
   A. undersea life.
   B. the father's funeral.
   C. what has happened to the father.
   D. the imaginary beings that live under the sea.

____ 3. What message is communicated by "Full Fathom Five"?
   A. The father is being honored in death by undersea creatures.
   B. The father should have known better than to go to sea.
   C. Undersea creatures have funerals just as humans do.
   D. Pearl diving can be a very dangerous undertaking.

____ 4. What does the speaker in "Full Fathom Five" suggest about the father in these lines?

Nothing of him that doth fade / But doth suffer a sea change / Into something rich and strange.

   A. The father's body has faded away to nothingness.
   B. The father has found vast stores of riches under the sea.
   C. The father has sailed away and is now out of sight.
   D. The father's body has changed into elements of the sea.

____ 5. If you were reading aloud these lines from "Onomatopoeia," where would you pause?

The rusty spigot / sputters, / utters / a splutter.

   A. after "sputters" and "utters"
   B. after "sputters" and "splutter"
   C. after "spigot," "sputters," and "utters"
   D. after "spigot," "sputters," "utters," and "splutter"

____ 6. Which of these words from "Onomatopoeia" is an example of onomatopoeia?
   A. "spigot"
   B. "gashes"
   C. "spurts"
   D. "clear"

____ 7. Listen to the sound of the word *splutter* in "Onomatopoeia." How might the sound best be described?
   A. soft and smooth
   B. high-pitched
   C. continuous
   D. loud and jerky

____ 8. Which of these lines from "Onomatopoeia" contains alliteration?
   A. "The rusty spigot / sputters"
   B. "gashes wider / slash"
   C. "gushes rushes splashes"
   D. "clear water dashes"

____ 9. What is happening in "Onomatopoeia"?
   A. A rusty faucet hesitates but then allows water to run.
   B. A rusty faucet sputters and then stops working altogether.
   C. A person tries to fill a sink with water from a rusty faucet.
   D. A person succeeds in getting water from a rusty faucet.

____ 10. Which poetic devices are used in these lines from "Train Tune"?
   Back through clouds / Back through clearing

   A. alliteration and onomatopoeia
   B. repetition and onomatopoeia
   C. repetition and alliteration
   D. repetition and rhyme

____ 11. The sound devices in "Train Tune" are meant to imitate the experience of a moving train. What effect might those sound devices have on the passengers of a moving train?
   A. They might teach them about trains.
   B. They might make them hungry.
   C. They might keep them awake.
   D. They might make them sleepy.

____ 12. Which words in "Train Tune" suggest that the train has traveled a great distance?
   A. "silence" and "love"
   B. "mountains" and "plains"
   C. "lightning" and "rain"
   D. "clouds" and "birds"

____ 13. Imagine someone reading aloud this verse from "Train Tune." Where should the reader pause?
   Back through plains / Back through flowers / Back through birds / Back through rain

   A. The reader should not pause at all.
   B. The reader should pause at the end of each line.
   C. The reader should pause at the end of the second and fourth lines.
   D. The reader should pause at the end of the verse.

Vocabulary and Grammar

_____ 14. In which sentence is the word *spigot* used correctly?
   A. Water flows from a faucet to a *spigot*.
   B. Water flows through the *spigot* slowly.
   C. A *spigot* holds the gutters in place.
   D. A *spigot* makes the blender work.

_____ 15. In which sentence is the word *groves* used correctly?
   A. Five *groves* of pigeons landed in the square.
   B. The carrier delivered three *groves* of papers.
   C. The guitar was fitted with half a dozen *groves*.
   D. The storm wiped out six *groves* of fruit trees.

_____ 16. Which of the following is a subordinate clause?
   A. Many consider Shakespeare the greatest writer.
   B. Merriam was enthralled by the sound of words.
   C. Which led her to write poems, fiction, and plays.
   D. Bogan had written poetry throughout her career.

_____ 17. Which sentence contains a subordinate clause?
   A. In the back yard on a hot summer day, Jane uncovered a rusty old spigot.
   B. All at once, when he was twelve years old, Sean wrote an excellent poem.
   C. Entranced by the rhythm of the moving train, Thomas felt himself being lulled to sleep.
   D. Anna noted the alliteration in "Full Fathom Five" and the repetition in "Train Tune."

Essay

18. Look again at the poem "Onomatopoeia." In an essay, suggest why Eve Merriam might have varied the lengths of the lines the way she did. First, describe how the line lengths vary. Then, tell how the variation relates to the event described in the poem.

19. In an essay, explain how the alliteration in "Full Fathom Five" helps convey the atmosphere of the poem. Think about where the poem is set and what is described. Then, give two examples of alliteration in the poem, and describe how they add to the atmosphere.

20. In an essay, discuss the meaning of the words that end each line of "Train Tune"— "clouds," "clearing," "distance," and so on. What idea or ideas do you think the words are meant to communicate?

21. **Thinking About the Big Question: What is the best way to communicate?** Think about the rhythm of the sound devices used in "Full Fathom Five," "Onomatopoeia," and "Train Tune." In an essay, compare the rhythm in at least two of the poems. In your answer, explain which rhythm you found most effective, and why.

Vocabulary Warm-up Word Lists

Study these words from the poetry of Edgar Allan Poe, Raymond Richard Patterson, and Emily Dickinson. Then, apply your knowledge to the activities that follow.

Word List A

age [AYJ] *n.* a period of time in history
   The <u>age</u> of chivalry, famous for its knights and daring deeds, began in the 12th Century.

darling [DAHR ling] *n.* someone who is deeply loved
   My uncle always called my aunt his <u>darling</u>.

dreary [DREER ee] *adj.* dull and gloomy
   The <u>dreary</u> weather made me want to stay home and read.

maiden [MAYD en] *n.* a young woman or girl who is not married
   The shepherd asked the young <u>maiden</u> to be his wife.

reason [REE zuhn] *n.* the cause or motive behind an action
   Unusually deep snow was the <u>reason</u> for the avalanche.

worth [WERTH] *n.* the quality that makes someone or something valuable or important
   The number of inventions that came from the mind of Thomas Edison is just one measure of his <u>worth</u>.

Word List B

aside [uh SYD] *adv.* to one side, sideways
   Mrs. Peters turned <u>aside</u> to let the principal pass.

envying [EN vee ing] *v.* desiring something possessed by someone else
   We were all <u>envying</u> the violinist's grace and talent.

kinsmen [KINZ muhn] *n.* relatives
   Many <u>kinsmen</u> joined in the ceremony, marking William's passage from boyhood to manhood.

passion [PASH uhn] *n.* very strong feeling; enthusiasm
   The actor's deep <u>passion</u> moved the audience to tears.

public [PUHB lik] *adj.* made or done openly for all to see
   We attended a <u>public</u> meeting for better schools.

wiser [WYZ er] *adj.* having or showing better judgment
   In his decision to return the money, Ben made a <u>wiser</u> choice than his partner.

Name _____ Date _____

Poetry Collection: Edgar Allan Poe, Raymond Richard Patterson, and Emily Dickinson
Vocabulary Warm-up Exercises

Exercise A *Fill in each blank in the paragraph below with an appropriate word from Word List A. Use each word only once.*

Before the Revolution, Marie Antoinette was the [1] _____ of the French court. She was just a young [2] _____ when she married the king. At first she did not like her new life. It was boring and [3] _____. The fact that she had no friends at court was one [4] _____ for her unhappiness. Another was her husband, King Louis, who Marie believed was undeserving of her love. Eventually, the French court embraced her and recognized the [5] _____ of Marie as their queen. The peasants did not, however. During the French Revolution, both Marie and Louis lost their heads, and the [6] _____ of the French Monarchy ended.

Exercise B *Find a synonym for each word in the following vocabulary list. Use each synonym in a sentence that makes the meaning of the word clear.*

Example: Vocabulary word: *public*   Synonym: *open*
    Sentence: *Celebrities' private thoughts are often made __open__ to the world.*

1. kinsmen

   _____

2. passion

   _____

3. wiser

   _____

4. envying

   _____

5. aside

   _____

Unit 4 Resources: Poetry
© Pearson Education, Inc. All rights reserved.
167

Poetry Collection: Edgar Allan Poe, Raymond Richard Patterson, and Emily Dickinson

Reading Warm-up A

Read the following passage. Pay special attention to the underlined words. Then, read it again, and complete the activities. Use a separate sheet of paper for your written answers.

Writing about true love is really hard to do. Many famous writers have tried and failed. There is a <u>reason</u> for this. Ordinary language cannot express the experience of deep love. Only words that go beyond the ordinary can do that. That's why the true language of love is found most often in poetry where all the elements of language deliver a single emotional punch.

In the mid-1800s, Edgar Allan Poe wrote *Annabel Lee,* a poem about a lovely young <u>maiden</u> who died. Although the subject seems <u>dreary</u>, the poem is quite beautiful. It speaks of a dear one's <u>worth</u>, her everlasting importance to the poet.

The first thing a reader notices is the musical quality of the poem. Poe created the musical language by repeating the letter "l" throughout the poem. You can hear it when you say the words out loud.

In poetry, love is often described in exaggerated language. In *Annabel Lee,* Poe claims the angels became so jealous of him and his beloved they stole away his <u>darling</u>. It is this claim that raises the poem's subject above the ordinary.

Poe's use of dark and light images also adds to the poem's powerful punch. Annabel's beauty is described with images of light: the heavens, the stars, and the moon. Annabel's death is described in dark images: *sepulchers,* or tombs; demons; and night clouds. Joy and sadness, love and loss, life and death—the light and dark images in the poem represent all of these.

Poe wrote *Annabel Lee* during an <u>age</u> when death was a popular subject in art and literature, making it a poem for its time. The reason for its continuing popularity, however, is easily explained. The poem is not about death. It's about undying love, which makes *Annabel Lee* a poem for every age and for all time.

1. Underline the sentence that gives the <u>reason</u> why many writers have failed to capture true love. Give one *reason* why you think writers continue to try.

2. Circle the words that name the lovely young <u>maiden</u>. Rewrite the sentence, using a synonym for *maiden*.

3. Circle a nearby word that means the opposite of <u>dreary</u>. Write a sentence using the word *dreary*.

4. Circle the words that give a clue to the meaning of <u>worth</u>. Is it possible to put a price or dollar value on a person's *worth*? Explain your answer.

5. Circle the word that is a synonym for <u>darling</u>. Write a sentence using the word *darling*.

6. Underline the words that describe the <u>age</u> in which Poe wrote Annabel Lee. Give a synonym for *age* as it is used in this passage.

Name _____ Date _____

Poetry Collection: Edgar Allan Poe, Raymond Richard Patterson, and Emily Dickinson
Reading Warm-up B

Read the following passage. Pay special attention to the underlined words. Then, read it again, and complete the activities. Use a separate sheet of paper for your written answers.

Before Martin Luther King Jr. became a hero, he had heroes of his own. One was his father, the Reverend Martin Luther King Sr., who preached love and tolerance. Another was Mahatma Gandhi, a Hindu leader preached social change through nonviolent protest. The teachings of these men helped to form Martin's <u>passion</u> for justice. It was this passion that made him a powerful leader.

During the 1960s, America needed a leader such as Martin. Although many young people sang about love and peace, much of what was going on was neither loving nor peaceful. President John F. Kennedy was assassinated. Shortly afterward, his brother Robert was assassinated, too. The Civil Rights Movement challenged attitudes toward blacks and other people of color. <u>Public</u> violence tore communities apart. An unpopular war in Vietnam became increasingly hated, as more and more soldiers died. The nation seemed to be spinning out of control.

Martin didn't have easy solutions for these problems, but he knew violence was not the answer. He believed nonviolent protests were the <u>wiser</u> way. Martin began to speak out for racial equality. He was attacked, thrown in jail, and even threatened. Still, he urged his followers to turn <u>aside</u> from riots and violent acts. His followers responded with sit-ins, marches, and public speeches. His enemies, fearing Martin's power and <u>envying</u> his success, continued to attack him. Still Martin encouraged only peaceful acts of protest. Soon people of every color, along with Martin's wife and <u>kinsmen</u>, joined him in marches that drew the attention of the entire nation.

During the March on Washington in 1963, whites and blacks together cheered Martin's now-famous speech. In it, he told of his dream of equal rights for all Americans. Martin Luther King Jr. became a national hero.

1. Circle the word tells what Martin had a <u>passion</u> for. Write about something for which you have a *passion*.

2. Circle the words that describe what <u>public</u> violence did. Write a sentence describing a *public* event you've attended.

3. Underline the words that tell what was <u>wiser</u> than violence. Give a synonym for *wiser*.

4. Underline the words that tell from what Martin urged his followers to turn <u>aside</u>. Write a sentence using an antonym for *aside*.

5. Circle the words that tell what Martin's enemies were <u>envying</u>. Explain what *envying* means in your own words.

6. According to this passage, who might Martin's <u>kinsmen</u> be? Circle another word in the passage that could replace *kinsmen* in this sentence.

Poetry Collection: Edgar Allan Poe, Raymond R. Patterson, Emily Dickinson

Writing About the Big Question

What is the best way to communicate?

Big Question Vocabulary

communicate	contribute	enrich	entertain	express
inform	learn	listen	media	produce
react	speak	teach	technology	transmit

A. *Use one or more words from the list above to complete each sentence.*

1. An argument with someone can _____ feelings of anger, or it can work out problems.

2. Arguing can actually be a good way to _____.

3. When you argue, you need to _____ yourself clearly.

4. Use positive words and a calm tone of voice when you _____.

B. *Respond to each item with a complete sentence.*

1. Describe an argument you have had in which you were able to communicate with the other person. Use at least two Big Question vocabulary words.

   _____

   _____

   _____

2. Explain how you expressed yourself in the argument, describing the words you used and your tone of voice.

   _____

   _____

   _____

C. *In "Poetry Collection 7," the poets present people and ideas about which they feel passionate. Complete these sentences. Then, write a short paragraph connecting the sentences to the Big Question.*

Words can be used to **produce** _____

_____

The way people **react** can _____

_____

Poetry Collection: Edgar Allan Poe, Raymond Richard Patterson, Emily Dickinson

Reading: Reread in Order to Paraphrase

To **paraphrase** means to restate or explain something in your own words. When you paraphrase lines of poetry, you make the meaning clear to yourself. If you are unsure of a poem's meaning, **reread** the parts that are difficult. Follow these steps:

- Look up unfamiliar words, and replace them with words you know.
- Restate the line or passage using your own everyday words.
- Reread the passage to make sure that your version makes sense.

Look at these lines from the poem "Martin Luther King":

He came upon an age / Beset by grief, by rage

The first line tells you that King "came upon an age." If you look up "come upon" in a dictionary, you will learn that it means "meet by chance." In this case, you might use a looser definition: "happen to live in." *Age* can refer to the number of years a person has lived or to a period in history. In this case, it refers to a period of history when African Americans did not have the same rights as white Americans.

If you looked up *beset,* you would discover that one of its meanings is "troubled." You probably know that *grief* is a synonym for *sorrow* or *sadness* and that *rage* is a synonym for *anger.* Now you have all the ingredients for a paraphrase of the line. It might look like this:

He happened to live at a time that was troubled by sorrow and anger.

DIRECTIONS: *Read these passages from "Annabel Lee," "Martin Luther King," and "I'm Nobody." Following the process described above, write a paraphrase of each passage.*

1. "A wind blew out of a cloud by night / Chilling my Annabel Lee; /
So that her highborn kinsmen came / And bore her away from me, /
To shut her up in a sepulcher / In this kingdom by the sea."

_____

_____

_____

2. "He came upon an age / Beset by grief and rage—
His love so deep, so wide / He could not turn aside."

_____

_____

_____

3. "How dreary to be Somebody! / How public like a Frog /
To tell your name the livelong June / To an admiring Bog!"

_____

_____

Poetry Collection: Edgar Allan Poe, Raymond Richard Patterson, Emily Dickinson
Literary Analysis: Rhythm, Meter, and Rhyme

Rhythm and rhyme make poetry musical. **Rhythm** is a poem's pattern of stressed (ˊ) and unstressed (ˇ) syllables.

Meter is a poem's rhythmical pattern. It is measured in *feet*, or single units of stressed and unstressed syllables. In the examples below, stressed and unstressed syllables are marked, and the feet are separated by vertical lines (|). The first line of "Annabel Lee" contains four feet, and the second line contains three feet. The two lines of "Martin Luther King" contain three feet each.

Rhyme is the repetition of sounds at the ends of lines. The two words that rhyme in the lines from "Martin Luther King" are underlined.

It was MAN | -y and MAN | -y a YEAR | a-GO. | / In a KING | -dom BY | the SEA.

He CAME | up-ON | an AGE | be-SET | by GRIEF, | by RAGE.

A. DIRECTIONS: *Mark the stressed (ˊ) and unstressed (ˇ) syllables in these lines. Then, show the meter by drawing a vertical rule after each foot.*

1. But our love it was stronger by far than the love / Of those who were older than we

2. His passion, so profound, / He would not turn around.

B. DIRECTIONS: *The words that end each line of "Annabel Lee" and "Martin Luther King" are listed in the following items. In each item, circle each word that rhymes with another word. Then, draw lines to connect all the words that rhyme with each other in that item.*

1. ago sea know Lee thought me

2. child sea love Lee Heaven me

3. ago sea night Lee came me sepulcher sea

4. Heaven me know sea chilling Lee

5. love we we above sea soul Lee

6. dreams Lee Lee side bride sea sea

7. age rage / wide aside / profound around / Earth worth / be free

Poetry Collection: Edgar Allan Poe, Raymond Richard Patterson, Emily Dickinson

Vocabulary Builder

Word List

banish   coveted   envying   kinsmen   passion   profound

A. DIRECTIONS: *Read each sentence, and think about the meaning of the italicized word from the Word List. Then, answer the question, and explain your answer.*

1. The speaker in "Annabel Lee" says that the angels *coveted* the love between him and Annabel Lee. Did the angels criticize their love?

_____

2. The speaker in "Martin Luther King" says that King's feeling was *profound*. Did King feel very strongly?

_____

3. The speaker in "I'm Nobody" says that "they" will *banish* her if they find out that she is a Nobody. Will "they" accept her in their social circle?

_____

4. The speaker in "Annabel Lee" says the angels were *envying* the love he and Annabel shared. Did the angels want love for themselves?

_____

5. Annabel Lee's *kinsmen* took her away from the speaker. Were they related to her?

_____

6. The speaker of "Martin Luther King" says that King felt a deep *passion*. Was King's feeling one of despair?

_____

B. WORD STUDY: *The Latin prefix im- means "in, into, toward." Use the meaning of the italicized word in each question to write an answer.*

1. If someone had a tooth *implanted*, what would the result be?

_____

2. What would it look like if you *imprinted* a picture on a T-shirt?

_____

3. If your car is *impounded*, what has happened to it?

_____

Name _____ Date _____

Enrichment: Art

Visual art forms come in many shapes and sizes. One art form is a **collage,** a composition that is created by attaching different materials to a surface. Some materials such as photographs, postcards, parts of a letter or an e-mail message, or words, pictures, or articles clipped from magazines or newspapers are one-dimensional. Other materials such as cloth, yarn, wood, shells, beads, or leaves have texture.

DIRECTIONS: *Follow these steps to make a collage based on one of the poems in this collection: "Annabel Lee," "Martin Luther King," or "I'm Nobody."*

1. Reread the poem you have chosen to illustrate. Select ten to fifteen words that appeal to you. Choose words that name things you might illustrate ("sea," "winged seraphs," "moon," "Martin Luther King," "Frog") and words that name or describe ideas or actions ("love," "envying," "profound," "Man's worth," "Nobody," "Somebody"). List your words here:

   _____

   _____

   _____

2. Gather materials. You will need one sheet of paper that is heavy enough to attach the other materials to. Do a scavenger hunt to see what you can come up with. Be sure that you use only materials that may be cut up. Here are some ideas: paper in different colors, paper of different textures, glossy magazines, newspapers.

3. Write the words you have chosen on the paper you have collected. Write the words in different styles and different sizes. You might write the words on newsprint, so that your words have words on them. You might generate words with a computer program. You might also write each letter of a word on a different kind of paper.

4. Be sure that you spell every word correctly. Cut out the words and letters.

5. Decide on an arrangement. Here are some ideas for arranging the letters and words on the page: Overlap words, or pair short words with long ones. Place the words in a circle or in a spiral. Arrange the words against blocks of different-colored paper. Arrange the words alphabetically.

6. If other materials—fabric, seashells, beads—are available, you might plan on adding them to your collage.

7. Now, carry out your plan: Paste or glue the letters and words onto the paper you saved for attaching your materials to.

8. When you have finished your collage, share it with your class.

Name _____ Date _____

Open-Book Test

Short Answer *Write your responses to the questions in this section on the lines provided.*

1. Rhyme is the repetition of sounds at the ends of words. In the first stanza of "Annabel Lee," there are two groups of lines that rhyme. Reread the stanza, and write the words that rhyme. Look at the end of each line to help you respond.

   _____

   _____

2. Reread lines 6–13 of "Annabel Lee." How and why was Annabel Lee taken away from the man who loved her? Use details from these lines to help you answer. You may include details from other lines to support your response.

   _____

   _____

   _____

3. In lines 17–19 of "Annabel Lee," the speaker describes an experience. Paraphrase these lines. Use your understanding of the poem, along with details from these lines, to help you tell what the speaker experiences in your own words.

   _____

   _____

4. In the final line of "Annabel Lee," there are stressed and unstressed syllables. Use your understanding of rhythm to tell which syllables are stressed and why they are stressed.

   _____

   _____

5. How does the poet use rhyme in "Martin Luther King"? Use the graphic organizer to list the pairs of words that rhyme in the poem. Circle the pair that is not an exact rhyme. Then, explain why the poet might have chosen to end the rhyme in this manner.

Rhyming Pairs in "Martin Luther King"				

   _____

6. In "Martin Luther King," the poet describes King's passion as "profound." Based on this description, would you have expected King to stay committed to his cause if he had lived longer? Use your understanding of *profound* to help you answer.

_____

_____

_____

7. Reread the final line of "Martin Luther King." Why does the poet say that King will "come again"? Explain what the poet might mean. Use specific examples from the poem to support your answer.

_____

_____

_____

8. Notice that "I'm Nobody" has punctuation in the middle of many of its lines. How does that affect the rhythm of the poem? Identify the rhythm of "I'm Nobody" as regular or irregular. Explain your answer, using a line or two from the poem as support.

_____

_____

_____

_____

9. In line 4 of "I'm Nobody," the speaker suggests that she and the listener run the risk of being banished. Why is being banished something to fear? Use the definition of *banish* in your answer.

_____

_____

10. In "I'm Nobody," why does the poet choose a frog to represent a "Somebody"? In your answer, explain whether you think a frog is really a "Somebody."

_____

_____

_____

Essay

Write an extended response to the question of your choice or to the question or questions your teacher assigns you.

11. What is the poet's main message in "Martin Luther King"? In a brief essay, explore the main idea that the poet is trying to communicate. Select important words or phrases that support your opinion about the main idea.

12. Would you describe the mood of "Annabel Lee" as depressing, or do you think there is another way to characterize the poem? In a short essay, express your opinion about the feelings the poem expresses. Use details from "Annabel Lee" to support your analysis.

13. In "I'm Nobody," how does the speaker feel about being a nobody? In an essay, explore the comparison she makes between a nobody and a somebody. Include in your answer an explanation for why she feels that being one is better than being the other.

14. **Thinking About the Big Question: What is the best way to communicate?** "Annabel Lee," "Martin Luther King," and "I'm Nobody" each tell a story about someone. Would the same story be as effective if it were told in prose form? In an essay, explore how one of the poems in this collection might tell a more or less effective story in prose form.

Oral Response

15. Go back to question 2, 3, or 10 or to the question your teacher assigns you. Take a few minutes to expand your answer and prepare an oral response. Find additional details in the poem or poems that support your points. If necessary, make notes to guide your oral response.

Poetry Collection: Edgar Allan Poe, Raymond Richard Patterson, Emily Dickinson
Selection Test A

Critical Reading *Identify the letter of the choice that best answers the question.*

____ 1. There are eight unstressed syllables in this line from "Annabel Lee." How many stressed syllables are there?

   It was many and many a year ago

   A. two
   B. four
   C. six
   D. eight

____ 2. According to the speaker in "Annabel Lee," where does the action described in the poem take place?

   A. in a city
   B. in heaven
   C. under the sea
   D. by the sea

____ 3. What is the best paraphrase of this passage from "Annabel Lee"?

   her highborn kinsmen came / And bore her away from me, / To shut her up in a sepulcher

   A. Her tallest family members kidnapped her and imprisoned her in a cell.
   B. Her aristocratic relatives carried away her corpse and buried it in a tomb.
   C. Her royal relatives carried her from me and imprisoned her in a room.
   D. Her oldest family members carried away her corpse and buried it in a tomb.

____ 4. How many syllables are stressed in this line from "Martin Luther King"?

   He came upon an age

   A. two
   B. three
   C. four
   D. six

____ 5. What poetic technique is illustrated by the use of the words "age" and "rage" in "Martin Luther King"?

   A. meter
   B. rhyme
   C. rhythm
   D. rhythmic pattern

_____ 6. What is the meaning of these lines from "Martin Luther King"?

> His love so deep, so wide, / He could not turn aside. /
> His passion, so profound, / He would not turn around.

   A. Martin Luther King was too loving and passionate to work effectively.

   B. Martin Luther King was too stubborn to change the way he worked.

   C. Martin Luther King's love and passion kept him going in a straight line.

   D. Martin Luther King's love and passion drove him to accomplish his mission.

_____ 7. In writing "Martin Luther King," what was the poet most likely trying to do?

   A. tell about the grief that Martin Luther King felt

   B. persuade readers of the worth of Martin Luther King

   C. praise the passion and commitment of Martin Luther King

   D. criticize people's lack of interest in the grief and rage around them

_____ 8. Who are the subjects of "I'm Nobody"?

   A. frogs and people

   B. Nobodies and Somebodies

   C. individuals and pairs

   D. land dwellers and bog dwellers

_____ 9. What is the best paraphrase of these lines from "I'm Nobody"?

> Are you—Nobody—too? / Then there's a pair of us!

   A. Do you have no name? Then we are a pair without names.

   B. If you are also no one important, then there are two of us.

   C. If your name is also Nobody, then we make a pair.

   D. Are you named Nobody also? There are two of us.

_____ 10. What does the speaker in "I'm Nobody" say is dreary?

   A. being well known

   B. being a frog

   C. being a bog

   D. being unknown

Vocabulary and Grammar

_____ 11. In which sentence is the word *coveted* used correctly?

   A. The princess *coveted* the queen's jewelry.

   B. The queen threw her *coveted* possessions into the fire.

   C. Taylor *coveted* the lowest grade on the test.

   D. John *coveted* the paper because it was full of bad news.

_____ 12. In which sentence does the word *profound* make sense?

    A. Feeling a *profound* disappointment, Anthony began to sing.

    B. Our surprise at being awarded the prize was *profound*.

    C. Her feeling was so *profound* that it lasted just ten minutes.

    D. Jessica fell into a *profound* sleep, waking several times in the night.

_____ 13. Which of the following is a simple sentence—a single independent clause?

    A. Annabel Lee was a child, and the speaker was a child.

    B. Not only did Edgar Allan Poe write poetry, but he also wrote stories.

    C. Martin Luther King was born in 1929, and he was assassinated in 1968.

    D. Emily Dickinson was not well known in her lifetime.

_____ 14. Which of the following is a compound sentence?

    A. Edgar Allan Poe wrote poetry, but he is also known for his short stories.

    B. Martin Luther King was a student of the teachings of Mohandas Gandhi.

    C. In 1964, Martin Luther King was awarded the Nobel Prize for Peace.

    D. Emily Dickinson hardly ever traveled far from her home in Massachusetts.

Essay

15. The poems "Annabel Lee" and "Martin Luther King" are very different in subject matter, rhythm, and rhyme. Which poem do you like better? In an essay, state which poem you prefer. Paraphrase the main idea of the poem. Then, tell why you like it.

16. The speaker of "I'm Nobody" makes it clear that she thinks it is better to be a nobody than a somebody. Do you agree or disagree? In an essay, give your opinion, and explain why you believe the way you do. Refer to two details in the poem in your explanation.

17. **Thinking About the Big Question: What is the best way to communicate?** Each of the poems in this section—"Annabel Lee," "Martin Luther King," and "I'm Nobody"—tells a story about someone. Would the same story be as effective if it were told in prose form? In an essay, explore how one of the poems in this collection might work better or not as well in prose form.

Poetry Collection: Edgar Allan Poe, Raymond Richard Patterson, Emily Dickinson
Selection Test B

Critical Reading *Identify the letter of the choice that best completes the statement or answers the question.*

_____ 1. Which of the following words from "Annabel Lee" form a rhyme?
A. "ago," "sea," "thought," "child"
B. "child," "love," "Lee," "Heaven"
C. "ago," "sea," "know," "Lee"
D. "heaven," "me," "know," "chilling"

_____ 2. What is the pattern of metrical feet in this passage from "Annabel Lee"?
It was many and many a year ago, / In a kingdom by the sea.

A. four feet in each line
B. three feet in each line
C. four feet in the first line, three feet in the second line
D. three feet in the first line, four feet in the second line

_____ 3. When does the speaker in "Annabel Lee" dream of and see Annabel Lee?
A. when he is near the sea
B. when the moon beams and the stars rise
C. when he visits her tomb
D. when the weather is stormy and chilly

_____ 4. Where does Annabel Lee live?
A. in a distant kingdom
B. in her lover's memory
C. in a beautiful castle
D. under the sea

_____ 5. What is the best summary of the speaker's basic message in "Annabel Lee"?
A. I am heartbroken, and I will never stop loving Annabel Lee.
B. I am heartbroken, and I will get revenge for Annabel Lee's death.
C. Annabel Lee and I were friends from the time we were children.
D. Annabel Lee is buried by the sea because she loved the sea.

_____ 6. What is the pattern of stressed and unstressed syllables in each metrical foot in the following passage from "Martin Luther King"?
His love so deep, so wide, / He could not turn aside.

A. stressed, unstressed
B. unstressed, stressed
C. stressed, unstressed, unstressed
D. unstressed, unstressed, stressed

____ 7. What is the best paraphrase of these lines from "Martin Luther King"?
He taught this suffering Earth / The measure of Man's worth.

A. He taught people in trouble the meaning of human dignity.
B. He taught that suffering could be ended on earth.
C. He taught that dignity goes hand in hand with suffering.
D. He taught that suffering is something to be desired.

____ 8. Which word best describes the speaker's view of the human experience in "Martin Luther King"?
A. blessed
B. peaceful
C. doomed
D. troubled

____ 9. What is the basic message of "Martin Luther King"?
A. Martin Luther King was set free by death.
B. Martin Luther King lived during troubled times.
C. Martin Luther King was a loving and passionate teacher.
D. Martin Luther King taught people what they could achieve.

____ 10. Which lines rhyme in this verse from "I'm Nobody"?
I'm Nobody! Who are you? / Are you—Nobody—too? /
Then there's a pair of us! / Don't tell! they'd banish us—you know!

A. the first and second
B. the first and third
C. the first, second, and fourth
D. the second and fourth

____ 11. What is the speaker in "I'm Nobody" saying?
A. She thinks that frogs need to be protected.
B. She believes that bogs are noisy places.
C. She wants to remain hidden and unknown.
D. She cannot be heard when she speaks in public.

____ 12. What is the best paraphrase of "an admiring Bog" in the last line of "I'm Nobody"?
A. an overcrowded pond
B. a cheering crowd
C. a restored wetland
D. a summer audience

____ 13. The speaker in "I'm Nobody" regards fame as
A. a good thing.
B. the American dream.
C. a bad thing.
D. a reward for hard work.

Vocabulary and Grammar

____ 14. In which sentence does the word *profound* make sense?

A. The mourners, deeply moved by the man's death, expressed their *profound* sympathy.

B. The candidate, not caring if she won or lost, showed a *profound* interest in the race.

C. Hearing that the test did not count, the students showed *profound* interest in their scores.

D. The man showed a *profound* sadness, shedding one tear and then breaking into laughter.

____ 15. In which sentence does the word *banish* make sense?

A. The king wishes to *banish* his brother because he loves him greatly.

B. If I tell you this sad story, it will surely *banish* your bad mood.

C. If the man betrays his friends, they will surely *banish* him.

D. The people begged the emperor to *banish* the popular official.

____ 16. Which of the following is a compound sentence?

A. Although Annabel Lee has died, the speaker in the poem still loves her.

B. The speaker and Annabel Lee loved each other passionately even when they were young.

C. The speaker continues to see Annabel Lee in his memory, and he always will.

D. The angels envied the lovers and therefore caused Annabel Lee to die.

____ 17. Which of these is a complex sentence?

A. Emily Dickinson rarely left Amherst, Massachusetts, where she was born.

B. Dickinson lived quietly, and she wrote hundreds of poems in her lifetime.

C. Dickinson did not wish to be famous, but she did become famous after her death.

D. Along with Walt Whitman, Dickinson is considered one of America's greatest poets.

Essay

18. Some people say that "Annabel Lee" tells a story. Others say that it communicates a mood. What do you think? In an essay, argue for one view or the other, or present an argument that combines the two views. Refer to at least three details in the poem to support your opinion.

19. Even though it is a short poem, "I'm Nobody" tells a great deal about the poet, Emily Dickinson. In an essay, use elements of the poem to describe what Dickinson might have been like. Then, tell how Dickinson might have reacted had she known that she would be famous after her death.

20. The poets of "Annabel Lee" and "Martin Luther King" use rhythm, rhyme, and meter, as well as other poetic devices, to create verbal music. In an essay, compare and contrast the ways in which the poets create their poetry. Consider how the poems are alike and how they are different. Refer to two instances of rhythm, rhyme, and/or meter in each poem to support your points.

21. **Thinking About the Big Question: What is the best way to communicate?** "Annabel Lee," "Martin Luther King," and "I'm Nobody" each tell a story about someone. Would the same story be as effective if it were told in prose form? In an essay, explore how one of the poems in this collection might tell a more or less effective story in prose form.

Vocabulary Warm-up Word Lists

Study these words from the poetry of Gwendolyn Brooks, Lewis Carroll, and Robert Frost. Then, complete the activities that follow.

Word List A

awfully [AW flee] *adv.* very
 Edward was <u>awfully</u> glad the bad weather didn't delay his flight.

enough [ee NUF] *adj.* as much or as many as necessary
 The farmer had <u>enough</u> seed to plant a hundred acres of lettuce.

hardly [HAHRD lee] *adv.* only just; scarcely
 The surfer could <u>hardly</u> believe the size of the giant wave.

replied [ri PLYD] *v.* gave an answer
 The quiz show contestant <u>replied</u> correctly to the $100,000 question.

steady [STED ee] *adj.* firm or stable, not shaky
 The pilot kept the plane <u>steady</u> on its course in spite of the high winds.

suppose [suh POHZ] *v.* to imagine that something is possible or true
 I <u>suppose</u> Maggie will win the cheerleader trophy again this year.

Word List B

argued [AHR gyood] *v.* to present reasons or opinions to prove something
 The defense lawyer <u>argued</u> for a verdict of *not guilty*.

clever [KLEV uhr] *adj.* able to think quickly and creatively
 The <u>clever</u> writer has won many prizes for her poetry.

medicine [MED i sin] *n.* a substance used for treating illness
 The patient had to take <u>medicine</u> for his cough three times a day.

ointment [OINT muhnt] *n.* soft, oily substance rubbed on the skin to heal a rash or wound
 The doctor prescribed an <u>ointment</u> to treat Sharon's skin rash.

promises [PRAHM is ez] *n.* statements that something will definitely be done or something will definitely happen
 Raymond made several <u>promises</u> to his mom that he would be more helpful around the house.

youth [YOOTH] *n.* the time of life, before adulthood, when someone is young
 The elderly man misses the strength and energy he had in his <u>youth</u>.

Poetry Collection: Gwendolyn Brooks, Lewis Carroll, and Robert Frost
Vocabulary Warm-up Exercises

Exercise A *Fill in each blank in the paragraph below with an appropriate word from Word List A. Use each word only once.*

Jessica's mom began packing the vacation clothes. "I [1] _____ you're disappointed that we're leaving the resort early," she said.

"I am," Jessica [2] _____, climbing onto a chair to reach a high shelf. "We've [3] _____ been here a week, and you know me. I can never get [4] _____ of the beach."

"That chair is not very [5] _____," her mother warned. "See how it wobbles?" At that moment the chair collapsed, throwing Jessica to the floor.

"Ouch!" Jessica cried, clutching her ankle. "I think I broke something."

Her mom helped her up. "You broke a chair!" she said laughing, "You must want to stay [6] _____ bad if you're willing to break a leg to do so!"

Exercise B *Revise each sentence so that the underlined vocabulary word is used in a logical way. Be sure to keep the vocabulary word in your revision.*

Example: Many children have happy memories of their <u>youth</u>.
Many adults have happy memories of their <u>youth</u>.

1. The teacher was very disappointed with the student's <u>clever</u> answers.

   _____

2. Because the two friends agreed about everything, they <u>argued</u> constantly.

   _____

3. The <u>ointment</u> helped to clear up the man's stomach problems.

   _____

4. People who keep their <u>promises</u> are usually very unreliable.

   _____

5. The patient took the <u>medicine</u> to pay her hospital bill.

   _____

Poetry Collection: Gwendolyn Brooks, Lewis Carroll, and Robert Frost

Reading Warm-up A

Read the following passage. Pay special attention to the underlined words. Then, read it again, and complete the activities. Use a separate sheet of paper for your written answers.

Last summer my grandmother got sick and moved into our house. I became her nurse because Mom and Dad both work. I was the only one available until Gram's insurance approved <u>enough</u> money for a real nurse. The job wasn't hard. I only had to help her in and out of bed, fix her lunch, and make sure she took her pills. The rest of the day I just watched TV. Sometimes my friends would call, but I <u>hardly</u> ever had company except for Bobby Standish. He'd come over to play video games, but Bobby didn't enjoy that very much. He's into baseball.

One afternoon, Bobby called and said his team's second-base player was sick. He wanted me to help out with the game. "Come on," he begged. "You'll only be gone an hour or so. You'll be home before your parents."

"I don't think so," I <u>replied</u>, but I really wanted to go. "Wait a minute." I checked on Gram. She was sleeping and it looked as if she was out for the afternoon. I went back to the phone. "Bobby, I <u>suppose</u> it will be all right; that is, I guess, if I'm not gone too long."

While I was waiting for Bobby to pick me up I started to worry. What if Gram woke up while I was out? She was <u>awfully</u> weak and very frail. She might fall trying to get out of bed and break a bone. By the time Bobby came to get me, I had changed my mind. I told him I couldn't leave after all. Bobby was pretty angry, even though I apologized. Anyway, I know it was the right decision because, soon after he left, Gram did wake up and she called for me.

"Rudy? Rudy, I need to get up, but my legs don't feel very <u>steady</u>."

I was there to answer, "I'm here, Gram. I'm right here." It felt really good.

1. Circle the word that tells what Gram needed <u>enough</u> of to hire a nurse. Write the definition of *enough*.

2. Circle the word that tells what Rudy <u>hardly</u> ever had. Rewrite the sentence using a synonym for *hardly*.

3. Underline the words that tell how Rudy <u>replied</u> to Bobby. Find and circle a synonym for *replied* in the next paragraph.

4. Underline the word that means about the same thing as <u>suppose</u>. Write a sentence, using the word *suppose*.

5. Circle the word that is a synonym for <u>awfully</u>. Write a sentence about a sport that you think is *awfully* dangerous.

6. Circle the word that tells what wasn't <u>steady</u>. Rewrite the sentence without changing the meaning, using an antonym for *steady*.

Poetry Collection: Gwendolyn Brooks, Lewis Carroll, and Robert Frost
Reading Warm-up B

Read the following passage. Pay special attention to the underlined words. Then, read it again, and complete the activities. Use a separate sheet of paper for your written answers.

When you are young, it is difficult to imagine yourself as old. It's equally difficult to imagine an old person as ever being young. <u>Youth</u> and old age, however, mark the beginning and end of the same life. If you live long, you will grow old. That is one of life's <u>promises</u> you can count on!

Not too long ago, the average lifetime lasted about 30 to 40 years. Disease and lack of effective <u>medicine</u> almost guaranteed a short life. Fortunately, in recent times, scientists have developed preventive medicines and cures for many life-threatening diseases. We have a pill, an <u>ointment</u>, or a medical procedure to ease many ailments. Because of this and other factors, people now expect to live at least 25 years longer than their ancestors.

Today, a person is considered a youth for the first 20 years of life and an active adult for the next 45 years. During the active years, a person usually works at a job or profession. Beyond the age of 65, though, most people retire from demanding jobs and engage in lighter activities.

People over 65 are often very wise. Perhaps, this is because older people tend to think a lot about their past. They remember important events, successes and failures, and all the joys and sorrows of their lives. Looking back on a lifetime of experiences, the elderly person begins to understand, at last, how life works. So, although the young are valued for their quick and <u>clever</u> minds, it can be <u>argued</u> that elderly minds offer something of value, too. They have the wisdom that comes after long life.

It will be many years before you retire. Until then, here is a wish for you. Live well, live long, and grow wise!

1. Circle the words that mean the opposite of <u>youth</u>. Write a sentence using a synonym for *youth*.

2. Underline the sentence that reveals one of life's <u>promises</u>. Write about two *promises* you have made to yourself.

3. Underline the words that tell what a lack of <u>medicine</u> almost guaranteed. Write the meaning of *medicine*.

4. Underline the words that tell the purpose of an <u>ointment</u>. Write a sentence using the word *ointment*.

5. Circle the nearby word that means almost the same thing as <u>clever</u>. Describe someone you know who has a *clever* mind.

6. Underline the words that tell what can be <u>argued</u>. Write the definition of *argued*.

Poetry Collection: Lewis Carroll, Robert Frost, Gwendolyn Brooks

Writing About the Big Question

What is the best way to communicate?

Big Question Vocabulary

communicate	contribute	enrich	entertain	express
inform	learn	listen	media	produce
react	speak	teach	technology	transmit

A. *Use one or more words from the list above to complete each sentence.*

1. When you take part in a poetry slam, you can _____ an audience with poetry.

2. You _____ yourself through your poetry to the audience.

3. Your audience can _____ about you as they _____ to your poems.

B. *Respond to each item with a complete sentence.*

1. Describe a poem you have listened to or read that you found moving or entertaining.

   _____

   _____

   _____

2. Explain why the poem entertained you, and explain what you learned from it. Use at least two Big Question vocabulary words in your response.

   _____

   _____

   _____

C. *In "Poetry Collection 8," each poem uses rhythm and rhyme to create a musical quality. Complete this sentence. Then, write a short paragraph connecting the sentences to the Big Question.*

Messages that **entertain** as well as **inform** _____

_____

_____

Poetry Collection: Gwendolyn Brooks, Lewis Carroll, Robert Frost

Reading: Reread in Order to Paraphrase

To **paraphrase** means to restate or explain something in your own words. When you paraphrase lines of poetry, you make the meaning clear to yourself. If you are unsure of a poem's meaning, **reread** the parts that are difficult. Follow these steps:

- Look up unfamiliar words, and replace them with words you know.
- Restate the line or passage using your own everyday words.
- Reread the passage to make sure that your version makes sense.

Look at these lines from "Father William":

"In my youth," said his father, "I took to the law

    And argued each case with my wife;

And the muscular strength which it gave to my jaw

    Has lasted the rest of my life."

The first line tells you that Father William "took to the law." If you look up *law* in a dictionary, you will learn that one of its meanings is "the legal profession." Father William is saying that he was a lawyer. That knowledge will help you understand the second line: Father William prepared for his legal cases by arguing them with his wife. You probably know or can guess that *muscular* has to do with muscles. Now you have all the ingredients to write a paraphrase of the verse. It might look like this:

"When I was young," Father William said, "I was a lawyer

    And I talked over every case with my wife;

And as a result, I developed strong jaw muscles

    That I still have today."

DIRECTIONS: *Read these passages from "Jim," "Father William," and "Stopping by Woods on a Snowy Evening." Following the process described above, write a paraphrase of each passage.*

1. The sun should drop its greatest gold / On him.

    _____

2. "In my youth," said the sage, as he shook his gray locks, / "I kept all my limbs very supple / By the use of this ointment—one shilling the box—/ Allow me to sell you a couple?"

    _____

    _____

    _____

3. He gives his harness bells a shake / To ask if there is some mistake. / The only other sound's the sweep / Of easy wind and downy flake.

    _____

    _____

    _____

Poetry Collection: Gwendolyn Brooks, Lewis Carroll, Robert Frost
Literary Analysis: Rhythm, Meter, and Rhyme

Rhythm and rhyme make poetry musical. **Rhythm** is a poem's pattern of stressed (´) and unstressed (˘) syllables.

Meter is a poem's rhythmical pattern. It is measured in *feet*, or single units of stressed and unstressed syllables. In the examples below, stressed and unstressed syllables are marked, and the feet are separated by vertical lines (|). The first line of "Father William" contains four feet, and the second line contains three feet. The two lines of "Stopping by Woods on a Snowy Evening" contain four feet each.

"You are OLD, | Fa-ther WILL- | iam," the YOUNG | man SAID, |

And your HAIR | has be-COME | ver-y WHITE" |

Rhyme is the repetition of sounds at the ends of lines. The two words that rhyme in the lines from "Stopping by Woods on a Snowy Evening" are underlined.

My LIT- | tle HORSE | must THINK | it <u>QUEER</u> |

to STOP | with-OUT | a FARM- | house <u>NEAR</u> |

A. DIRECTIONS: *Mark the stressed (´) and unstressed (˘) syllables in these lines. Then, show the meter by drawing a vertical rule after each foot.*

1. "You are old," said the youth, "as I mentioned before. / And have grown most uncommonly fat."

2. He gives his harness bells a shake / To ask if there is some mistake. / The only other sound's the sweep / Of easy wind and downy flake.

B. DIRECTIONS: *The words that end each verse of "Jim," "Father William," and "Stopping by Woods on a Snowy Evening" are listed in the following items. In each item, circle each word that rhymes with another word. Then, draw lines to connect all the words that rhyme with each other in that item.*

1. boy Jim gold him / sick in bread medicine / room see baseball Terribly

2. said white head right / son brain none again before fat door that

3. locks supple box couple / weak suet beak do it law wife jaw life

4. suppose ever nose clever / enough airs stuff downstairs

5. know though here snow / queer near lake year

6. shake mistake sweep flake / deep keep sleep sleep

Poetry Collection: Gwendolyn Brooks, Lewis Carroll, Robert Frost
Vocabulary Builder

Word List

downy   harness   incessantly   sage   supple   uncommonly

A. DIRECTIONS: *Read each item, and think about the meaning of the italicized word from the Word List. Then, answer the question, and explain your answer.*

1. Father William stands on his head *incessantly*. Does he stand on his head for an hour at a time, taking breaks when he gets tired?

   _____

2. Father William is a *sage*. Would he be likely to do well on a quiz show?

   _____

3. Father William used an ointment to keep his joints *supple*. Was he likely to have had trouble bending down to tie his shoes?

   _____

4. The snow falls in *downy* flakes. Is the snow heavy?

   _____

5. The horse wears a *harness* with bells. Does the harness keep it warm?

   _____

6. Father William has grown *uncommonly* fat. Is it usual for someone to become so fat?

   _____

B. WORD STUDY: *The Latin prefix* un- *means "not." Answer each question by adding* un- *to each italicized word and using the new word in your response.*

1. What would happen if you were not *prepared* for a test?

   _____

2. Is a fantasy movie likely to have only *realistic* characters?

   _____

3. Is it hard to sleep in a *comfortable* bed?

   _____

Poetry Collection: Gwendolyn Brooks, Lewis Carroll, Robert Frost
Enrichment: Healthy Living

Lewis Carroll does not tell us how old "Father William" is, but he creates a picture of a vigorous old man. Father William stands on his head, turns backward somersaults, chews his food without a problem, and balances an eel on his nose. How unusual is Father William?

Today, people are living longer than ever. People are living healthy, vigorous lives into their eighties and nineties. Many people are still active in their hundreds. Consider the accomplishments of some older people and think about what you might want to accomplish eighty or even ninety years from now.

DIRECTIONS: *Do research in a book or on the Internet to answer these questions about the accomplishments of a few older people.*

1. Who is the oldest living man? How old is he, and where does he live? What are one or two things he has done in his life?

   _____

   _____

2. Who is the oldest living woman? How old is she, and where does she live? What are one or two things she has done in her life?

   _____

   _____

3. Who was the oldest man to complete a marathon? What marathon was it, and how old was he when he did it?

   _____

4. Who was the oldest woman to complete a marathon? What marathon was it, and how old was she when she did it?

   _____

5. Who was the oldest man to climb Mount Everest? How old was he when he did it?

   _____

6. Who was the oldest woman to win an Academy Award for Best Actress? How old was she when she did it?

   _____

7. Describe an active older person whom you admire, someone you know personally or have read about. How old is he or she? What about this person do you admire? Is the person doing anything remarkable, given his or her age?

   _____

   _____

Poetry Collections: Edgar Allan Poe, Raymond Richard Patterson, Emily Dickinson; Gwendolyn Brooks, Lewis Carroll, Robert Frost

Integrated Language Skills: Grammar

Sentence Structure

A **simple sentence** is an independent clause. That is, it is a group of words that has a subject and a verb and can stand by itself as a complete thought.

A **compound sentence** consists of two or more independent clauses that are joined by a conjunction such as *and, but, or,* or *for.*

> Lewis Carroll was a mathematician, <u>but</u> he also wrote stories and poetry.

A **complex sentence** contains one independent clause and one or more subordinate clauses. In this sentence, the subordinate clause is underlined:

> <u>Although he was a mathematician</u>, Lewis Carroll also wrote novels.

A. DIRECTIONS: *Identify each sentence below by writing* Simple, Compound, *or* Complex.

1. Gwendolyn Brooks lived in an area of Chicago known as Bronzeville, and one of her volumes of poetry is called *A Street in Bronzeville.*

   _____

2. Although she was primarily a poet, Brooks published a novel, *Maud Martha.*

   _____

3. Gwendolyn Brooks served as the poet laureate of Illinois.

   _____

4. Lewis Carroll's *Alice's Adventures in Wonderland* has been translated into more than thirty languages.

   _____

5. Carroll liked to write nonsense verse, and he invented nonsense characters, such as the Snark, the Jabberwock, and the twins Tweedledee and Tweedledum.

   _____

B. Writing Application: *Write a short paragraph in which you describe your reaction to one of the poems in these collections. Tell what you liked most about the poem and why it appeals to you. Use at least one simple sentence, one compound sentence, and one complex sentence. Label your sentences by writing* Simple, Compound, *or* Complex *in parentheses after each one.*

_____

_____

_____

_____

_____

Poetry Collections: Edgar Allan Poe, Raymond Richard Patterson, Emily Dickinson; Gwendolyn Brooks, Lewis Carroll, Robert Frost

Integrated Language Skills: Support for Writing a Paraphrase

Use these charts to draft a **paraphrase** of one of the six poems you have read. In the first chart, write down unfamiliar words from the poem, their dictionary definition, and the definition restated in your own words. In the second chart, write each line of the poem in the first column. In the second column, restate the meaning of the line in your own words. If you are paraphrasing "Father William," finish your paraphrase on a separate sheet of paper.

Title of poem: _____

Word to Look Up	Dictionary Definition	Definition in My Own Words

Poem, Line by Line	Paraphrase, Line by Line

Now, read over your paraphrase to make sure it has the same meaning as the original. Make your revisions as you prepare your final draft.

Poetry Collections: Edgar Allan Poe, Raymond Richard Patterson, Emily Dickinson; Gwendolyn Brooks, Lewis Carroll, Robert Frost

Integrated Language Skills: Support for Extend Your Learning

Research and Technology

As you gather information for your **survey,** use tally marks to enter the results. (With tally marks, each line stands for one vote. Draw every fifth line diagonally through the four preceding lines: ||||.) Using tally marks, you can easily count by fives to figure out which poem received the most votes in each category.

Category	"Annabel Lee"	"Martin Luther King"	"I'm Nobody"
Best character description			
Best overall use of language			
Best rhythm			
Best rhyme			
Best meter			

Category	"Jim"	"Father William"	"Stopping by Woods on a Snowy Evening"
Best character description			
Best overall use of language			
Best rhythm			
Best rhyme			
Best meter			

Now, circle the winning tally in each category. Which poem is the winner in the most categories? That poem is the class favorite. Write its title here. (If it's a tie, write both titles.)

Winner of Class-Favorite-Poem Award: _____

Name _____   Date _____

Poetry Collection: Gwendolyn Brooks, Lewis Carroll, Robert Frost
Open-Book Test

Short Answer *Write your responses to the questions in this section on the lines provided.*

1. Rhyme is the repetition of sounds at the ends of words. Reread "Jim" and look for rhyme. Which word does the poet rhyme with the word *see* in line 10? In your answer, explain why the rhyme works.

_____

_____

_____

2. Reread lines 5–8 of "Jim." Write a brief paraphrase of these lines. Include the main idea of the lines rather than every detail.

_____

_____

_____

3. Reread lines 3 and 4 of "Jim." Is the speaker's high opinion of Jim deserved? Explain your answer, using details from the rest of the poem as support.

_____

_____

_____

_____

4. In the first stanza of "Father William," we learn that the title character incessantly stands on his head. Based upon this description, would you expect him to be a typical senior citizen? Use the definition of *incessantly* in your answer.

_____

_____

_____

5. In line 14 of "Father William," the title character explains that his body is very supple. Why does he need to be supple? Use details from the poem and the definition of *supple* in your answer.

_____

_____

_____

_____

Name _____ Date _____

6. Reread the fourth stanza of "Father William," which begins on line 17. Think about the rhythm and rhyme of the lines. On the graphic organizer, list the rhyming word pairs from the stanza and whether the words have one or two syllables. Then, on the line, tell how the two-syllable pair changes the rhythm of those lines.

Rhyming Pairs	Syllables

_____

7. In "Father William," the title character explains that he has an exceptionally strong jaw. Why is his explanation especially humorous? Use details from lines 20–25 to support your response.

_____

_____

_____

_____

8. In the first four lines of "Stopping by Woods . . . ," the speaker has chosen to briefly stop. Why has he stopped? Use your understanding of the entire poem to help you respond.

_____

_____

_____

9. "Stopping by Woods . . ." has a rhyming pattern that changes in the last stanza. Look at lines 9–16. Explain how this rhyme pattern is different from the other three stanzas and why the poet might have chosen to make it different.

_____

_____

_____

_____

10. At the end of "Stopping by Woods . . . ," the speaker decides to leave the woods. Why does he decide to go? Use details from lines 13–16 to support your answer.

_____

_____

_____

Essay

Write an extended response to the question of your choice or to the question or questions your teacher assigns you.

11. Reread lines 10–12 from "Jim." In a brief essay, explain how he behaves in these lines and why he behaves that way. Include in your answer a description of Jim's character. Use details that support your explanation.

12. Reread the final stanza of "Stopping by Woods . . . ." In a brief essay, explore the meaning of these lines. Consider whether the poem is only about a ride on a snowy night. Include in your answer an explanation for why the poet may have repeated the last line.

13. Even though "Father William" is a humorous poem, it has a message. In a short essay, explain the main message of the poem. Use details from the poem to support your opinions.

14. Thinking About the Big Question: What is the best way to communicate? "Jim," "Father William," and "Stopping by Woods . . ." each has a character. Which of the poems does the best job of communicating what the character truly feels or thinks? In an essay, compare how the characters are presented in each poem. Explain why you think one poem best explores a particular character.

Oral Response

15. Go back to question 3, 7, or 9 or to the question your teacher assigns you. Take a few minutes to expand your answer and prepare an oral response. Find additional details in the poem or poems that support your points. If necessary, make notes to guide your oral response.

Poetry Collection: Gwendolyn Brooks, Lewis Carroll, Robert Frost

Selection Test A

Critical Reading *Identify the letter of the choice that best answers the question.*

___ 1. What is the meaning of this line from "Jim"?

   The sun should drop its greatest gold / On him.

   A. The sun should always shine on Jim.

   B. Jim should be rewarded for his goodness.

   C. The sun should keep rain from falling on Jim.

   D. Jim should wear a medal the color of the sun.

___ 2. Which lines rhyme in this verse from "Jim"?

   Because, when Mother-dear was sick, / He brought her cocoa in. /
   And brought her broth, and brought her bread. / And brought her medicine.

   A. every line

   B. the second and fourth lines

   C. the first and third lines and the second and fourth lines

   D. the first and second lines and the third and fourth lines

___ 3. What is the best paraphrase of the last verse of "Jim"?

   A. Jim walks on tiptoes as he cleans his mother's room and thinks about
      baseball.

   B. Jim, neatening his mother's room on tiptoes, is terribly sorry he cannot play
      baseball.

   C. Jim walks on tiptoes, cleans up his mother's room, and misses playing
      baseball.

   D. Jim quietly neatens his mother's room and does not let on that he misses
      playing baseball.

___ 4. What is the pattern of stressed and unstressed syllables in this line from
      "Father William"?

   "And your hair has become very white"

   A. stressed, unstressed, stressed

   B. stressed, unstressed, unstressed

   C. unstressed, stressed, unstressed

   D. unstressed, unstressed, stressed

_____ **5.** Which lines rhyme in this verse from "Father William"?

> "In my youth," said the sage, as he shook his gray locks,
>> "I kept all my limbs very supple
> By the use of this ointment—one shilling the box—
>> Allow me to sell you a couple?"

    A. every line

    B. the first and fourth lines

    C. the first and third lines and the second and fourth lines

    D. the first and second lines and the third and fourth lines

_____ **6.** "Father William" conveys a serious message. How would that message best be expressed?

    A. Young people cannot understand what old people want out of life.

    B. Old people can do many of the things they did when they were young.

    C. Young people ask some very ridiculous questions and anger their parents.

    D. Old people do some very ridiculous things and embarrass their children.

_____ **7.** What do Father William's final words to his son show about him?

    A. He loves his son deeply.

    B. He is about to fall asleep.

    C. He is running out of patience.

    D. He is funnier than he ever was.

_____ **8.** Which lines rhyme in this verse from "Stopping by Woods on a Snowy Evening"?

> Whose woods these are I think I know. / His house is in the village, though; /
> He will not see me stopping here / To watch his woods fill up with snow.

    A. every line

    B. the first, second, and fourth lines

    C. the first, third, and fourth lines

    D. the second, third, and fourth lines

_____ **9.** Why has the speaker in "Stopping by Woods on a Snowy Evening" stopped his horse?

    A. because he is lost

    B. to avoid responsibilities and promises

    C. because his horse is tired

    D. to appreciate the beauty of the woods

____ **10.** What is the best paraphrase of these lines from "Stopping by Woods on a Snowy Evening"?

My little horse must think it queer / To stop without a farmhouse near

A. My small horse must think it peculiar to stop without a farmhouse.

B. My small horse must think it odd that we have stopped far from any farmhouse.

C. My miniature horse must find it odd to come to a stop without a farmhouse.

D. My tiny horse must find it peculiar to stop someplace that does not have a farmhouse.

Vocabulary and Grammar

____ **11.** In which sentence does the word *sage* make sense?

A. The *sage* gave advice to all who came in search of wisdom.

B. A *sage* won the game with a last-minute touchdown.

C. Our uncle is a *sage* with a local insurance company.

D. The class *sage* is doing poorly in math and social studies.

____ **12.** Which of the following is a simple sentence?

A. When we were walking in the park, we found a stray cat.

B. It seemed healthy, although it was skinny and muddy.

C. We looked for the cat's owner even though it did not have a tag.

D. After feeding it for several days, we decided to keep the cat.

____ **13.** Which of the following is a compound sentence?

A. We took a trip to Arizona and saw the Grand Canyon.

B. Visitors can ride into the canyon even though it is hot.

C. The ride is extremely safe, but the trail is pretty narrow.

D. At the bottom, the Colorado River rushes right by your feet.

Essay

14. Both "Jim" and "Father William" are about a child and his parent. In an essay, contrast the two poems. State at least one way in which the young people are different and at least one way in which the old people are different.

15. Based on your reading of "Stopping by Woods on a Snowy Evening," what would you say was Robert Frost's view of the natural world? In an essay, respond to that question. Give two examples from the poem to support your viewpoint.

16. **Thinking About the Big Question: What is the best way to communicate?**
Each of the poems in this section—"Jim," "Father William," and "Stopping by Woods . . ."—features a main character. Which of the poems does the best job of communicating what the character truly feels or thinks? In an essay, explain why you think one poem best explores a particular character.

Poetry Collection: Gwendolyn Brooks, Lewis Carroll, Robert Frost
Selection Test B

Critical Reading *Identify the letter of the choice that best completes the statement or answers the question.*

___ 1. How many stressed syllables are there in this line from "Jim"?
    There never was a nicer boy

    A. two
    B. three
    C. four
    D. eight

___ 2. What is the pattern of stressed and unstressed syllables in this line from "Jim"?
    The sun should drop its greatest gold

    A. stressed, unstressed
    B. unstressed, stressed
    C. stressed, stressed
    D. unstressed, unstressed

___ 3. What is the meaning of these lines from "Jim"?
    The sun should drop its greatest gold / On him

    A. The sun should shine on Jim always.
    B. Jim is as accomplished as an Olympic gold medalist.
    C. The sun should allow Jim to become wealthy.
    D. Jim should be rewarded for his good deeds.

___ 4. What is the best paraphrase of the last verse of "Jim"?
    A. Jim tiptoes around while his mother is sick, caring for her and thinking of baseball.
    B. Jim, neatening his mother's room on tiptoes, is terribly sorry he is not playing baseball.
    C. Jim tiptoes, cleans his mother's room, and feels terribly sorry he is not playing baseball.
    D. Jim quietly neatens his mother's room and does not let on that he misses playing baseball.

___ 5. What is the pattern of stressed and unstressed syllables in this line from "Father William"?
    "You are old, Father William," the young man said

    A. stressed, unstressed, stressed
    B. stressed, unstressed, unstressed
    C. unstressed, stressed, unstressed
    D. unstressed, unstressed, stressed

_____ 6. Father William's son asks Father William about the goose he has eaten because he thinks that people as old as his father
   A. should eat only suet.
   B. need a balanced diet.
   C. can chew only the softest foods.
   D. should not be eating such rich foods.

_____ 7. Which statement best summarizes the main idea of "Father William"?
   A. Old people are often ridiculous.
   B. Young people are usually insensitive.
   C. Society's views on what is age-appropriate are silly.
   D. There will always be quarrels between parents and children.

_____ 8. How many metrical feet are there in each of these lines from "Stopping by Woods on a Snowy Evening"?
   Whose woods these are I think I know. / His house is in the village, though; /
   He will not see me stopping here / To watch his woods fill up with snow.
   A. two
   B. three
   C. four
   D. five

_____ 9. Where does the speaker in "Stopping by Woods on a Snowy Evening" halt his horse?
   A. by a farmhouse
   B. on a dirt road
   C. in the village
   D. by the woods

_____ 10. Why does the speaker in "Stopping by Woods on a Snowy Evening" hear so few sounds?
   A. It is the darkest evening of the year.
   B. The horse's bells drown out other sounds.
   C. The snow muffles most noise.
   D. The village is very far away.

_____ 11. What is the best paraphrase of these lines from "Stopping by Woods on a Snowy Evening"?
   The woods are lovely, dark, and deep, / But I have promises to keep
   A. I would like to stay, but I have too many other responsibilities.
   B. I made a promise that I would not take the road past the woods.
   C. The woods are beautiful, but they are owned by someone else.
   D. The woods are beautiful, but my horse is tired and hungry.

_____ 12. On a symbolic level, what does the speaker in "Stopping by Woods on a Snowy Evening" mean when he says, "And miles to go before I sleep"?
   A. He has a long way to go before he can go to bed.
   B. He has much to do before the end of his life.
   C. He is too far from home to get much sleep that night.
   D. He hopes he will not fall asleep on his way home.

Vocabulary and Grammar

____ 13. In which sentence does the word *incessantly* make sense?
A. The woodpecker tapped *incessantly* at the hard tree.
B. Our cat chased a mouse *incessantly* while she slept.
C. The rain fell *incessantly* during the long drought.
D. One should speak *incessantly* during a study period.

____ 14. In which sentence does the word *supple* make sense?
A. This *supple* sheetrock will not bend easily.
B. The *supple* branch broke under the weight of the snow.
C. This willow branch is *supple* enough to bend easily.
D. The dancer's *supple* movements were jerky.

____ 15. Which of the following is a compound sentence?
A. The poet stops at the woods, though his horse wants to keep going.
B. The speaker says that the woods are lovely, dark, and deep.
C. The poet wishes to stay, but he has promises to keep.
D. The horse gives its harness bells a shake.

____ 16. Which of the following is a complex sentence?
A. The son insults Father William, but the old man responds cleverly.
B. The old man replies to the young man's questions with good humor.
C. The young man asks questions, and the old man answers them.
D. The son insults Father William even though he should respect him.

____ 17. Which of the following is *not* a complex sentence?
A. When Jim's mother is sick, he brings her cocoa, broth, bread, and medicine.
B. In the view of the speaker in the poem, there is no one nicer than Jim.
C. Because his mother is ill, Jim must care for her and miss his baseball game.
D. The reader is inclined to admire Jim because the speaker praises him.

Essay

18. In the poems in this collection—"Jim," "Father William," and "Stopping by Woods on a Snowy Evening"—consider Jim, Father William, Father William's son, and the speaker in Frost's poem. Which of these characters do you find most interesting? In an essay, name the character you like best, and explain your opinion. Refer to three details in the poem to support your opinion.

19. Think about the dialogue between Father William and his son. In an essay, discuss what this poem has to tell the modern reader about youth and old age. In making your points, cite three details from the poem.

20. In an essay, analyze the different levels of meaning in "Stopping by Woods on a Snowy Evening." Cite one passage in the poem. First, tell the literal meaning of the passage. Then, present a different interpretation: the symbolic meaning of the passage. You might consider any of the lines in the last verse.

21. **Thinking About the Big Question: What is the best way to communicate?** "Jim," "Father William," and "Stopping by Woods. . ." each has a character. Which of the poems does the best job of communicating what the character truly feels or thinks? In an essay, compare how the characters are presented in each poem. Explain why you think one poem best explores a particular character.

Vocabulary Warm-up Word Lists

Study these words from the poetry of Walt Whitman and E. E. Cummings. Then, complete the activities that follow.

Word List A

balloonman [buh LOON man] *n.* a person who sells balloons
   The balloonman carried a huge bundle of colorful balloons into the park.

delicate [DEL i kit] *adj.* beautifully fine in texture, quality, or appearance
   The delicate lace of the gown was very pretty.

lame [LAYM] *adj.* having an injured foot or leg that causes one to limp
   The dog's lame foot made it difficult for the animal to take a walk.

Manhattan [man HAT en] *n.* an island forming one of the boroughs of New York City
   The downtown section of Manhattan is a popular tourist attraction.

motion [MOH shuhn] *n.* a movement
   The motion of the dancer was filled with leaps and kicks.

sight [SYT] *n.* the act of seeing with one's eyes
   Matt's sight was directed toward the sailboat on the horizon.

Word List B

continual [kuhn TIN yoo uhl] *adj.* ongoing, happening over and over again
   The continual passing of the seasons happens each year.

insects [IN sektz] *n.* members of a large class of small creatures, such as ants and termites
   The insects swarmed around the campers in the forest.

light [LYT] *n.* the daylight hours
   We saw pink light fill the sky as we watched the sunrise.

miracle [MEER uh kuhl] *n.* a marvel, a remarkable, unexplained event
   The kitten's sudden recovery from its illness seemed like a miracle.

spring [SPRING] *n.* the season of the year that follows winter, when the weather begins to warm
   Joan enjoyed the blooming flowers during spring.

whistles [HWIS uhlz] *v.* makes a note, tones, or a tune by blowing through the lips
   Dave always whistles a tune when he is busy painting the walls.

Poetry by Walt Whitman and E. E. Cummings
Vocabulary Warm-up Exercises

Exercise A *Fill in each blank in the paragraph below with an appropriate word from Word List A. Use each word only once.*

Norm went to [1] _____ in New York City to see the circus. After he

went inside the arena, he saw a [2] _____ selling balloons that had

been twisted into animal shapes. Then he looked upward and directed his

[3] _____ to acrobats tumbling through the air. One acrobat performed

a back-and-forth swinging [4] _____ on a rope before springing into the

air and being caught by another performer. In one ring, a chimp dressed as a hospital

patient pretended to have a [5] _____ leg and used a crutch to walk.

Next a baby elephant dressed in a tutu made of [6] _____ material did a

dance for them. Norm had a very entertaining time!

Exercise B *Revise each sentence so that the underlined vocabulary word is used in a logical way. Be sure to keep the vocabulary word in your revision.*

Example: It is unusual to hear the <u>continual</u> sound of the waves at the seashore.
  It is common to hear the <u>continual</u> sound of the waves at the seashore.

1. Most people enjoy being bitten by <u>insects</u>, such as flies.
   _____

2. If someone <u>whistles</u>, he uses his feet to make a noise.
   _____

3. It will more difficult to find the lost ring in the <u>light</u> of day.
   _____

4. It was a <u>miracle</u> that Dean passed the test when he studied so much for it.
   _____

5. This <u>spring</u> the leaves will be pretty colors.
   _____

Poetry by Walt Whitman and E. E. Cummings
Reading Warm-up A

Read the following passage. Pay special attention to the underlined words. Then, read it again, and complete the activities. Use a separate sheet of paper for your written answers.

Jill lived in <u>Manhattan</u>, one of the most exciting parts of New York City. She loved to watch the people, hurrying on their way to classes or work. The city was filled with activity and <u>motion</u>. Jill imagined the lives of the people she saw. She enjoyed sketching them in her journal and writing about those who caught her interest. Her imagination soared as she made up all kinds of things about these strangers.

School, however, was another matter. There, the other kids seemed to know how to joke and talk with each other. It was hard for Jill to join in, so she often worked by herself during lunch, refining the <u>delicate</u> lines of her sketches and writing more stories.

Her quiet world was about to change when her teacher, Mr. Flanagan, asked Jill if she would help Terri, a new girl in school, with her writing. Mr. Flanagan suggested the two spend some time together. He knew about Jill's journal, and he asked her to share some of it with Terri. He thought Terri might be encouraged to write by Jill's example.

At first, Jill didn't want to. Terri was very talkative and good at sports. Would they have anything in common?

Reluctantly, she agreed to meet Terri after school. They walked around the park. A <u>balloonman</u> stood, selling his colorful wares. The girls giggled at the funny shapes of the balloons. Then their <u>sight</u> turned to a little old lady lovingly feeding a <u>lame</u> pigeon. Jill and Terri decided to sketch her. Then Jill suggested they both write about the old woman's life. Terri wanted to go skating at the rink in the park next. At first, Jill was cautious on her skates, but with Terri's help she gained confidence.

Jill was surprised by how fast the afternoon passed. The two agreed to meet again the next day. As she walked home, Jill realized sharing her "make-believe" friends with a real friend was more fun than she ever could have imagined.

1. Circle the words that tell what <u>Manhattan</u> is. What would you like to see if you lived in or visited *Manhattan*?

2. Underline the word that is another word for <u>motion</u>. Use *motion* in a sentence.

3. Underline the words that <u>delicate</u> describes. Define *delicate*.

4. Underline the words that tell what the <u>balloonman</u> stood in the park doing. Where else might you see a *balloonman*?

5. Circle the words that tell what the girls saw when their <u>sight</u> turned to something else. What does *sight* mean?

6. Circle the word in the story that tells what was <u>lame</u>. Use *lame* in a sentence.

Poetry by Walt Whitman and E. E. Cummings
Reading Warm-up B

Read the following passage. Pay special attention to the underlined words. Then, read it again, and complete the activities. Use a separate sheet of paper for your written answers.

Spring is a beautiful season of the year. It is the season that comes after winter and before summer. In spring, birds are busy building nests. Their chirping often sounds like someone who happily whistles a tune. Many baby animals are born in the spring. The plants seem to come alive again, too. Grass turns green, and flowers bud and burst into bloom. This lovely season also brings longer daylight hours, and the temperature begins to warm.

What causes the season of spring? This season of new life seems like a miracle, but it is actually the result of the position of the Earth in relation to the sun. The Earth is on a continual trip around the sun. This never-ending journey is called Earth's orbit. As the Earth orbits the sun, the Earth is also tilting. Imagine a rubber ball with a stick through it. Then imagine holding the stick at a slight angle. That is how the Earth is tilting as it travels.

In spring, the northern part of the world tilts toward the sun while on its journey, causing this part of the Earth to have spring. This happens about March 21 each year, which is the beginning of spring. Earth receives the sun's rays more directly at this time, bringing more hours of light and more warmth from the sun.

The extra light and warmth of spring are a signal to plants and animals to start a new cycle of life. Insects, such as ants, swarm. They have come out of a dormant, or sleeping state, and are ready to gather food and build their colony. Animals, such as skunks and chipmunks that hibernate during the cold of winter when food is hard to find, awaken now. These creatures begin to look for food, such as berries and nuts, which the plants are now producing. As flowers bloom and leaves sprout on the trees, they, too, are beginning a new cycle of life on the planet Earth.

1. Underline the words that describe when spring takes place. Use *spring* in a sentence.

2. Circle the words that tell what the story compares to the sound of someone who whistles a tune. Tell what *whistles* means.

3. Circle the words that tell what seems like a miracle. Define *miracle*.

4. Circle the words that are synonyms for continual trip. What other things can you think of that are *continual*?

5. Underline the words that explain why there are more hours of light in spring. Define *light* as it is used in this passage.

6. Underline the kind of insects mentioned in the story. Name a few more kinds of *insects*.

Name _____ Date _____

Writing About the Big Question

What is the best way to communicate?

Big Question Vocabulary

communicate	contribute	enrich	entertain	express
inform	learn	listen	media	produce
react	speak	teach	technology	transmit

A. *Use one or more words from the list above to complete each sentence.*

1. You can _____ with others by speaking, writing, or through the arts.

2. All communication helps you _____ about other people.

3. Communication can _____ your life and the lives of others.

B. *Respond to each item with a complete sentence.*

1. Describe your favorite way to communicate and tell when you are likely to use it. Use at least two Big Question vocabulary words.

   _____

   _____

   _____

2. Explain why you prefer to communicate in the way you have chosen. Tell how it helps you express yourself and learn about other people.

   _____

   _____

   _____

C. In the poetry of Whitman and Cummings, the writers use imagery to paint vivid pictures in the minds of readers. Think about the Big Question as you complete the sentence.

   Descriptive words can enrich a piece of writing because _____ .

   _____

   _____

   _____

Name _____ Date _____

Poetry by Walt Whitman and E. E. Cummings
Literary Analysis: Comparing Imagery

In poetry, an **image** is a word or phrase that appeals to one or more of the five senses. Writers use **imagery** to bring poetry to life with descriptions of how their subjects look, sound, feel, taste, and smell.

Both "Miracles" and "in Just—" contain images that appeal to the senses. For example, "wade with naked feet along the beach" appeals to the sense of touch, and "the little lame balloonman" appeals to sight.

DIRECTIONS: *Read each image in the first column, and mark an X in the column or columns to indicate the sense or senses that the image appeals to. The first fifteen images are from "Miracles"; the last nine are from "in Just—."*

Image	Sight	Hearing	Touch	Taste	Smell
1. "walk the streets of Manhattan"					
2. "dart my sight over the roofs"					
3. "stand under trees in the woods"					
4. "talk by day with any one I love"					
5. "sit at table at dinner with the rest"					
6. "look at strangers opposite me"					
7. "honeybees busy around the hive"					
8. "animals feeding in the fields"					
9. "birds, or . . . insects in the air"					
10. "the sundown"					
11. "stars shining so quiet and bright"					
12. "thin curve of the new moon"					
13. "fishes that swim the rocks"					
14. "the motion of the waves"					
15. "the ships with men in them"					
16. "the world is mud-luscious"					
17. "little lame balloonman whistles"					
18. "eddieandbill come running"					
19. "from marbles and piracies"					
20. "the world is puddle-wonderful"					
21. "queer old balloonman whistles"					
22. "bettyandisbel come dancing"					
23. "from hop-scotch and jump-rope"					

Name _____ Date _____

Poetry by Walt Whitman and E. E. Cummings
Vocabulary Builder

Word List
    distinct   exquisite

A. DIRECTIONS: *Complete these word maps by writing synonyms, antonyms, and an example sentence for each vocabulary word.*

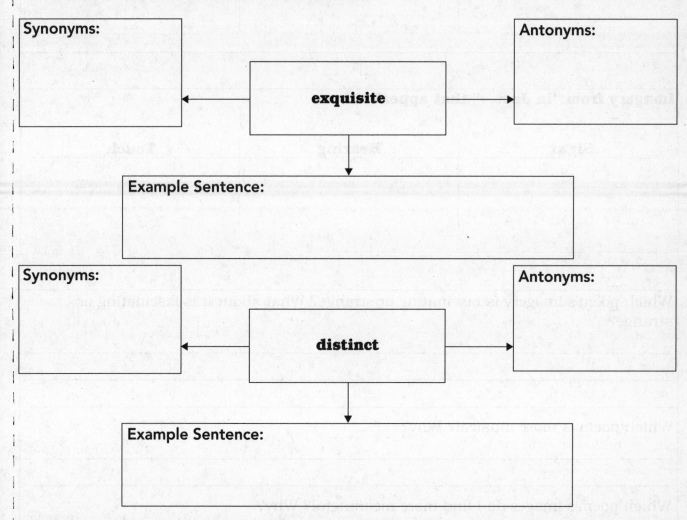

B. DIRECTIONS: *Write the letter of the word or words whose meaning is most nearly* the same as *the word from the Word List.*

____ 1. exquisite
    A. quaint   B. significant   C. costly   D. beautiful

____ 2. distinct
    A. blurry   B. separate   C. similar   D. pure

Name _____ Date _____

Integrated Language Skills: Support for Writing to Compare Literary Works

Use the following graphic organizers as you prepare to write an essay recommending either "Miracles" or "in Just—" to someone your age.

Imagery from "Miracles" that appeals to me:		
Sight	**Hearing**	**Touch**

Imagery from "in Just—" that appeals to me:		
Sight	**Hearing**	**Touch**

Which poem's imagery is fascinating or strange? What about it is fascinating or strange?

_____

_____

Which poem is more musical? Why?

_____

_____

Which poem's images do I find more meaningful? Why?

_____

_____

_____

Now, use your notes to write an essay about the poem that you would recommend.

Poetry by Walt Whitman and E. E. Cummings
Open-Book Test

Short Answer *Write your responses to the questions in this section on the lines provided.*

1. In "Miracles," the speaker describes the thin curve of the new moon as "exquisite." Read line 5 and line 13. Which line describes something that could be called exquisite? Explain your answer.

   _____

   _____

2. In "Miracles," the speaker says that all of what he describes are miracles, yet they are all distinct. Why would it be easy to find your umbrella among many umbrellas if it were distinct?

   _____

   _____

3. In each blank box, write one of the miracles from the poem "Miracles." Then, on the line, tell the main message of the poem.

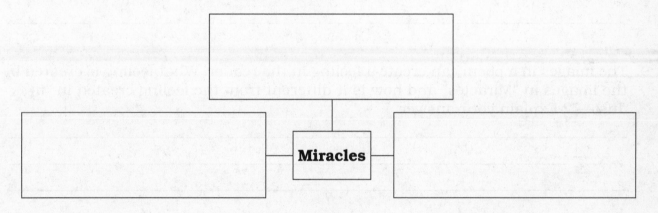

   _____

4. The speaker of "in Just—" uses made-up words to describe the weather. What is the speaker trying to say about spring by using descriptions such as "mud-luscious" and "puddle-wonderful"? Explain your answer.

   _____

   _____

   _____

5. In "in Just—," how do eddieandbill and bettyandisbel feel about the coming of spring and the balloonman? Support your answer with details from the poem.

   _____

   _____

   _____

6. On one level, the balloonman in "in Just—" is simply a man who sells balloons. What does he stand for on a deeper level? Use details from the poem to support your answer.

_____

7. An image is a word or phrase that appeals to the five senses. Think about the images in both "Miracles" and "in Just—." To which sense do both poems appeal most strongly? Support your answer with details from the poems.

_____

_____

_____

8. One image in "Miracles" is "talk by day with any one I love." Give an image from "in Just—" that appeals to the same sense. Explain your answer.

_____

_____

_____

9. The images in a poem can create a feeling in the reader. What feeling is created by the images in "Miracles" and how is it different from the feeling created in "in Just—"? Explain your answer.

_____

_____

_____

_____

10. The images in "Miracles" and those in "in Just—" describe very different scenes. How are the scope and size of the scenes different? Explain.

_____

_____

Essay

11. Poets often use language that appeals to the five senses—sight, hearing, taste, touch, and smell. Choose the sense from "Miracles" on which you think the poet focuses. In an essay, explain how focusing on this sense helps the poet express the meaning of the poem. Give at least two examples from the poem to support your ideas.

12. In both "Miracles" and "in Just—," the poets use images that appeal to the senses. In an essay, compare the use of imagery in the two poems. First, present images in each poem that appeal to the senses of sight, sound, and touch. Then, state at least one way in which the imagery in the two poems is different and one way that it is the same. Include details from the poems in your essay.

13. In both "Miracles" and "in Just—," the poets express a view about nature. In an essay, compare and contrast the poets' attitudes toward nature as reflected in their poems. Focus on what the poets are saying about nature and how they feel about nature. Use images from the poems to support your ideas.

14. **Thinking About the Big Question: What is the best way to communicate?** Think about the communication that takes place in both "Miracles" and "in Just—." In an essay, explain how the speaker of both poems would answer the question "What is the best way to communicate?" Use details from the poems to support your ideas.

Oral Response

15. Go back to question 1, 5, 7, or 9 or to the question your teacher assigns you. Take a few minutes to expand your answer and prepare an oral response. Find additional details in "Miracles" and "in Just—" that will support your points. If necessary, make notes to guide your response.

Name _____ Date _____

Poetry by Walt Whitman and E. E. Cummings
Selection Test A

Critical Reading *Identify the letter of the choice that best answers the question.*

____ 1. Which quotation from "Miracles" contains an image?
   A. "who makes much of a miracle?"
   B. "I know of nothing else"
   C. "honeybees busy around the hive"
   D. "What stranger miracles are there?"

____ 2. To what sense does this image from "Miracles" most appeal?
   wade with naked feet along the beach
   A. sight
   B. touch
   C. sound
   D. smell

____ 3. Where does the speaker in "Miracles" see miracles?
   A. only in nature
   B. only in his family
   C. only in the sea
   D. everywhere

____ 4. What time of year is the speaker in "in Just—" describing?
   A. spring
   B. summer
   C. autumn
   D. winter

____ 5. To what sense does this image from "in Just—" most appeal?
   the little lame balloonman
   A. sight
   B. touch
   C. sound
   D. smell

____ 6. In "in Just—," how does the balloonman attract the children's attention?
   A. He sings.
   B. He calls out.
   C. He whistles.
   D. He carries balloons.

____ 7. In "in Just—," what do the children do when they hear the balloonman coming?

   A. They come dancing and singing.

   B. They remain playing and singing.

   C. They remain dancing and jumping.

   D. They come running and dancing.

____ 8. What does the speaker in "in Just—" mean when he says that "the world is puddle-wonderful"?

   A. The world is full of puddles.

   B. Spring is rainy and wet.

   C. Winter's drought has ended.

   D. The balloonman fell into a puddle.

____ 9. In what way are "Miracles" and "in Just—" alike?

   A. Both poems contain images.

   B. Both poems contain rhymes.

   C. Both poems are playful.

   D. Both poems are mournful.

____ 10. In what way are the speaker in "Miracles" and the speaker in "in Just—" alike?

   A. Both appreciate country life.

   B. Both appreciate the joy of childhood.

   C. Both have a positive outlook.

   D. Both have a negative outlook.

____ 11. In what way are "Miracles" and "in Just—" different?

   A. "Miracles" contains images, but "in Just—" does not.

   B. "Miracles" contains rhymes, but "in Just—" does not.

   C. "Miracles" deals with people and nature, while "in Just—" deals only with nature.

   D. "Miracles" deals with the whole world, while "in Just—" describes a single scene.

Vocabulary

____ 12. In which sentence does the word *distinct* make sense?

   A. The assembly line produced a series of identical toys, each *distinct* from the next.

   B. Because of the man's *distinct* appearance, he easily got lost in the crowd.

   C. The singer's voice is so *distinct* that it blends in with every other singer's voice.

   D. There were many umbrellas in the foyer, but I recognized mine because it is *distinct*.

___ **13.** In which sentence does the word *exquisite* make sense?

    A. The critics called the singer's monotonous, off-key voice *exquisite*.

    B. The delicate antique teacup is an example of *exquisite* craftsmanship.

    C. The *exquisite* work of art was thought to be coarse and primitive.

    D. The roughly carved stone is an example of *exquisite* workmanship.

Essay

14. Both "Miracles" and "in Just—" refer to nature. In an essay, compare and contrast the ways in which the two poems do this. Consider these questions: What is the poet saying in each poem? Do both poets treat nature as a miracle? How can you tell? How important is nature to each poem? Refer to at least two details in each poem as you make your points.

15. Both "Miracles" and "in Just—" contain images that appeal to the senses. In an essay, compare the use of imagery in the two poems. First, point to images in each poem that appeal to the senses of sight, sound, and touch. Then, state one way in which the imagery in the two poems is different. Finally, name the poem whose imagery you like better, and explain why you prefer it.

16. Thinking About the Big Question: What is the best way to communicate?
Think about the communication with nature that takes place in both "Miracles" and "in Just—." In an essay, explain how the speaker of each poem would answer the question "What is the best way to communicate?" Use details from the poems to support your ideas.

Poetry by Walt Whitman and E. E. Cummings
Selection Test B

Critical Reading *Identify the letter of the choice that best completes the statement or answers the question.*

_____ 1. According to the following lines from "Miracles," when does the speaker experience a miracle?

Or talk by day with any one I love . . . / Or sit at table at dinner with the rest. / Or look at strangers opposite me riding in the car.

A. only when he talks with people he loves
B. only when he eats with people he knows
C. only when he sits with strangers in a car
D. whenever he is with anybody at all

_____ 2. Which quotation from "Miracles" contains an image that primarily appeals to the sense of touch?
A. "dart my sight over the roofs of houses"
B. "wade with naked feet along the beach just in the edge of the water"
C. "stand under trees in the woods"
D. "talk by day with anyone I love . . . / Or sit at table at dinner with the rest"

_____ 3. Which quotation from "Miracles" contains an image that primarily appeals to the sense of sight?
A. "wade with naked feet"
B. "riding in the car"
C. "delicate thin curve of the new moon"
D. "What stranger miracles are there?"

_____ 4. What is the most likely explanation for the poet's ending "Miracles" with this line?
What stranger miracles are there?

A. He wishes to tell the reader that miracles are strange occurrences.
B. He wishes to tell the reader that he has described all the miracles there are.
C. He wishes to encourage the reader to see everyday things and events as miracles.
D. He wishes to encourage the reader to think about the way in which the sea is a miracle.

_____ 5. Which statement best describes "Miracles"?
A. It is the story of the speaker's life.
B. It is a definition of the word *miracle.*
C. It is a list of things the speaker considers miracles.
D. It is a description of the world in the speaker's time.

_____ 6. What is the main message of "Miracles"?
A. Cities have wondrous qualities.
B. The ocean is a mysterious essence.
C. Nature is wonderful.
D. All of life is wondrous.

____ 7. In "in Just—," what is the meaning of the words "In Just— / spring"?
  A. Spring has only recently arrived.
  B. Spring has not quite arrived.
  C. Spring is the most reasonable season.
  D. Spring is all right but not a special time.

____ 8. What is the best explanation of *mud-luscious,* as it is used by the speaker in "in Just—"?
  A. The mud probably tastes sweet, like chocolate pudding.
  B. It is annoying to sink into mud wherever you go in spring.
  C. It is time to plant gardens and put away winter clothes.
  D. The mud is a delightful reminder that spring has come.

____ 9. To what senses do these lines from "in Just—" appeal?
    when the world is mud- / luscious the little / lame balloonman / whistles
  A. sight and taste
  B. taste and smell
  C. smell and hearing
  D. sight and hearing

____ 10. On a literal level, the balloonman in "in Just—" is simply a man who sells balloons. What might he stand for on a symbolic, or deeper, level?
  A. the coming of spring
  B. the success of small businesses
  C. the desire to succeed
  D. the complexity of the universe

____ 11. In "in Just—," what are eddieandbill and bettyandisbel doing when they hear the balloonman's whistle?
  A. running home from school
  B. playing
  C. arguing
  D. starting their homework

____ 12. Which word best describes eddieandbill and bettyandisbel as they are presented in "in Just—"?
  A. frightened
  B. hostile
  C. happy
  D. mischievous

____ 13. Which quotation from "in Just—" contains an image that appeals to the sense of hearing?
  A. "the world is mud- / luscious"
  B. "the little / lame balloonman / whistles"
  C. "bettyandisbel come dancing"
  D. "it's spring"

____ 14. In what way are the speaker in "Miracles" and the speaker in "in Just—" alike?
  A. Both appreciate rural scenes.
  B. Both appreciate the joy of childhood.
  C. Both have a positive outlook.
  D. Both have a negative outlook.

____ 15. In what way are "Miracles" and "in Just—" different?
  A. "Miracles" contains images, but "in Just—" does not.
  B. "Miracles" contains rhyme and rhythm, but "in Just—" does not.
  C. "Miracles" deals with people and nature, whereas "in Just—" deals only with nature.
  D. "Miracles" deals with the whole world, whereas "in Just—" describes only a single scene.

____ 16. The tone of a poem is the speaker's attitude toward his or her subject matter and audience. Which statement accurately compares the tone of "Miracles" and "in Just—"?
  A. Both "Miracles" and "in Just—" are reflective.
  B. Both "Miracles" and "in Just—" are playful.
  C. "Miracles" is reflective, whereas "in Just—" is playful.
  D. "Miracles" is playful, whereas "in Just—" is reflective.

Vocabulary

____ 17. Which object would most likely be described as *exquisite*?
  A. a delicate blossom   C. a rugged landscape
  B. a rough sketch   D. a prickly rosebud

____ 18. Which statement is *not* true of something that is *distinct*?
  A. It is in some way different from all other things.
  B. It may be confused with other things that are similar to it.
  C. It is recognizable because it is separate and different from other things.
  D. It may be similar to other things, but in some way it is different from them.

Essay

19. To a degree, Walt Whitman in "Miracles" and E.E. Cummings in "in Just—" are expressing their views of the natural world. In an essay, describe each poet's attitude toward nature as it is reflected in these poems. Begin by describing two images of nature that appear in "Miracles" and one that appears in "in Just—." Then, briefly summarize what the poets are saying about nature, and tell how each poet seems to feel about nature.

20. Both "Miracles" and "in Just—" contain images that appeal to the senses. In an essay, explain which poem's imagery you like better. Consider these questions: Which images in the two poems appeal to the sense of sight? Which appeal to the sense of hearing? Do any appeal to the sense of touch, smell, or taste? Which images are more meaningful to you? Why? Support your opinion with at least two examples from each poem.

21. **Thinking About the Big Question: What is the best way to communicate?** Think about the communication that takes place in both "Miracles" and "in Just—." In an essay, explain how the speaker of each poem would answer the question "What is the best way to communicate?" Use details from the poems to support your ideas.

Name _____ Date _____

Writing Workshop—Unit 4, Part 2
Persuasion: Persuasive Essay

Prewriting: Gathering Details

Use the following graphic organizer to gather facts, statistics, anecdotes, and quotations from authorities as you conduct research on your topic.

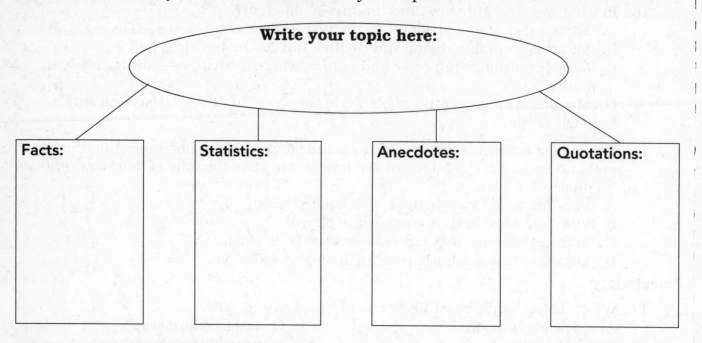

Drafting: Organizing Your Arguments

Use the following graphic organizer to list the supporting evidence you have gathered, starting with your least important points at the top and building toward your most important ones.

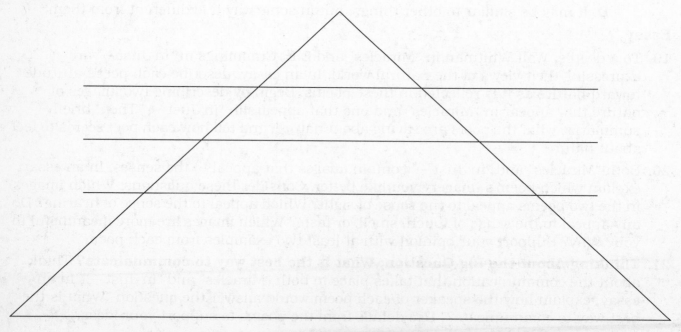

Writing Workshop—Unit 4, Part 2
Persuasive Essay: Integrating Grammar Skills

Revising Fragments and Run-On Sentences

A **fragment** is a group of words that does not express a complete thought. It is punctuated as if it is a sentence, but it is only part of a sentence. Often it is missing a subject, a verb, or both. To correct a fragment, build a sentence that has a subject and a verb and that expresses a complete thought.

A **run-on sentence** is two or more complete thoughts that are not properly joined or separated. They may have no punctuation between them, or they may have the wrong punctuation. To correct a run-on sentence, use the proper punctuation, and add a conjunction or a conjunctive adverb if necessary.

Run-On with No Punctuation	The birds sang the alarm clock rang.
Run-On with Incorrect Punctuation	The birds sang, the alarm clock rang.
Corrected as Two Sentences	The birds sang. The alarm clock rang.
Corrected with Coordinating Conjunction	The birds sang, and the alarm clock rang.
Corrected with Semicolon	The birds sang; the alarm clock rang.
Corrected with Semicolon and Conjunctive Adverb	The birds sang; afterward, the alarm clock rang.

Identifying Fragments and Run-On Sentences

A. DIRECTIONS: *On the line before each sentence, write* F *if it is a sentence fragment,* R *if it is a run-on sentence, or* S *if it is a complete, properly punctuated sentence.*

____ 1. In winter I always have oatmeal for breakfast today was no exception.

____ 2. My mom prefers bran cereal, I usually have that in summer.

____ 3. Raisins floating in the milk.

____ 4. My brother has eggs once a week; otherwise, he has oatmeal.

Fixing Fragments and Run-On Sentences

B. DIRECTIONS: *On the lines provided, correct the fragments and run-on sentences. If a sentence is correct as presented, write* correct.

1. The school bus usually arrives at seven, sometimes it is late.

_____

2. Waiting on the corner with my sister and brother.

_____

3. My brother takes one bus my sister and I take another.

_____

4. At school by seven-thirty.

_____

Unit 4 Vocabulary Workshop—1
Connotation and Denotation

A word's **denotation** is its literal, or dictionary, definition. Some words also have **connotations,** or shades of meaning, attached to them. Those shades of meaning might suggest positive or negative feelings. The words *unusual, rare,* and *peculiar* have the same denotation. But, as this chart shows, they have different connotations.

Word	unusual	rare	peculiar
Denotation	not ordinary or common		
Connotation	none; *Unusual* is a "neutral" word.	positive feelings; Something that is rare is usually valuable or desirable.	negative feelings; Something that is peculiar is often considered weird or odd.

A. DIRECTIONS: *The words in these sets have the same denotations. Some are neutral words, but others have positive or negative connotations. Add them to the correct columns of the chart.*

1. clever, sly
2. boastful, proud
3. reckless, brave, heroic

4. large, hearty, fat
5. immature, youthful
6. alone, lonely, independent

Neutral Words	Words with **Positive** Connotations	Words with **Negative** Connotations

Unit 4 Vocabulary Workshop—2
Connotation and Denotation

B. DIRECTIONS: *The words in these pairs have the same denotation, but some have positive or negative connotations. In the spaces following each pair, identify the "positive" and "negative" word. Then write sentences that show the shades of meaning attached to each word.*

Example: *invited, begged*

Positive: invited	Sentence: Shyly, she invited Beth to the party.
Negative: begged	Sentence: She begged Beth to give her some food.

1. challenging, confusing

Positive:	Sentence:
Negative:	Sentence:

2. discipline, punishment

Positive:	Sentence:
Negative:	Sentence:

3. nosy, curious

Positive:	Sentence:
Negative:	Sentence:

4. tiptoeing, sneaking

Positive:	Sentence:
Negative:	Sentence:

5. demanded, requested

Positive:	Sentence:
Negative:	Sentence:

Name _____ Date _____

Evaluating Advertisements

After choosing your commercial, fill out the following chart to evaluate the content and delivery of what you see.

Title of commercial: _____

What claims are made on this product?
What reliable information or logical reasoning is given about this product?
What persuasive techniques are used to try to persuade you to buy the product?
What questions do you have about the item being advertised?
How would you rate this commercial?

Unit 4: Poetry
Benchmark Test 8

MULTIPLE CHOICE

Reading Skill: Paraphrase

1. What does it mean to paraphrase a poem?
   A. to restate the poem in your own words
   B. to sum up the poem's main points
   C. to interpret the poem's meaning
   D. to restate the poem in complex language

2. Which of the following strategies will best help you paraphrase a poem?
   A. asking and answering questions
   B. rereading and reading aloud
   C. ignoring less important details
   D. ignoring the punctuation

3. Which of the following resources would most likely help you paraphrase a poem?
   A. a dictionary
   B. an encyclopedia
   C. a biographical reference
   D. a book of poetry

Read this selection from a poem by Henry Wadsworth Longfellow. Then, answer the questions that follow.

> 1 I shot an arrow into the air,
> 2 It fell to earth, I know not where;
> 3 For, so swiftly it flew, the sight
> 4 Could not follow it in its flight.
>
> —from "The Arrow and the Song"
> by Henry Wadsworth Longfellow

4. If you were paraphrasing the selection by Longfellow, which of these words would you most likely replace?
   A. I
   B. shot
   C. arrow
   D. swiftly

5. Which statement best paraphrases the second line of the selection?
   A. I do not know where it knocked out a piece of earth.
   B. I do not know where the arrow landed.
   C. It traveled the planet Earth to a place unknown to me.
   D. I don't know where the bird it hit landed.

6. Which statement best paraphrases the third and fourth lines of the selection?
   A. After it flew out of my sight, I soon forgot about it.
   B. Because it shined so brightly, my eyes could not spot it.
   C. Because it flew so close to me, I was too frightened to look at it.
   D. Because it flew so quickly, my eyes could not follow it.

Reading Skill: Determine Main Idea

Read the selection. Then, answer the questions that follow.

People have been making maps for hundreds of years. Christopher Columbus used maps when he sailed to the New World. At that time, people thought the Earth was flat, and all of the maps they used were flat, too. Of course, Columbus's maps were not accurate, but would you be surprised to know that many of the maps we use today are still not accurate?

Today, even though we know that the Earth is almost round, most of the world maps we see are flat. Consequently, it is impossible to represent the Earth without some kind of error. Some flat maps do not show distances correctly. Others have errors in directions or in the size and shape of land forms.

A globe, on the other hand, is very accurate. Many people do not consider a globe to be a map, but that is precisely what it is. Because it comes closer to the real shape of the Earth, a globe can show direction, distance, size, and shape with great accuracy.

7. What would be the best title for the selection?
   A. Flat Maps
   B. Maps of the Past
   C. The Accuracy of Maps
   D. Why a Globe Is a Map

8. Which of these best states the main idea of the selection?
   A. While the Earth is almost round, most maps are flat.
   B. Unlike a flat map, a globe is an accurate map of the world.
   C. Maps in the time of Christopher Columbus were not accurate.
   D. It is not possible to show the Earth on a flat map without error.

9. Which detail from the selection best supports the main idea?
   A. People have been making maps for hundreds of years.
   B. Christopher Columbus used maps when he sailed to the New World.
   C. Many people do not consider a globe to be a map, but that is precisely what it is.
   D. Because it comes closer to the real shape of the Earth, a globe can show direction, distance, size, and shape with great accuracy.

Literary Analysis

10. Which of the following are sound devices used in poetry?
    A. onomatopoeia, repetition, and imagery
    B. repetition, meter, and rhyme
    C. meter, rhyme, and imagery
    D. alliteration, rhythm, and imagery

11. Which of the following lines contains the best example of onomatopoeia?
    A. She glowed like a candle on a cold clear night.
    B. The child made a wish on the evening star.
    C. The buzz saw sputtered and droned.
    D. The tiger came closer—and closer—and closer.

12. Which of the following lines contains the best example of alliteration?
    A. Down he dove into the dreary dismal dungeon.
    B. April is an amazing and admirable month.
    C. A blue moon loomed in a darker blue sky.
    D. He went in the tent and met a friend.

13. How many feet does this line contain?

    I met a man who wasn't there.

    A. three   B. four   C. six   D. eight

14. What do you call a single unit of stressed and unstressed syllables?
    A. meter   B. rhythm   C. an image   D. a foot

15. Which statement is true?
    A. Meter is a type of rhythm.
    B. Rhythm is a type of meter.
    C. Rhyme is a type of alliteration.
    D. Alliteration is a type of rhyme.

16. Which of the following words rhyme exactly?
    A. *break* and *braid*
    B. *break* and *hate*
    C. *break* and *ache*
    D. *break* and *breakfast*

17. To which senses does this image appeal?

    The thick fog smothered the little homes.

    A. sight and sound
    B. sound and touch
    C. smell and touch
    D. sight and touch

18. Which of the following images appeals most strongly to the sense of sound?
    A. The wind raced through the trees.
    B. The wind howled and hissed.
    C. The wind froze my nose.
    D. The wind was calm and still.

19. Which of the following is the opposite of an image?
    A. a simile   B. a symbol   C. personification   D. an abstract idea

Vocabulary: Suffixes and Prefixes

20. What is the meaning of the word formed by adding the suffix -*ancy* to the root of the word *vacant*?
    A. emptiness   B. abundance   C. closeness   D. freedom

21. Using your knowledge of the suffix -*ancy*, what does *relevancy* mean in the following sentence?

    I did not understand the relevancy of her argument.

    A. foundation   B. significance   C. strength   D. objective

22. The suffix -*less* means "without." Using this knowledge, which of the following words means "unkind"?
    A. emotionless
    B. careless
    C. heartless
    D. helpless

23. Based on your knowledge of the prefix *un-*, which would best describe someone who is *unfortunate*?

    A. not lucky   **B.** very lucky   **C.** lucky again   **D.** close to being lucky

24. Based on your knowledge of the prefix *im-*, what happens when something *implodes*?

    A. It blows up.   **C.** It causes no damage.

    B. It makes no sound.   **D.** It bursts inward.

25. What is the meaning of the word formed by adding the prefix *im-* to *precise*?

    A. fictional   **B.** vague   **C.** truthful   **D.** uneventful

Grammar

26. What is a clause?

    A. a group of words with its own subject and verb

    B. a group of words with either a subject or a verb but not both

    C. a group of words that can stand alone as a sentence

    D. a group of words with a subject and verb that cannot stand alone as a sentence

27. Identify the independent clause in the following sentence.

Before electric lighting was invented, people used candles to light their homes at night.

    A. Before electric lighting was invented

    B. people used

    C. people used candles to light their homes at night

    D. to light their homes at night

28. Identify the subordinate clause in the following sentence.

Before the invention of refrigerators, people used ice when they needed to keep food cold.

    A. Before the invention of refrigerators

    B. people used ice

    C. people used ice when they needed to keep food cold

    D. when they needed to keep food cold

29. Which of the following is a simple sentence?

    A. When you exercise, you help build your muscles.

    B. You will keep the pounds off if you walk a few miles each day.

    C. Point your toes and stretch your muscles.

    D. After a long day, it feels incredibly good to relax.

30. Which of these sentences is a complex sentence?

    A. You can sometimes save money if you shop online.

    B. For online shopping, choose a reliable company.

    C. Some online companies charge for delivery, and some do not.

    D. Before buying, you should compare prices at different sources.

31. Which of the following is a compound sentence?

    A. The film is no longer in theaters but just came out as a DVD.

    B. You can buy the DVD, or you can rent it.

    C. Some libraries offer DVDs and video-cassettes for you to borrow.

    D. When a new DVD comes out, the wait at the library is long.

32. Which of the following is a sentence fragment?

    A. We were late for the party.
    B. As long as we didn't miss dinner.
    C. The party already started.
    D. Lateness is a bad characteristic.

33. Which of the following is the best correction for the run-on sentence below?

    We went to the park, we went swimming.

    A. We went to the park, but we went swimming.
    B. We went to the park but didn't go swimming.
    C. We went to the park and swimming.
    D. We went to the park, and we went swimming.

Spelling

34. Which of the following spelling rules is accurate?

    A. If adding a prefix to a word results in a double letter, drop one of the double letters.
    B. If adding a prefix to a word results in a double letter, keep both letters.
    C. If the last letter of a word is a silent *e*, keep the *e* before adding any suffix.
    D. If the last letters of a word are a consonant and *y*, keep the *y* before adding any suffix.

35. Identify the sentence in which the italic word is spelled correctly.

    A. Our mayor is *influential* in state politics.
    B. A *suspencion* bridge crosses the river at the foot of Wynkoop Street.
    C. My dad will *prearange* to have mom's birthday cake delivered at two.
    D. Be careful not to *mispell* any words.

36. Identify the word that is spelled correctly.

    A. unneccessary
    B. reinlist
    C. recognition
    D. musculer

ESSAY

Writing

37. Think of a time of year that you enjoy the most. Then, write a short poem about it using at least one sound device.

38. Write a paraphrase of the poem you wrote about your favorite time of year.

39. Imagine that there is a controversy about plans to build a new sports stadium in your community. You favor the plans and are writing a newspaper column expressing your support. You have written most of the column, explaining what you see as the benefits of the stadium. To show that you have thought fully about the issue, it is now time for your column to address some of the concerns of people who are against the stadium. On your paper or on a separate sheet, write a paragraph in which you address two of these concerns and offer counterarguments in response to them.

Vocabulary in Context

Identify the answer choice that best completes the statement.

1. Since our supplies are running low, it is time to_____ them.
   A. repeat
   B. resolute
   C. recollect
   D. replenish

2. The gems in the suitcase turned out to be worth a_____ .
   A. fortune
   B. gold
   C. lustrous
   D. grace

3. When asked questions, he always waited a minute and gave_____ answers.
   A. reliable
   B. unaltered
   C. uncertain
   D. thoughtful

4. When we stared out at the vast desert, we knew we were in_____ .
   A. process
   B. peril
   C. praise
   D. penance

5. Stir this water in slowly, and then add more water_____ .
   A. mildly
   B. faintly
   C. gradually
   D. obviously

6. Which one of you is that dog's_____ .
   A. master
   B. beggar
   C. merchant
   D. apprentice

7. During the storm, we used the cave as a_____ .
   A. refuge
   B. welfare
   C. resource
   D. workhouse

8. My business is on the main road and is_____ to the bus stop.
   A. bleak
   B. bound
   C. dismal
   D. convenient

9. After the war, he was their only_____ son.
   A. unique
   B. expected
   C. surviving
   D. preserved

10. Do you think that our society is too dependent on_____?
    A. newspapers
    B. machines
    C. impropriety
    D. prejudices

11. In our town, excellent dinners are served by many fine_____.
    A. energies
    B. varieties
    C. observations
    D. establishments

12. This recipe requires that the egg yolks and the egg whites be_____.
    A. bled
    B. labored
    C. separated
    D. neglected

13. He was paid fair_____ for his work.
    A. bulk
    B. wages
    C. issues
    D. budget

14. He has a_____ temper when people disagree with him.
    A. worn
    B. nasty
    C. comfortable
    D. tremendous

15. Just about every action can have either a good or a bad_____ .
   A. attention
   B. consequence
   C. complex
   D. menace

16. Greenland is one place where they have not yet_____ .
   A. adapted
   B. altered
   C. toured
   D. relived

17. That large box of crayons contains such a_____ of colors.
   A. charity
   B. variety
   C. production
   D. visuals

18. Dad and I plan to paint all of our apartment's_____ walls this summer.
   A. local
   B. initial
   C. interior
   D. silken

19. I have already heard her side of the story, so what is your_____ ?
   A. trait
   B. destiny
   C. version
   D. publication

20. The songs were sung by a large group of_____ .
   A. interpretations
   B. specters
   C. carolers
   D. populace

Diagnostic Tests and Vocabulary in Context
Use and Interpretation

The Diagnostic Tests and Vocabulary in Context were developed to assist teachers in making the most appropriate assignment of *Prentice Hall Literature* program selections to students. The purpose of these assessments is to indicate the degree of difficulty that students are likely to have in reading/comprehending the selections presented in the *following* unit of instruction. Tests are provided at six separate times in each grade level—a *Diagnostic Test* (to be used prior to beginning the year's instruction) and a *Vocabulary in Context*, the final segment of the Benchmark Test, appearing at the end of each of the first five units of instruction. Note that the tests are intended for use not as summative assessments for the prior unit, but as guidance for assigning literature selections in the upcoming unit of instruction.

The structure of all Diagnostic Tests and Vocabulary in Context in this series is the same. All test items are four-option, multiple-choice items. The format is established to assess a student's ability to construct sufficient meaning from the context sentence to choose the only provided word that fits both the semantics (meaning) and syntax (structure) of the context sentence. All words in the context sentences are chosen to be "below-level" words that students reading at this grade level should know. All answer choices fit *either* the meaning or structure of the context sentence, but only the correct choice fits *both* semantics and syntax. All answer choices—both correct answers and incorrect options—are key words chosen from specifically taught words that will occur in the subsequent unit of program instruction. This careful restriction of the assessed words permits a sound diagnosis of students' current reading achievement and prediction of the most appropriate level of readings to assign in the upcoming unit of instruction.

The assessment of vocabulary in context skill has consistently been shown in reading research studies to correlate very highly with "reading comprehension." This is not surprising as the format essentially assesses comprehension, albeit in sentence-length "chunks." Decades of research demonstrate that vocabulary assessment provides a strong, reliable prediction of comprehension achievement—the purpose of these tests. Further, because this format demands very little testing time, these diagnoses can be made efficiently, permitting teachers to move forward with critical instructional tasks rather than devoting excessive time to assessment.

It is important to stress that while the Diagnostic and Vocabulary in Context were carefully developed and will yield sound assignment decisions, they were designed to *reinforce*, not supplant, teacher judgment as to the most appropriate instructional placement for individual students. Teacher judgment should always prevail in making placement—or indeed other important instructional—decisions concerning students.

Diagnostic Tests and Vocabulary in Context
Branching Suggestions

These tests are designed to provide maximum flexibility for teachers. Your *Unit Resources* books contain the 40-question **Diagnostic Test** and 20-question **Vocabulary in Context** tests. At *PHLitOnline,* you can access the Diagnostic Test and complete 40-question Vocabulary in Context tests. Procedures for administering the tests are described below. Choose the procedure based on the time you wish to devote to the activity and your comfort with the assignment decisions relative to the individual students. Remember that your judgment of a student's reading level should always take precedence over the results of a single written test.

Feel free to use different procedures at different times of the year. For example, for early units, you may wish to be more confident in the assignments you make—thus, using the "two-stage" process below. Later, you may choose the quicker diagnosis, confirming the results with your observations of the students' performance built up throughout the year.

The **Diagnostic Test** is composed of a single 40-item assessment. Based on the results of this assessment, make the following assignment of students to the reading selections in Unit 1:

Diagnostic Test Score	Selection to Use
If the student's score is 0–25	more accessible
If the student's score is 26–40	more challenging

Outlined below are the three basic options for administering **Vocabulary in Context** and basing selection assignments on the results of these assessments.

1. For a one-stage, quicker diagnosis using the *20-item* test in the *Unit Resources:*

Vocabulary in Context Test Score	Selection to Use
If the student's score is 0–13	more accessible
If the student's score is 14–20	more challenging

2. If you wish to confirm your assignment decisions with a *two-stage* diagnosis:

Stage 1: Administer the 20-item test in the *Unit Resources*	
Vocabulary in Context Test Score	Selection to Use
If the student's score is 0–9	more accessible
If the student's score is 10–15	(Go to Stage 2.)
If the student's score is 16–20	more challenging

Stage 2: Administer items 21–40 from *PHLitOnline*	
Vocabulary in Context Test Score	Selection to Use
If the student's score is 0–12	more accessible
If the student's score is 13–20	more challenging

3. If you base your assignment decisions on the full 40-item **Vocabulary in Context** from *PHLitOnline:*

Vocabulary in Context Test Score	Selection to Use
If the student's score is 0–25	more accessible
If the student's score is 26–40	more challenging

Grade 7—Benchmark Test 7
Interpretation Guide

For remediation of specific skills, you may assign students the relevant Reading Kit Practice and Assess pages indicated in the far-right column of this chart. You will find rubrics for evaluating writing samples in the last section of your Professional Development Guidebook.

Skill Objective	Test Items	Number Correct	Reading Kit
Reading Skill			
Drawing Conclusions	1, 2, 3, 4, 5, 6, 7		pp. 150, 151
Follow Technical Directions	8, 9, 10		pp. 152, 153
Literary Analysis			
Forms of Poetry	11, 12, 13, 14, 15, 16		pp. 154, 155
Figurative Language	17, 18, 19, 20, 21		pp. 156, 157
Narrative Poetry	22, 23		pp. 158, 159
Vocabulary			
Roots and Suffixes -lum-, -gram-, -ly, -y	24, 25, 26, 27, 28, 29		pp. 160, 161
Grammar			
Infinitives and Infinitive Phrases	30, 31		pp. 162, 163
Appositives and Appositive Phrases	32, 33		pp. 164, 165
Identifying Verbals (Participles and Participial Phrases)	34, 35		pp. 166, 167
Writing			
Poem	37	Use rubric	pp. 168, 169
Metaphor	38	Use rubric	pp. 170, 171
Problem-and-Solution Essay	36	Use rubric	pp. 172, 173

Name _____   Date _____

Grade 7—Benchmark Test 8
Interpretation Guide

For remediation of specific skills, you may assign students the relevant Reading Kit Practice and Assess pages indicated in the far-right column of this chart. You will find rubrics for evaluating writing samples in the last section of your Professional Development Guidebook.

Skill Objective	Test Items	Number Correct	Reading Kit
Reading Skill			
Paraphrase	1, 2, 3, 4, 5, 6		pp. 174, 175
Determine Main Idea	7, 8, 9		pp. 176, 177
Literary Analysis			
Sound Devices	10, 11, 12		pp. 178, 179
Rhythm and Rhyme	13, 14, 15, 16		pp. 180, 181
Comparing Imagery	17, 18, 19		pp. 182, 183
Vocabulary			
Suffixes and Prefixes *-ancy, -less, im-, un-*	20, 21, 22, 23, 24, 25		pp. 184, 185
Grammar			
Independent and Subordinate clauses	26, 27, 28		pp. 186, 187
Sentences (Simple, Compound, and Complex), Fragments, and Run-ons	29, 30, 31, 32, 33		pp. 188, 189, 190, 191
Spelling			
Words with Prefixes and Suffixes	34, 35, 36		pp. 192, 193
Writing			
Poem (with alliteration)	37	Use rubric	pp. 194, 195
Paraphrase a poem	38	Use rubric	pp. 196, 197
Persuasive Essay	39	Use rubric	pp. 198, 199

ANSWERS

Big Question Vocabulary—1, p. 1

A. 1. listen
2. react
3. entertain
4. communicate
5. speak

B. 1. react
2. listen
3. speak
4. communicate
5. entertain

Big Question Vocabulary—2, p. 2

Answers will vary. Possible responses are shown.

1. smile, describe it in words, jump for joy

   Jim chose to express his happiness by jumping for joy.

2. how to write a poem, how to ride a bike, how to bake a cake

   My great aunt Sarah taught me how to write a haiku poem.

3. a short story, a drawing, a song

   Using a sharp pencil, Jenna produced a picture of a skyscraper.

4. help build a playground, make a community garden, pick up litter

   You can contribute to your neighborhood by picking up litter.

5. good manners, safety rules, how to make friends

   At a very young age, children need to learn safety rules.

Big Question Vocabulary—3, p. 3

A. Answers will vary. Possible responses are shown.

1. laptop computers
2. an email over the Internet
3. Be a good listener when your friend needs help.
4. Cats cannot chew food; their teeth are designed only for biting.
5. CNN or PBS

B. Summaries will vary, but should include details mentioned in the assignment, as well as all five vocabulary words.

The Poetry of Pat Mora

Vocabulary Warm-up Exercises, p. 8

A. 1. glare
2. blend
3. sprinkles
4. spiked
5. tease
6. cactus

B. Sample Answers

1. If I *strummed* a guitar, I would not be likely to win a contest because strumming does not suggest any great talent or expertise.

2. Before someone blows out the candles on a birthday cake, I might sing the *melody* of "Happy Birthday to You."

3. If I were forming a musical *trio* with two friends, I would most like to have keyboards, guitar, and bass.

4. An audience *swaying* to music would not be moving fast; they would be moving slowly from side to side.

5. Since *partners* have to do things together, two squeamish people would not be likely to get things accomplished in a science lab. At least one person has to be bold and be willing to experiment.

6. No, I would not wear formal clothes to a *village* square dance because casual clothes like jeans and a flannel shirt would be more suitable.

Reading Warm-up A, p. 9

Sample Answers

1. (very little rain); The cook *sprinkles* spices into the bubbling stew.

2. cactus; *Spiked* means "with long, slender, pointy parts or projections."

3. (in the southwestern United States); A *cactus* is "a desert plant with a green pulpy trunk covered with spines or prickles instead of leaves and often having showy flowers."

4. of the sun's rays; The *glare* of the car's headlights was blinding.

5. (that water is near); Disguising your voice is a way to *tease* people into thinking you are someone else. Children often *tease* each other by tickling.

6. Areas that once supported human settlements; When Sofia was visiting New York, she tried to *blend* in as a local.

Reading Warm-up B, p. 10

Sample Answers

1. guitar; *Strummed* means "played (as a stringed instrument or a tune) in a careless or casual way."

2. They used the guitar to accompany themselves; One *melody* that I enjoy humming is "We Are the World."

3. get-togethers; A *village get-together* might have taken place in a barn or in a town square and probably included music, dancing, and food.

4. (moved around the floor); People need a sense of rhythm and movement to become good dance *partners*.

5. the Spanish rhythms in his music; *Swaying* means "moving from side to side."

6. (as a solo instrument), (in a larger group); A *trio* is a group of three.

Pat Mora

Listening and Viewing, p. 11

Sample responses:

Segment 1. The English and Spanish languages are both parts of Pat Mora that she needs to use in order to communicate; she is of Mexican American heritage and likes to share her two cultural realities with readers. Students may answer that it is important to read literature from different heritages in order to learn more about them and honor the diversity between cultures.

Segment 2. In this poem, Mora creates a conversation between the speaker of the poem and her home, the desert; the last line in Spanish creates a longer string of sounds and steady rhythm at the conclusion of the poem. Students may suggest that this line allows them to be brought closer to the world Pat Mora wants to put them in and makes the speaker of the poem more realistic.

Segment 3. Pat Mora reads poetry by other authors in order to build excitement and creativity. She also keeps a notebook and carries it around with her to record observations and ideas. Students may suggest that they would read other authors, take notes, try not to focus on the audience, and take risks by being honest in self-expression.

Segment 4. Pat Mora gets to personally see the reactions of her audience as she reads to them; she can also see that her writing efforts are worthwhile when she connects with a reader. Students may suggest certain books or stories that have taught, influenced, or related to them.

Learning About Poetry, p. 12

A. 1. A; 2. D; 3. B; 4. C

B. Sample Answers

1. The moon is a silver coin resting on black velvet.
2. My dog is as big as a barn.
3. The clock warned me that I was running late.
4. A green light stands for "go."

The Poetry of Pat Mora

Model Selection: Poetry, p. 13

A. 1. clap
2. round and round (Phrase appears in lines 2 and 5.)
3. onomatopoeia
4. alliteration

B. Poems should be written about a family member or friend and contain at least two examples of the figures of speech and sound devices covered.

Open-Book Test, p. 14

Short Answer

1. The poet is using the key as a symbol. A real key unlocks real things. It cannot unlock meaning.
   Difficulty: *Average* **Objective:** *Literary Analysis*

2. The poetic device being used is metaphor. A metaphor describes one thing as if it were something else. The sun is being described as if it were a balloon.
   Difficulty: *Easy* **Objective:** *Literary Analysis*

3. The words are all examples of onomatopoeia, or the use of words that imitate sounds. They are often used in poetry to help the poem come to life for the reader.
   Difficulty: *Average* **Objective:** *Literary Analysis*

4. An audience is applauding for a performer. This explanation is supported by lines 4 and 5, which read "again and again he bows/to stage lights and upturned faces."
   Difficulty: *Easy* **Objective:** *Interpretation*

5. Mora is using repetition. By repeating words such as "again and again," Mora adds emphasis. A musician must practice everything "again and again" and "note by note" until he becomes a maestro.
   Difficulty: *Challenging* **Objective:** *Literary Analysis*

6. A maestro is a great musician. The first stanza refers to "stage lights" and "rows of hands" that clap. Only a great musician would draw a large crowd to a large stage.
   Difficulty: *Average* **Objective:** *Vocabulary*

7. The phrase "I say" is repeated many times in the poem. The speaker sounds as if she is having a conversation with the desert, which makes the desert seem human.
   Difficulty: *Average* **Objective:** *Literary Analysis*

8. Line 2: "She serves red prickly pear"; Line 7: "She whispers, 'Lie in my arms'"; Line 16: "She chants her windy songs." The poet chose the comparison because a mother takes care of her children. She wants to show that the desert takes care of her in the same ways.
   Difficulty: *Average* **Objective:** *Interpretation*

9. The speaker is speaking to her "dear aunt" (line 12). She is celebrating her aunt's joy and beauty as a young woman and an old woman.
   Difficulty: *Challenging* **Objective:** *Interpretation*

10. The speaker's aunt is laughing at herself. She says "Estoy bailando" as though she is dancing instead of "tottering" when she walks. She is an old woman who still sees herself as young.
    Difficulty: *Challenging* **Objective:** *Interpretation*

11. Sample answer: The poet's use of personification is effective because she gives clear examples of how the desert behaves like a mother. The desert does whatever the speaker asks, whether it means feeding, teasing, frightening, or any other behavior that is requested.
    Difficulty: *Easy* **Objective:** *Essay*

12. Sample answer: In "Bailando," Pat Mora uses repetition with the phrases "spinning round and round," effectively conveying the feeling of someone dancing. She paints a continuous image that helps the reader picture a person who is dancing. In addition, she repeats certain words—"a young girl"/"a young woman" and "your long, black hair"/"your long, blue dress."

Because she paints such a clear picture of her aunt as a young person, the later image of her aunt as an older person provides a strong, effective contrast.

Difficulty: *Average*   **Objective:** *Essay*

13. Sample answer: I would use repetition to show the aunt's feeble walking as she attempts to dance, in order to convey a sense of motion. I might even write that she is still "spinning round and round" in her mind, even though she is only taking a few steps. To convey her relationship with the speaker, I might have them dance together, but this time with the aunt looking up into the speaker's eyes instead of the other way around.

Difficulty: *Challenging*   **Objective:** *Essay*

14. Sample answer: I think music is an excellent way to communicate feelings. In "Maestro," Mora shows that the career of the musician was greatly influenced by the early, close experiences he had playing music with his parents. Those feelings are communicated through him and to him in his playing.

Difficulty: *Average*   **Objective:** *Essay*

Oral Response

15. Oral responses should be clear, well organized, and well supported by appropriate examples.

Difficulty: *Average*   **Objective:** *Oral Interpretation*

Selection Test A, p. 17

Learning About Poetry

1. ANS: A	DIF: Easy	OBJ: Literary Analysis
2. ANS: B	DIF: Easy	OBJ: Literary Analysis
3. ANS: D	DIF: Easy	OBJ: Literary Analysis
4. ANS: B	DIF: Easy	OBJ: Literary Analysis
5. ANS: D	DIF: Easy	OBJ: Literary Analysis
6. ANS: B	DIF: Easy	OBJ: Literary Analysis

Critical Reading

7. ANS: C	DIF: Easy	OBJ: Comprehension
8. ANS: A	DIF: Easy	OBJ: Comprehension
9. ANS: D	DIF: Easy	OBJ: Interpretation
10. ANS: A	DIF: Easy	OBJ: Comprehension
11. ANS: C	DIF: Easy	OBJ: Literary Analysis
12. ANS: A	DIF: Easy	OBJ: Literary Analysis
13. ANS: C	DIF: Easy	OBJ: Literary Analysis
14. ANS: B	DIF: Easy	OBJ: Literary Analysis
15. ANS: A	DIF: Easy	OBJ: Literary Analysis

Essay

16. Students will probably say the speaker feels affection and respect for the desert because of all the things

(food, mystery, beauty) that it gives to her, and for the way it can tease, teach, and caress her.

Difficulty: *Easy*

Objective: *Essay*

17. Students should clearly state a preference and effectively support their preference with reasons.

Difficulty: *Easy*

Objective: *Essay*

18. Sample answer: I think music is an excellent way to communicate feelings. In "Maestro," Mora shows that the career of the musician was greatly influenced by the early, close experiences he had playing music with his parents. Those feelings are communicated through him and to him in his playing.

Difficulty: *Average*

Objective: *Essay*

Selection Test B, p. 20

Learning About Poetry

1. ANS: B	DIF: Average	OBJ: Literary Analysis
2. ANS: C	DIF: Average	OBJ: Literary Analysis
3. ANS: A	DIF: Challenging	OBJ: Literary Analysis
4. ANS: D	DIF: Average	OBJ: Literary Analysis
5. ANS: C	DIF: Challenging	OBJ: Literary Analysis
6. ANS: B	DIF: Challenging	OBJ: Literary Analysis

Critical Reading

7. ANS: D	DIF: Challenging	OBJ: Literary Analysis
8. ANS: B	DIF: Average	OBJ: Comprehension
9. ANS: D	DIF: Average	OBJ: Comprehension
10. ANS: B	DIF: Average	OBJ: Interpretation
11. ANS: D	DIF: Average	OBJ: Comprehension
12. ANS: B	DIF: Average	OBJ: Literary Analysis
13. ANS: B	DIF: Average	OBJ: Interpretation
14. ANS: A	DIF: Challenging	OBJ: Interpretation
15. ANS: B	DIF: Average	OBJ: Literary Analysis
16. ANS: C	DIF: Average	OBJ: Literary Analysis
17. ANS: C	DIF: Challenging	OBJ: Interpretation
18. ANS: B	DIF: Average	OBJ: Literary Analysis
19. ANS: D	DIF: Average	OBJ: Literary Analysis

Essay

20. Students should select appropriate and accurate onomatopoeic words, such as *pitter patter, splash, drip* (rainstorm); *crash, boom, thud* (thunder); and *howl, screech, whoosh* (wind).

Difficulty: *Average*

Objective: *Essay*

21. Students should accurately identify the main idea of one of the poems and describe what it is about (for example, a great musician's childhood memories, an elderly aunt who has always loved to dance, or the desert).
Difficulty: *Average*
Objective: *Essay*

22. Sample answer: I think music is an excellent way to communicate feelings. In "Maestro," Mora shows that the career of the musician was greatly influenced by the early, close experiences he had playing music with his parents. Those feelings are communicated through him and to him in his playing.
Difficulty: *Average*
Objective: *Essay*

Poetry Collection: Naomi Shihab Nye, William Jay Smith, Buson

Vocabulary Warm-up Exercises, p. 24

A. 1. watery
2. plunges
3. float
4. darts
5. flick
6. deep

B. Sample Answers

1. A *champion* probably feels very proud and happy after achieving a big <u>victory</u>.

2. A friend and I would probably be *panting* after pedaling our *bicycles* uphill because it takes a lot of strength and effort to ride up an incline, which would make us breathe more heavily than if we were resting.

3. It is important to be at the dock on time if only one ferry boat *departs* each day because that is the only chance to leave the island for home.

4. I have *desperately* tried to succeed at being more prompt in completing my homework before it is due.

Reading Warm-up A, p. 25

Sample Answers

1. <u>into the water from the highest rock</u>; *Plunges* means "throws oneself or rushes into something."

2. (to get the fish the guide had tossed there); Maria was *deep* in thought as she wondered how to solve the problem.

3. (one . . . exhibit after another); *Watery* means "full of water."

4. (a school of fish); The mouse *darts* to its hole to escape the cat.

5. <u>a baby beluga whale; this whitish whale</u>; Other things that can *float* are a boat on the water, a leaf in a puddle, or a twig in a stream.

6. (caught rings on their noses); *Flick* means "a quick, snapping motion."

Reading Warm-up B, p. 26

Sample Answers

1. <u>Tour de France</u>; Have you and a friend ever raced your *bicycles* down a hill?

2. <u>from a point in France</u>; *Departs* means "leaves or sets out for somewhere."

3. (to achieve the best time in each event every day); *Desperately* means "with intense need."

4. <u>short of breath</u>; Someone might be *panting* after running or doing hard exercise.

5. (wins the race); A *champion* is a winner.

6. (at a special ceremony, which takes place in Paris); The chess player celebrated an important *victory* in the tournament.

Writing About the Big Question, p. 27

A. 1. learn
2. teach
3. transmit
4. technology

B. Sample Answers

1. I helped my sister **learn** how to cook pasta. I also **informed** a classmate how to solve word problems in math.

2. I used a recipe and showed my sister when I taught her to cook. I used technology – email – to teach my classmate.

C. Sample Answer

Through poetry, writers **communicate** their thoughts and feelings. I most enjoy reading poems that **express** strong feelings about nature.

Reading: Ask Questions to Draw a Conclusion, p. 28

Sample Answers

Question / Details Relating to Question / Conclusion

"The Rider": How is the boy's remark about rollerskating away from his loneliness related to the way the speaker feels? / The speaker wonders "if it translates to bicycles." / The speaker also feels lonely.

"Seal": Why does the poet mention "Sting Ray and Shark"? / The seal swims past those creatures and comes out of the water with "a zoom, / A whoop, a bark." / The seal is not afraid of them.

"O foolish ducklings": Why does the speaker call the ducklings foolish? / A weasel is watching the pond. / The baby ducks are foolish because they do not realize that they may be eaten by the weasel.

"Deep in a windless wood": Why is "something" afraid to move? / It is "windless"; not even the leaves are moving. / Perhaps it is the calm before a storm, and the creature is frightened because it senses trouble.

Literary Analysis: Forms of Poetry, p. 29

Sample Answers

1. I would use the shape of an arrow to suggest motion.
2. "Quicksilver-quick he swims past"
3. I would focus on the "windless wood" because I would like to explore the mystery of what is afraid.
4. "A lonely skater"
5. I would focus on my own thoughts and feelings about the seal, because viewing an image or idea from the poet's point of view is what a lyric poem is supposed to do.

Vocabulary Builder, p. 30

A. Sample Answers

1. Yes, I could see luminous stars on a clear night because they would be bright.
2. No, someone who did not speak would not be able to win a debate.
3. No, a weasel is a small mammal, so it would not be housed with the large mammals.
4. Yes, a driver would likely steer a car in a curve to avoid hitting something in the road.
5. No, a minnow is a small fish.
6. Yes, it would no longer be in a foreign language.

B. Possible responses:

1. An *illuminated* field is lighted, so the game is probably being played at night.
2. A *bioluminescent* fish gives off light, so it probably lives in the darkest, deepest part of the ocean.
3. A *luminary* in medicine is probably considered by others to be a brilliant doctor—a bright star.

Enrichment: Seals, p. 31

Sample Answers

Type of seal: Northern elephant seal

Physical characteristics/life span: They have no external ears and silvery gray fur that darkens with age. Males weigh up to 5,060 pounds and may reach a length of 13.5 feet; females weigh up to 1,980 pounds and may reach a length of 10 feet. They can dive to a depth of 3,000 feet. They live about 14 years.

Social behavior/breeding habits: It is not known whether seals live in groups or alone year-round, but during mating season they live in groups. A male may mate with as many as 80 females. Gestation period is 11 months. Females give birth to one pup, which they nurse for a month, then they mate again.

Habitat/migration patterns: Seals live off the coast of California and migrate as far north as southern Alaska.

Diet: Seals feed on fish and squid.

Natural enemies: sharks

Poetry Collection: Naomi Shihab Nye, William Jay Smith, Buson

Open-Book Test, p. 32

Short Answer

1. It is a lyric poem. It expresses the poet's thoughts on one idea, trying to outrace loneliness.
   Difficulty: *Average* **Objective:** *Literary Analysis*
2. Something that is *luminous* gives off light. In the poem, the azaleas help chase away feelings of loneliness, a dark feeling.
   Difficulty: *Average* **Objective:** *Vocabulary*
3. Nye makes loneliness seem like a human opponent in a race. She says a victory is leaving your loneliness "panting behind you on some street corner."
   Difficulty: *Easy* **Objective:** *Interpretation*
4. A concrete poem creates a visual image that suggests the poem's subject. "Seal" is shaped like a curve. It makes sense because it shows the curved shape of the seal and its motion.
   Difficulty: *Average* **Objective:** *Literary Analysis*
5. Sample details: zoom, darts, flip of the flipper, quicksilver-quick, plunges, whoop. Conclusion: The seal is playful and full of energy.
   Difficulty: *Average* **Objective:** *Reading*
6. A swerve is a curving motion. The word is appropriate in the poem because it suggests the shape of the seal as well as tells how it moves.
   Difficulty: *Easy* **Objective:** *Vocabulary*
7. The poet seems to expect that the ducklings will get eaten by the weasel. He calls them "foolish," so they must be on or near the pond already.
   Difficulty: *Average* **Objective:** *Interpretation*
8. Each poem has three lines with five, seven, and five syllables, which is true of haiku. Each poem is about something in nature (ducklings, a wood, the setting moon). Haiku is often about nature.
   Difficulty: *Easy* **Objective:** *Literary Analysis*
9. The poet draws the conclusion "Something is afraid." He uses the details "windless" and "not one leaf dares to move."
   Difficulty: *Challenging* **Objective:** *Reading*
10. The second haiku conveys the strongest feelings because it focuses on fear. The first haiku seems more humorous, and the third haiku has a quiet, controlled feeling.
    Difficulty: *Challenging* **Objective:** *Interpretation*

Essay

11. Sample answer: The seal starts out diving from the rocks, down into the water past other sea creatures and

plants. He twists and turns as he swims, and he swims away very quickly. He soon returns with fish he has caught. As he starts his journey, he is probably hungry. At the end of it, he is glad to have found food, and excited about his swim.

Difficulty: *Easy*   **Objective:** *Essay*

12. Students may say they like the treatment of nature in "Seal" better than in the haiku because of the playful, lively quality of the poem. The seal seems to leap off the page as it darts, twists, and flips. Others may prefer the quieter imagery and the sparseness of the haiku.

Difficulty: *Average*   **Objective:** *Essay*

13. Sample answer: The poem explores Nye's feelings about loneliness. The rider wonders whether she can escape her loneliness by pedaling harder on her bike, as if loneliness is something she can beat in a race. She calls leaving it behind a victory, and seems envious of the pink petals "that have never felt loneliness."

Difficulty: *Challenging*   **Objective:** *Essay*

14. Students may say they find the concrete poem most effective because both the shape and the words contribute to the idea of motion. Others may find the haiku effective because of the simple images the short lines present, or they may find the lyric poem effective because of its concentration on a single emotion. Students should use detailed examples from the chosen poem as support.

Difficulty: *Average*   **Objective:** *Essay*

Oral Response

15. Oral responses should be clear, well organized, and well supported by appropriate examples from the poems.

Difficulty: *Average*   **Objective:** *Oral Interpretation*

Selection Test A, p. 35

Critical Reading

1. ANS: B	DIF: Easy	OBJ: Comprehension
2. ANS: B	DIF: Easy	OBJ: Interpretation
3. ANS: B	DIF: Easy	OBJ: Literary Analysis
4. ANS: D	DIF: Easy	OBJ: Comprehension
5. ANS: A	DIF: Easy	OBJ: Literary Analysis
6. ANS: D	DIF: Easy	OBJ: Interpretation
7. ANS: A	DIF: Easy	OBJ: Comprehension
8. ANS: A	DIF: Easy	OBJ: Reading
9. ANS: D	DIF: Easy	OBJ: Reading
10. ANS: B	DIF: Easy	OBJ: Interpretation
11. ANS: C	DIF: Easy	OBJ: Interpretation

Vocabulary and Grammar

12. ANS: C	DIF: Easy	OBJ: Vocabulary
13. ANS: B	DIF: Easy	OBJ: Vocabulary

14. ANS: A	DIF: Easy	OBJ: Grammar
15. ANS: C	DIF: Easy	OBJ: Grammar

Essay

16. Students should cite passages from both poets' work and explain why one poet is more successful than the other at communicating his feelings about nature or his observations of the natural world.

Difficulty: *Easy*

Objective: *Essay*

17. Students should recognize that Nye is writing about the idea of escaping from one's loneliness. They should mention the images of rollerskating or bicycling to escape loneliness and the pink petals of an azalea blossom, which seem to represent victory over loneliness.

Difficulty: *Easy*

Objective: *Essay*

18. Students should pick one poem that they responded to more than the others, and explain why that poem's form communicated more effectively to them. Their answers should be supported by specific examples from the text.

Difficulty: *Average*

Objective: *Essay*

Selection Test B, p. 38

Critical Reading

1. ANS: B	DIF: Challenging	OBJ: Literary Analysis
2. ANS: A	DIF: Average	OBJ: Interpretation
3. ANS: A	DIF: Challenging	OBJ: Reading
4. ANS: C	DIF: Challenging	OBJ: Interpretation
5. ANS: A	DIF: Average	OBJ: Literary Analysis
6. ANS: C	DIF: Average	OBJ: Literary Analysis
7. ANS: B	DIF: Average	OBJ: Comprehension
8. ANS: C	DIF: Average	OBJ: Interpretation
9. ANS: D	DIF: Average	OBJ: Interpretation
10. ANS: D	DIF: Challenging	OBJ: Interpretation
11. ANS: A	DIF: Average	OBJ: Interpretation
12. ANS: D	DIF: Challenging	OBJ: Literary Analysis
13. ANS: C	DIF: Average	OBJ: Literary Analysis

Vocabulary and Grammar

14. ANS: C	DIF: Challenging	OBJ: Vocabulary
15. ANS: B	DIF: Average	OBJ: Vocabulary
16. ANS: D	DIF: Average	OBJ: Vocabulary
17. ANS: A	DIF: Average	OBJ: Grammar
18. ANS: D	DIF: Average	OBJ: Grammar

Essay

19. Students should recognize that the speaker in "The Rider" suggests that loneliness can be outrun: It can be escaped by rollerskating or bicycling at great speed. The speaker suggests that racing to escape loneliness is "the best reason [she] ever heard / for trying to be a champion."

    Difficulty: *Average*
    Objective: *Essay*

20. Students should note that in "The Rider," motion is a way to escape loneliness. The bicycle rider's movement results in a feeling of joyous victory, in which she "float[s] free into a cloud of sudden azaleas." In "Seal," motion creates a rhythm and a feeling of grace, playfulness, and lightheartedness; it is also symbolized by the actual arrangement of the lines on the page.

    Difficulty: *Challenging*
    Objective: *Essay*

21. Students may say they find the concrete poem most effective because both the shape and the words contribute to the idea of motion. Others may find the haiku effective because of the simple images the short lines present, or the lyric poem effective because of its concentration on a single emotion. Students should use detailed examples from the chosen poem as support.

    Difficulty: *Average*
    Objective: *Essay*

Poetry Collection: Nikki Giovanni, Mary Ellen Solt, Matsuo Bashō

Vocabulary Warm-up Exercises, p. 42

A. 1. winter
   2. collect
   3. layers
   4. mountain
   5. oatmeal
   6. remain

B. Sample Answers

1. The carefully tended rose garden had many colorful blossoms.
2. We liked smelling the fragrant, freshly baked bread.
3. Did you ever hear the saying "mighty oaks from tiny acorns grow"?
4. Anna wanted everything to be perfect for the party, so she spent a lot of time preparing for it.
5. The warm days of spring are a welcome treat after the long winter.

Reading Warm-up A, p. 43

Sample Answers

1. (season); The season that comes before *winter* is fall, and the season after *winter* is spring.
2. (hot breakfasts); Laura cooked *oatmeal* with honey and milk in it.

3. hours of daylight; *Remain* means "to stay or be left behind when the rest has gone away."
4. acorns; *Collect* means "to gather together."
5. (This extra-thick coat will keep them warm on cold winter days.); The many *layers* of snow meant the trails were good for skiing.
6. (skunks and bears); A *mountain* is a "natural formation of the earth that rises sharply from the surrounding land and is larger than a hill."

Reading Warm-up B, p. 44

Sample Answers

1. The bitter, cold days of winter have drawn to an end. The northern part of the earth is beginning to tilt toward the sun at this time. This means the daylight hours are getting longer, and the weather is warmer.; *Spring* is the "season after winter when plants begin to grow and the weather warms."
2. (plants), (buds for new leaves), (grass), (flowers and other plants); Other things that *grow* are hair, fingernails, babies, trees.
3. (the beauty and colors); *Blossoms* are "flowers."
4. bright yellow flowers; one of the first signs of the spring season, This shrub, which is a member of the olive family, looks like a fountain of color when it blooms. Its green leaves emerge only after the yellow flowers have bloomed; Jean painted a colorful picture of a yellow *forsythia* in bloom.
5. (Roses and lilacs); Other fragrant things are cookies that are baking, soap, fresh-cut lumber.
6. the plant to make new seeds; *Preparing* means "making ready or suitable for some event."

Writing About the Big Question, p. 45

A. 1. speak
   2. listen
   3. react
   4. express

B. Sample Answers

1. If you widen your eyes and open your mouth, you can **express** shock or surprise.
2. If you jump up and down, you can show that you **react** with excitement.

C. Sample Answer

Descriptive language can **contribute** *to an understanding of the feelings the poet is trying to communicate.*

Reading: Ask Questions to Draw a Conclusion, p. 46

Sample Answers

Question / Details Relating to Question / Conclusion

"*Winter*": What feeling do the details create? / The speaker describes frogs, snails, dogs, bears, and chipmunks, as well as people, preparing for winter. / The details create a feeling of calm anticipation and a sense of security.

"Forsythia": What is the meaning of "HOPE INSISTS ACTION"? / The first letter of each word is part of the word *forsythia*. / Perhaps the forsythia symbolizes hope. *Insists* and *action* are forceful words. The poet is saying that forsythia, or hope, insists on action.

"Has spring come indeed?": What is the speaker's attitude? / The speaker includes the word *indeed* in his question. / The speaker is scornful. Perhaps it is spring according to the calendar, but the weather indicates that it is still winter.

"Temple bells die out": What is the speaker's attitude? / The speaker declares the evening "perfect." / The speaker is content.

Literary Analysis: Forms of Poetry, p. 47

Sample Answers

1. I would rewrite "Has spring come indeed?" in the shape of a mountain, with some letters around it to represent the mist.
2. "Winter's coming; bears store fat."
3. I would focus on the feeling of hope I have when I see the yellow of the forsythia blossom because I find that color intense and inspiring.
4. "Loud yellow blossoms"
5. I would rewrite the second haiku, focusing on feeling deceived by the weather. I would use that focus because a lyric poem is supposed to express the poet's thoughts or feelings about a single image or idea.

Vocabulary Builder, p. 48

Sample Answers

A.
1. No, it is a spring flower.
2. No, it is a coded message with important information.
3. Yes, an animal could dig down to get out of sight.
4. Yes, roses have a very pleasant smell.

B.
1. An <u>electrocardiogram</u> might record the way your heart works.
2. A <u>grammarian</u> probably studies grammar, the rules of language and writing.
3. An <u>anagram</u> of "bat" would be "tab" because it uses the same letters to make a new word.

Enrichment: Preparing for Winter, p. 49

A. Sample Answers

Clothing: I would check to be sure my boots, coat, scarf, hat, and sweaters are still in good condition. I would make sure my boots are adequately waterproofed.

Outdoor sports: My friends and I would check on the condition of our skates, skis, snowboard, and sleds. I would see if my skates needed sharpening or my skis or snowboard needed waxing.

Indoor activities: I would make sure I had a supply of books and games.

Food: I would make sure I had cocoa, oatmeal, and some canned soup.

Health: I might get a flu shot. I might be sure I had tissues, cold medicine, and aspirin.

Emergency supplies: I would be sure there were batteries for the flashlight, candles, and a supply of bottled water.

B. Students should write a well-reasoned explanation of what they like, or imagine they would like, most and least about winter.

Poetry Collections: Naomi Shihab Nye, William Jay Smith, Buson; Nikki Giovanni, Mary Ellen Solt, Matsuo Bashō

Integrated Language Skills: Grammar, p. 50

A. Each infinitive is followed by the infinitive phrase, if there is one:

1. to air; to air her quilts
2. To create; to create a poem that looks like a forsythia bush
3. to escape; to escape his loneliness
4. to move (*no infinitive phrase*)
5. to swim; to swim fast

B. Sample Answers

1. After I read "The Rider," I wanted to get on my bicycle and ride fast.
2. "Seal" is a good poem to read out loud.
3. Reading Buson's haiku about the moon is like trying to solve a mystery.
4. Reading "Winter" makes me want to sit before a fire and read a book.
5. To read "Forsythia" is to see forsythia in bloom.
6. I wonder why something is afraid to move?

Poetry Collection: Nikki Giovanni, Mary Ellen Solt, Bashō

Open-Book Test, p. 53

Short Answer

1. A lyric poem directs the reader to a single idea or image. Here, the idea is that people or animals prepare themselves in different ways for the winter.
   Difficulty: *Easy* **Objective:** *Literary Analysis*
2. The word *burrow* means "to dig a hole for shelter." The frogs prepare for winter by digging a place that will help them stay comfortable in colder weather.
   Difficulty: *Easy* **Objective:** *Vocabulary*

3. Lines 3, 5, and 9 use all one-syllable words, so the rhythm feels very steady in these lines. They create a beat for the poem.
   Difficulty: *Challenging*   **Objective:** *Literary Analysis*

4. The poem seems to be about either a vase or a bush that has long stems and flowers coming off it, so readers can assume that forsythia is a kind of flower. Based on the page color, the flower is probably yellow in color.
   Difficulty: *Easy*   **Objective:** *Literary Analysis*

5. Sample answer: The poem seems to be saying that forsythias are a sign of springtime. The words "spring's yellow telegram" show that forsythias send a message that spring has come.
   Difficulty: *Average*   **Objective:** *Reading*

6. Sample answer: The lines go in several directions to show branches of forsythia flowers. Each branch of flowers is twisting and expressing the way forsythias grow.
   Difficulty: *Average*   **Objective:** *Reading*

7. Sample answer: The poet creates a feeling of happiness and peace. The use of "sweet" tells the reader that there is something to appreciate. The use of "blossoms" shows that nature is growing and in its prettiest phase.
   Difficulty: *Average*   **Objective:** *Interpretation*

8. The first and third lines of each of the three poems has five syllables. A haiku always has three lines, with five syllables in the first line and the third line.
   Difficulty: *Easy*   **Objective:** *Literary Analysis*

9. GO: Subject: Nature; Other circles: plum blossoms; sun; spring; mountain; mist; fragrant; evening
   The poet seems to value and appreciate nature.
   Difficulty: *Average*   **Objective:** *Literary Analysis*

10. The first haiku uses an exclamation point to show a sense of wonder at discovering a path. The second haiku asks the reader to join in the poet's discovery of a new season. The third haiku uses an exclamation point to emphasize the poet's pleasure and enjoyment of the evening.
    Difficulty: *Challenging*   **Objective:** *Interpretation*

Essay

11. Students should explain that the word "telegram" conveys the idea of something that sends a message. Forsythia acts as a "telegram" for spring—it is the first message that spring is on the way.
    Difficulty: *Easy*   **Objective:** *Essay*

12. Sample answer: The first haiku most intensely celebrates nature because it expresses a sense of joy, wonder, and discovery. The poet is in the moment, enjoying the sudden sunrise and the discovery of a path. The second poem has more of a questioning tone, wondering if indeed spring has come. The third poem expresses appreciation of a "perfect" evening, but it is calmer and less intense.
    Difficulty: *Average*   **Objective:** *Essay*

13. Sample answer: The poet talks about animals making preparations for food and warmth. They find places to live for the winter; they find ways to make themselves warm, and they store food. Humans get their quilts ready and take winter medicine. By preparing herself with quilts and books, the poet's attitude seems to be one of looking forward to a slower time of year.
    Difficulty: *Challenging*   **Objective:** *Essay*

14. Sample answer: The most effective poem for me is "Winter," because it uses so much imagery to convey an idea. I can see the animals digging in mud, burying themselves, and gathering food. I can also picture someone shaking out quilts, and I can imagine the faces of children who have to take medicine. All of these images work well together to suggest the coming of winter. The other forms worked less well for me because they do not have as many words that I could use to form a clear picture in my mind.
    Difficulty: *Average*   **Objective:** *Essay*

Oral Response

15. Oral responses should be clear, well organized, and well supported by appropriate examples from the poems.
    Difficulty: *Average*   **Objective:** *Oral Interpretation*

Selection Test A, p. 56

Critical Reading

1. ANS: A	DIF: Easy	OBJ: Interpretation
2. ANS: B	DIF: Easy	OBJ: Comprehension
3. ANS: D	DIF: Easy	OBJ: Comprehension
4. ANS: C	DIF: Easy	OBJ: Reading
5. ANS: C	DIF: Easy	OBJ: Literary Analysis
6. ANS: B	DIF: Easy	OBJ: Reading
7. ANS: B	DIF: Easy	OBJ: Interpretation
8. ANS: A	DIF: Easy	OBJ: Comprehension
9. ANS: D	DIF: Easy	OBJ: Literary Analysis
10. ANS: D	DIF: Easy	OBJ: Comprehension
11. ANS: B	DIF: Easy	OBJ: Interpretation
12. ANS: A	DIF: Easy	OBJ: Interpretation

Vocabulary and Grammar

13. ANS: B	DIF: Easy	OBJ: Vocabulary
14. ANS: A	DIF: Easy	OBJ: Grammar
15. ANS: B	DIF: Easy	OBJ: Grammar

Essay

16. Students should point to two or three details in the poem, show how they relate, and draw a conclusion about the speaker's attitude toward winter based on the details and their relationship. For example, they might point to the bears' storing fat, the chipmunks' gathering nuts, and the speaker's collecting books to conclude

that in the speaker's view, winter is a season for which preparation is required.

Difficulty: *Easy*
Objective: *Essay*

17. Students should support their opinions in well-reasoned essays. For example, those who pick "Winter" may stress the cozy feeling of the poem and the descriptions of the animals' preparations for cold weather. Those who choose "Forsythia" may point out that the poem's shape captures the unrestrained shape of a branch of forsythia in bloom. Those who discuss the haiku might note how Bashō uses vivid imagery—the sunrise suddenly illuminating a mountain path, a mist shrouding a mountain, the fragrance of a blossom seeming to relate to the tolling of temple bells—to evoke a glimpse of the natural world.

Difficulty: *Easy*
Objective: *Essay*

18. Students should pick one poem that they responded to more than the others, and explain why that poem communicated more effectively to them. Their answers should be supported by specific examples from the text.

Difficulty: *Average*
Objective: *Essay*

Selection Test B, p. 59

Critical Reading

1. ANS: C	DIF: Average	OBJ: Interpretation
2. ANS: C	DIF: Average	OBJ: Interpretation
3. ANS: C	DIF: Average	OBJ: Comprehension
4. ANS: A	DIF: Challenging	OBJ: Interpretation
5. ANS: D	DIF: Challenging	OBJ: Reading
6. ANS: C	DIF: Average	OBJ: Literary Analysis
7. ANS: C	DIF: Average	OBJ: Interpretation
8. ANS: B	DIF: Challenging	OBJ: Reading
9. ANS: A	DIF: Challenging	OBJ: Interpretation
10. ANS: D	DIF: Average	OBJ: Literary Analysis
11. ANS: A	DIF: Average	OBJ: Reading
12. ANS: D	DIF: Average	OBJ: Interpretation
13. ANS: D	DIF: Average	OBJ: Interpretation
14. ANS: C	DIF: Challenging	OBJ: Reading

Vocabulary and Grammar

15. ANS: D	DIF: Average	OBJ: Vocabulary
16. ANS: C	DIF: Average	OBJ: Grammar
17. ANS: A	DIF: Challenging	OBJ: Grammar
18. ANS: C	DIF: Challenging	OBJ: Grammar

Essay

19. Students should support their viewpoints with at least two details from each poet's work. Those who choose

Giovanni may point out that "Winter" deals more with the relationship between people and nature than the other poem does. Those who choose Solt might point to her poem's exuberance. Those who choose Bashō are likely to point to the delicacy of the haiku.

Difficulty: *Average*
Objective: *Essay*

20. Students might note that the speaker in the first haiku registers surprise, the speaker in the second haiku seems doubtful and disappointed, and the speaker in the third haiku seems content. In pointing to a similarity, students might note that in all the haiku the speaker is attuned to nature.

Difficulty: *Challenging*
Objective: *Essay*

21. Sample answer: The most effective poem for me is "Winter" because it uses so much imagery to convey an idea. I can see the animals digging in mud, burying themselves, and gathering food. I can also picture someone shaking out quilts, and I can imagine the faces of children who have to take medicine. All of these images work well together to suggest the coming of winter. The other forms worked less well for me because they do not have as many words that I could use to form a clear picture in my mind.

Difficulty: *Average*
Objective: *Essay*

Poetry Collection: Naomi Long Madgett, Wendy Rose, Edna St. Vincent Millay

Vocabulary Warm-up Exercises, p. 63

A. 1. infant
2. amuse
3. instead
4. watch
5. spare
6. treasure

B. Sample Answers

1. The pyramids in Egypt are <u>centuries</u> old.
2. I put on extra clothing to keep from <u>trembling</u> from the cold.
3. To clean out a fireplace, I would shovel the <u>ashes</u> into a plastic bag and put the bag in the trash.
4. People are <u>fascinated</u> by celebrities because they are wealthy, and they live such exciting lives.
5. I believe that love is the <u>source</u> of all happiness.

Reading Warm-up A, p. 64

Sample Answers

1. (time); The digital *watch* told the time in hours, minutes, and seconds.
2. (bore); To *amuse* means "to keep somebody entertained."

3. the only picture I have of them together; I *treasure* an old stamp collection that belonged to my grandfather.

4. (baby); The *infant* cried all night long.

5. a loose photo of her mom; My grandmother's locket is so precious to me that I could not *spare* it.

6. look at family photos; I often read or listen to music *instead* of watching TV.

Reading Warm-up B, p. 65

Sample Answers

1. (volcano); The curtain went up in March 1980 when the volcano awoke, *shaking* from a series of earthquakes and steam explosions.

2. the terrifying force about to reveal itself; I was *fascinated* by the 2004 Baseball World Series.

3. steam and gas from the Earth's core that builds inside vents that lead to the Earth's surface; A synonym for *source* is "origin."

4. (as the pressure mounts); I *shudder* when I see scary movies and wait to see what will happen next.

5. (Volcanic); *Ashes* may be found in fireplaces and in forests after a fire.

6. The writer suggests that *centuries* from now Mount St. Helens may erupt again. That would be hundreds of years into the future.

Writing About the Big Question, p. 66

A. 1. media
2. inform;teach
3. enrich
4. produce

B. Sample Answers

1. I **learned** about the Muslim holiday of Ramadan from a newspaper story. A television program **informed** me about what children in Indonesia learn in school.

2. Learning about Ramadan **contributed** to a greater understanding of the Muslim religion. Finding out what Indonesians **learn** in school helped me understand their culture.

C. Sample Answer

When you make connections between unrelated things, you **enrich** your understanding of the things you are connecting and **learn** more about each of the things.

Reading: Connect the Details to Draw a Conclusion, p. 67

Sample Answers

"Life": The speaker is using the watch to talk about life and death.

"Loo-Wit": The speaker is describing a dormant volcano that is coming to life.

"The Courage That My Mother Had": The speaker admires her mother for the courage she had in life and wishes that instead of the brooch, she had her mother's courage.

Literary Analysis: Figurative Language, p. 68

Sample Answers

"Life": "Life is but a toy that swings on a bright gold chain / . . . And lets the watch run down.": extended metaphor

"Loo-Wit": "This old woman / . . . Loo-Wit sings and sings and sings!": extended metaphor; "spits her black tobacco," "stretching full length," "Finally up / she sprinkles ashes," "on her neck," "machinery growls, / snarls and plows / great patches / of her skin," "She crouches," "her trembling," "her slopes," "her arm," "She was sleeping / but she heard . . . / felt the pull . . . / from her thin shoulder. / With one free hand / she finds her weapons / and raises them high; / clearing . . . from her throat / she sings": personification; "like a blanket about her": simile

"The Courage That My Mother Had": "Rock from New England quarried": metaphor (for the mother's courage); "granite": symbol (of courage); "courage like a rock": simile

Vocabulary Builder, p. 69

A. Sample Answers

1. Explanation: To crouch is to stoop, so the sentence does not make sense. New sentence: The angry woman *crouches* as she picks up stones from the ground.

2. The sentence makes sense because stones that are *dislodged* are forced from the place where they were lying, so they might start an avalanche.

3. Explanation: It doesn't make sense because *fascinated* means "very interested." New sentence: Anita was so *fascinated* by the movie that she barely blinked.

4. Explanation: To *unravel* is to come undone, so the sentence does not make sense. New sentence: The sweater was so old that it began to *unravel*.

5. It makes sense because *prickly* means "scratchy."

6. Explanation: It doesn't make sense because *granite* is a very hard rock. New sentence: The hard rain ran off the piece of *granite*.

B. 1. A person who behaves *bravely* does something that is scary or dangerous.

2. A person might act *ambitiously* at work by working long hours and doing well.

3. You have to move *carefully* while hiking because it is easy to fall or twist an ankle.

Enrichment: Animated Film, p. 70

Sample Answers

A. Students should demonstrate an understanding of the "character."

B. Students should complete eight or more drawings of a character as directed in order to create an animation flip book.

Naomi Long Madgett,
Edna St. Vincent Millay, Wendy Rose

Open-Book Test, p. 71

Short Answer

1. The poet uses the metaphor that life is a toy (a watch). The poet seems to have chosen this metaphor to suggest that when we are young, the toy (life) amuses us, but when we are old, the toy (life) tires us.
   Difficulty: *Easy* **Objective:** *Literary Analysis*

2. In line 3, the keeper of the toy is an infant. In line 4, the keeper is an old man. Age, and the tiredness that goes along with age, affects the keeper. He cares less and less about the toy (life) the older he gets.
   Difficulty: *Average* **Objective:** *Interpretation*

3. Sample answer: Line 6 says that an old person "lets the watch run down." The use of the word "lets" suggests that we have some control over the length of our lives and that we let the watch run down (we die) when we are tired of living.
   Difficulty: *Challenging* **Objective:** *Reading*

4. The poet compares her mother's courage to a rock—specifically, granite. A reason that courage and granite might be compared is that they both represent strength.
   Difficulty: *Average* **Objective:** *Literary Analysis*

5. The speaker says that the brooch is important to her in line 7, but that she would be able to part with it in line 8. Her feelings are complicated. She is saying that although she cares about the brooch, she would rather have had some of her mother's courage left to her instead.
   Difficulty: *Average* **Objective:** *Reading*

6. The speaker seems to feel both longing for her mother and frustration that she is not as courageous as her mother was. By saying "Oh, if . . ." she expresses her disappointment. She also says that her mother no longer needs courage, but she does.
   Difficulty: *Challenging* **Objective:** *Interpretation*

7. Sample answers: Line 2: this old woman; Line 5: spits her black tobacco; Line 50: she sings

   By creating an image of an old woman to represent a volcano, the poet adds energy and emotion to an event that occurs in the natural world.
   Difficulty: *Average* **Objective:** *Literary Analysis*

8. The volcano erupted because she was tired of being mistreated by humans whose "machinery growls,/ snarls and plows/great patches" and whose footsteps wake her up.
   Difficulty: *Average* **Objective:** *Interpretation*

9. The volcano that the woman represents is not actually *crouching*, because a mountain cannot bend or stoop like a person.
   Difficulty: *Easy* **Objective:** *Vocabulary*

10. As the stones *dislodge*, they will move from their place. They are part of a volcano that erupts, causing stones to crash and fall from the side of a mountain.
    Difficulty: *Average* **Objective:** *Vocabulary*

Essay

11. Sample answer: The poet describes an old woman who has lived long enough that she doesn't care about others' opinions. As an example, she spits her tobacco in any direction she pleases. She is cranky after having been "bound" to the earth for such a long time, and she "sings" when she explodes. I would be very uncomfortable being around such an angry, explosive person.
    Difficulty: *Easy* **Objective:** *Essay*

12. Sample answer: The poet chose to make the poem short for a few reasons. First, the poet is saying that life is less complicated than we think, so it can be summed up in a few lines. The poet is also emphasizing that life is short, even though we don't always realize it. The length of the poem serves the poet's purpose of sending a message that life is basically simple and short.
    Difficulty: *Average* **Objective:** *Essay*

13. Sample answer: The speaker seems to have deeply loved her mother. She misses her mother's strength—the "rock" of her courage. She also misses her mother's presence, as expressed in the final line, when the speaker says that she now needs courage (perhaps to face the loss she feels after her mother's death).
    Difficulty: *Challenging* **Objective:** *Essay*

14. Sample answer: The personification used in "Loo-Wit" is especially powerful in communicating the poet's message because the imagery is very strong. With every activity of the woman—her spitting, stretching, crouching, and finally, "clearing the twigs from her throat"—the power of the volcano builds and builds. As the woman "sings" at the end of poem, it is easy to imagine a volcano exploding with great power.
    Difficulty: *Average* **Objective:** *Essay*

Oral Response

15. Oral responses should be clear, well organized, and well supported by appropriate examples from the poems.
    Difficulty: *Average* **Objective:** *Oral Interpretation*

Selection Test A, p. 74

Critical Reading

1. ANS: C	DIF: Easy	OBJ: Literary Analysis
2. ANS: B	DIF: Easy	OBJ: Comprehension
3. ANS: B	DIF: Easy	OBJ: Interpretation
4. ANS: A	DIF: Easy	OBJ: Literary Analysis
5. ANS: A	DIF: Easy	OBJ: Interpretation
6. ANS: C	DIF: Easy	OBJ: Reading
7. ANS: C	DIF: Easy	OBJ: Comprehension
8. ANS: C	DIF: Easy	OBJ: Reading
9. ANS: B	DIF: Easy	OBJ: Comprehension
10. ANS: A	DIF: Easy	OBJ: Literary Analysis

Vocabulary and Grammar

11. ANS: B   DIF: Easy   OBJ: Vocabulary
12. ANS: B   DIF: Easy   OBJ: Vocabulary
13. ANS: B   DIF: Easy   OBJ: Grammar

Essay

14. Students should write well-reasoned explanations of their preference. Those who choose "Life" may relate to the idea of life as a toy watch whose keeper, "a very old man / Becomes tired of the game / and lets the watch run down." Those who choose "Loo-Wit" may say that the poem makes them think about volcanoes in a new way, citing such vivid descriptions as "Around her / machinery growls / snarls and plows."
   Difficulty: *Easy*
   Objective: *Essay*

15. Students should recognize that the speaker compares her mother to granite. They may cite such lines as "Rock from New England quarried; / Now granite in a granite hill." They should point out that the comparison characterizes the mother as courageous and firm in her beliefs.
   Difficulty: *Easy*
   Objective: *Essay*

16. Students should pick one poem that they responded to more than the others, and explain why that poem's figurative language communicated more effectively to them. Their answers should be supported by specific examples from the text.
   Difficulty: *Average*
   Objective: *Essay*

Selection Test B, p. 77

Critical Reading

1. ANS: B   DIF: Challenging   OBJ: Literary Analysis
2. ANS: B   DIF: Challenging   OBJ: Reading
3. ANS: B   DIF: Average   OBJ: Interpretation
4. ANS: C   DIF: Average   OBJ: Literary Analysis
5. ANS: D   DIF: Challenging   OBJ: Comprehension
6. ANS: C   DIF: Challenging   OBJ: Comprehension
7. ANS: B   DIF: Average   OBJ: Reading
8. ANS: A   DIF: Average   OBJ: Literary Analysis
9. ANS: D   DIF: Average   OBJ: Interpretation
10. ANS: D   DIF: Average   OBJ: Comprehension
11. ANS: D   DIF: Average   OBJ: Literary Analysis
12. ANS: B   DIF: Average   OBJ: Interpretation

Vocabulary and Grammar

13. ANS: B   DIF: Average   OBJ: Vocabulary
14. ANS: B   DIF: Average   OBJ: Vocabulary
15. ANS: B   DIF: Average   OBJ: Grammar
16. ANS: B   DIF: Average   OBJ: Grammar

17. ANS: B   DIF: Average   OBJ: Grammar
18. ANS: C   DIF: Average   OBJ: Grammar

Essay

19. Students should define simile, metaphor, personification, and symbol as they are defined in their textbooks. For an example of a simile, they might cite the line "shaking the sky / like a blanket around her" from "Loo-Wit"; for an example of a metaphor, they might cite "Life is but a toy" from "Life"; for personification, they might cite any number of lines from "Loo-Wit"; and for symbol, they might cite the granite, which stands for the speaker's mother's courage in "The Courage That My Mother Had."
   Difficulty: *Average*
   Objective: *Essay*

20. Students should note that the speaker in both poems seems to indicate that life is short and tenuous. Students might note that the speaker in "The Courage That My Mother Had" appears regretful, whereas the speaker in "Life" is less serious.
   Difficulty: *Challenging*
   Objective: *Essay*

21. Sample answer: The personification used in "Loo-Wit" is especially powerful in communicating the poet's message because the imagery is very strong. With every activity of the woman—her spitting, stretching, crouching, and finally, "clearing the twigs from her throat"—the power of the volcano builds and builds. As the woman "sings" at the end of poem, it is easy to imagine a volcano exploding with great power.
   Difficulty: *Average*
   Objective: *Essay*

Poetry Collection: Langston Hughes, Henry Wadsworth Longfellow, Carl Sandburg

Vocabulary Warm-up Exercises, p. 81

A.
1. rejoice
2. harbor
3. fog
4. task
5. crystal
6. deed

B. Sample Answers
1. No, creating our own *fortunes*, or destiny, involves much more than making a lot of money.
2. If my *brow* is shaded from the sun, it is likely I'm wearing a hat because I wear my hat above my forehead.
3. If soldiers are moving *onward*, they are not in retreat, because to retreat means the opposite of moving forward.
4. If my job is to repair tires, I would not likely use an *anvil*, because an anvil is used for shaping iron.

5. If the *forge* is cold, it is likely the blacksmith is not in the shop, because he uses the fire in his forge for his work.

Reading Warm-up A, p. 82

Sample Answers

1. a misty cloud; I like the *fog* because it makes the world look dreamy.
2. (boats); A *harbor* is "a place near land where people keep their boats safe."
3. to count the number of young sea lions for the Marine Institute.; One of my *tasks* is to mow the lawn on the weekend.
4. (one act of kindness); I consider giving blood to the Red Cross a good *deed.*
5. (celebrate); I *rejoice* each time I get good grades.
6. (sparkling); *Crystal* is "sparkling glass."

Reading Warm-up B, p. 83

Sample Answers

1. He was a muscular man covered in soot from his head to his toes. *Brow* means "forehead."
2. his job, heavy labor; I'm covered in sweat after *toiling* in the hot sun in my mom's vegetable garden.
3. red-hot metal; Another word for *forge* is "fireplace" or "oven."
4. a large chunk of metal on which the blacksmith pounded the hot iron into shape; The old *anvil* was too heavy to move.
5. (time); *backward*
6. the honesty of their labors; I think hard work and a good education will help shape my *destiny.*

Writing About the Big Question, p. 84

A. 1. entertain
2. express
3. listen
4. produce

B. Sample Answers

1. I went to a concert and heard Beethoven's *Fifth Symphony*, which I found very moving. I also saw an amazing performance of *The Diary of Anne Frank*, which moved me.
2. When I watched *The Diary of Anne Frank*, I cried. I didn't know about the terrible things Anne Frank had faced, and I was moved by her courage and strength.

C. Sample Answer

Words that **express** strong emotions help readers understand how the poet feels about his or her subject.

Reading: Connect the Details to Draw a Conclusion, p. 85

Sample Answers

"Mother to Son": The speaker is determined that she will not be intimidated by setbacks; she keeps going no matter what.

"The Village Blacksmith": The blacksmith is an honorable, trustworthy, hardworking man.

"Fog": The fog is like a cat, arriving soundlessly, sitting watchfully, and then moving on.

Literary Analysis: Figurative Language, p. 86

"Mother to Son": "Life for me ain't been no crystal stair / . . . And life for me ain't been no crystal stair": extended metaphor (with "tacks" and "splinters" representing hardship, bare boards representing poverty, the landings representing achievements, the corners turned representing choices, darkness representing extreme hardship, and sitting down on the steps representing giving in to obstacles); "crystal stair": symbol (of an easy, luxurious life)

"The Village Blacksmith": "the muscles of his brawny arms / Are strong as iron bands": simile; "You can hear him swing his heavy sledge / . . . Like a sexton ringing the village bell": simile; "the burning sparks that fly / Like chaff from a threshing floor": simile; "at the flaming forge of life / Our fortunes must be wrought; / Thus on its sounding anvil shaped / Each burning deed and thought": extended metaphor (for the hardships, thoughts, and deeds that shape our lives)

"Fog": "The fog comes / . . . And then moves on": extended metaphor (comparing the fog to a cat)

Vocabulary Builder, p. 87

A. Sample Answers

1. It makes sense that a cheetah would push off from its upper legs and hips to gather speed.
2. It makes sense that the blacksmith would be able to lift the hammer, because *brawny* means "muscular and strong."
3. Explanation: The sentence does not make sense because *sinewy* means "tough and strong." New sentence: The *sinewy* construction worker could carry the heaviest loads.
4. It makes sense because *crystal* is very breakable.
5. Explanation: It doesn't make sense because a *parson* is a preacher. New sentence: The *parson* was a wonderful speaker and moved his audience with his words.
6. It makes sense because *wrought* means carefully shaped.

B. 1. An irate person might yell or throw something *angrily.*

2. Someone who learns *easily* would probably do well in school.

3. Writing *messily* on your test paper can bring down your grade.

Enrichment: Inspiring People, p. 88

A. Students should note vivid details and then recast them in figurative language.

B. Students should incorporate their figurative language into a well-written, coherent paragraph describing a person who has inspired them.

Poetry Collections: Naomi Long Madgett, Wendy Rose, Edna St. Vincent Millay; Langston Hughes, Henry Wadsworth Longfellow, Carl Sandburg

Integrated Language Skills: Grammar, p. 89

Sample Answers

A. The word that the appositive phrase identifies or explains follows the appositive phrase:

1. a volcano; Loo-Wit.
2. an old man; Death
3. a region in the northeast; New England
4. a hard rock; granite
5. a singer in the choir; daughter
6. a poem by Langston Hughes; "Mother to Son"

B. 1. In "The Courage That My Mother Had," the speaker's mother has given the speaker a brooch, a beautiful golden pin.

2. In "Fog," fog, a blanket of white mist, covers a harbor.

3. The mother in "Mother to Son" speaks of the crystal stair, a symbol of an easy life.

Poetry Collection: Langston Hughes, Henry Wadsworth Longfellow, Carl Sandburg

Open-Book Test, p. 92

Short Answer

1. The poet uses a worn staircase with "tacks in it, And splinters, And boards torn up."

   Difficulty: *Easy* **Objective:** *Literary Analysis*

2. They tell about the speaker's life—she has kept going through better times ("reachin' landin's") and worse times ("sometimes goin' in the dark").

   Difficulty: *Average* **Objective:** *Literary Analysis*

3. She is strong and determined. Even though her life has not been easy, she has kept "climbin" even "where there ain't been no light." She expects her son to do the same.

   Difficulty: *Average* **Objective:** *Reading*

4. A crystal stair would be smooth with no splinters or tacks to hurt your feet. It would be nice to look at,

without bare patches. It would also be something associated with wealth, which would make life easier.

Difficulty: *Challenging* **Objective:** *Interpretation*

5. The word *sinewy* means "tough and strong." The blacksmith must have strong hands in order to work as hard as he does every day.

Difficulty: *Average* **Objective:** *Vocabulary*

6. The blacksmith is a man who is honorable and hard-working and who feels a strong sense of family duty. He works "from morn til night," "goes on Sunday to the church," and rejoices at the sound of his daughter's voice.

Difficulty: *Average* **Objective:** *Reading*

7. The poet's metaphor for life is a "flaming forge." Like life, a forge can be difficult to endure, but it also has the power to shape an individual and make him or her stronger.

Difficulty: *Challenging* **Objective:** *Literary Analysis*

8. The word *haunches* means "upper legs and hips of an animal." The poet offers an image of a fog that rests quietly, as a cat might when it is observing something.

Difficulty: *Challenging* **Objective:** *Vocabulary*

9. Sample answer: GO: Line 2: little cat feet; Line 3: sits; Line 6: moves on

The metaphor for the fog is a cat. It is effective because, like a cat, the fog comes in quietly, rests for a while, and then moves quietly away.

Difficulty: *Average* **Objective:** *Literary Analysis*

10. The poem is short and easy to remember, and it creates a perfect image in the reader's mind of fog creeping in and out.

Difficulty: *Easy* **Objective:** *Interpretation*

Essay

11. Students should point out that the shortness of the poem adds to the image of a cat that may appear briefly ("sits looking on silent haunches") and then disappear without a sound. Like the fog, a cat can be almost an invisible presence, so the image works very well.

Difficulty: *Easy* **Objective:** *Essay*

12. Students should note that the poet describes the blacksmith as a model of hard work and dedication to his family and his life. He is at the forge week in and week out, with "honest sweat" on his brow. He takes his children to church and weeps for his dead wife. "Onward through life he goes," earning his night's rest with a day's work. In the final stanza, the speaker thanks the blacksmith for teaching us that we are shaped by what we do—each "burning deed and thought" shapes us on the "flaming forge of life."

Difficulty: *Average* **Objective:** *Essay*

13. Students should note that the informal dialect used in the poem supports the familiar tone a mother would use when speaking to her child. The dialect also suggests that the mother is relatively uneducated and thus

probably fairly poor, so it suggests the limits and difficulties of her life. She says, "I'se still goin', honey/ I'se still climbin'," suggesting that she knows that her life will always be difficult.

Difficulty: *Challenging* **Objective:** *Essay*

14. Students who choose "Mother to Son" may see the model of the mother in "Mother to Son" as very powerful, as she climbs the rough stairs of her life. The contrast between the "crystal stair" of others' lives and the steps she has to climb that have "boards torn up" is poignant and moving. Students who choose "The Village Blacksmith" may appreciate the power of the blacksmith contrasted with the gentleness of the man who sheds tears for his wife. Students who choose "Fog" may appreciate the simplicity of the image of the fog on little cat feet creeping in and out.

Difficulty: *Average* **Objective:** *Essay*

Oral Response

15. Oral responses should be clear, well organized, and well supported by appropriate examples from the poems.

Difficulty: *Average* **Objective:** *Oral Interpretation*

Selection Test A, p. 95

Critical Reading

1. ANS: D	DIF: Easy	OBJ: Interpretation
2. ANS: D	DIF: Easy	OBJ: Comprehension
3. ANS: B	DIF: Easy	OBJ: Reading
4. ANS: C	DIF: Easy	OBJ: Interpretation
5. ANS: A	DIF: Easy	OBJ: Interpretation
6. ANS: A	DIF: Easy	OBJ: Literary Analysis
7. ANS: D	DIF: Easy	OBJ: Comprehension
8. ANS: D	DIF: Easy	OBJ: Reading
9. ANS: C	DIF: Easy	OBJ: Interpretation
10. ANS: C	DIF: Easy	OBJ: Interpretation
11. ANS: B	DIF: Easy	OBJ: Comprehension
12. ANS: C	DIF: Easy	OBJ: Literary Analysis

Vocabulary and Grammar

13. ANS: B	DIF: Easy	OBJ: Vocabulary
14. ANS: B	DIF: Easy	OBJ: Vocabulary
15. ANS: B	DIF: Easy	OBJ: Grammar

Essay

16. Students should recognize that "Fog" is an extended metaphor, they should define the term, and they should refer to the lines in the poem that draw and extend the metaphor ("on little cat feet," "It sits looking," and "on silent haunches / and then moves on").

Difficulty: *Easy*

Objective: *Essay*

17. Students should recognize that the mother in "Mother to Son" teaches her son that he must never give up, even in the face of great hardship, or that the village blacksmith models the values of hard work, dependability, and love of family. They might cite any number of details from the poems to support their conclusions.

Difficulty: *Easy*

Objective: *Essay*

18. Students should pick one poem that they responded to more than the others, and explain why that poem communicated most effectively to them. Their answers should be supported by specific examples from the text.

Difficulty: *Average*

Objective: *Essay*

Selection Test B, p. 98

Critical Reading

1. ANS: A	DIF: Average	OBJ: Literary Analysis
2. ANS: D	DIF: Average	OBJ: Interpretation
3. ANS: C	DIF: Average	OBJ: Comprehension
4. ANS: B	DIF: Average	OBJ: Literary Analysis
5. ANS: B	DIF: Challenging	OBJ: Reading
6. ANS: A	DIF: Average	OBJ: Interpretation
7. ANS: C	DIF: Challenging	OBJ: Reading
8. ANS: B	DIF: Average	OBJ: Interpretation
9. ANS: C	DIF: Average	OBJ: Comprehension
10. ANS: B	DIF: Average	OBJ: Literary Analysis
11. ANS: B	DIF: Challenging	OBJ: Interpretation
12. ANS: D	DIF: Average	OBJ: Literary Analysis
13. ANS: B	DIF: Average	OBJ: Comprehension
14. ANS: A	DIF: Challenging	OBJ: Comprehension

Vocabulary and Grammar

15. ANS: B	DIF: Average	OBJ: Vocabulary
16. ANS: A	DIF: Average	OBJ: Vocabulary
17. ANS: A	DIF: Average	OBJ: Vocabulary
18. ANS: B	DIF: Average	OBJ: Grammar
19. ANS: C	DIF: Challenging	OBJ: Grammar

Essay

20. Students should recognize that the scene is a city and its harbor as fog arrives, settles in, and drifts off. The details they add should be in keeping with that scene— for example, tall buildings, city lights, ships, the smell of the water, the sound of a foghorn.

Difficulty: *Average*

Objective: *Essay*

21. Students should recognize similes and extended metaphors and demonstrate an understanding of the compo-

nents of each type of comparison. They should point to a simile in "The Village Blacksmith" (for example, "The muscles of his brawny arms / Are strong as iron bands," "You can hear him swing his heavy sledge, . . . / "Like a sexton ringing the village bell," "And catch the burning sparks that fly / Like chaff from a threshing floor") and to the extended metaphors in "Mother to Son" (life is a staircase with tacks and splinters, without carpeting, with landings and corners, and so on) or "Fog" (the fog is a cat that arrives, sits quietly, "and then moves on").

Difficulty: *Challenging*

Objective: *Essay*

22. Students who choose "Mother to Son" may see the model of the mother in "Mother to Son" as very powerful, as she climbs the rough stairs of her life. The contrast between the "crystal stair" of others' lives and the steps she has to climb that have "boards torn up" is poignant and moving. Students who choose "The Village Blacksmith" may appreciate the power of the blacksmith contrasted with the gentleness of the man who sheds tears for his wife. Students who choose "Fog" may appreciate the simplicity of the image of the fog on little cat feet creeping in and out.

Difficulty: *Average*

Objective: *Essay*

Poetry by Alfred Noyes and Gregory Djanikian

Vocabulary Warm-up Exercises, p. 102

A. 1. notions
   2. gusty
   3. clattered
   4. clutching
   5. dazed
   6. shattered

B. Sample Answers

   1. A ball might follow a high, steep *arc* if the batter hit a home run.
   2. Someone might use a locked door to *bar* entrance to a room.
   3. I would call a constant, naturally flowing *cascade* of water a waterfall.
   4. If driven by *desperation*, a basketball team might take some wild shots, hoping to score.
   5. If I were in a car at *dusk*, I would expect the driver to turn on the headlights because he wouldn't be able to see well without them.
   6. No, I would not describe someone with black hair as having *tawny* hair because *tawny* means light brown or brownish-orange.

Reading Warm-up A, p. 103

Sample Answers

   1. (a loud yell); in this passage, *shattered* means "broke through."

   2. (embraced); Pat stood *clutching* an umbrella as he waited for the storm to pass.
   3. Finally, the men fell to the ground and lay *stunned* by their discovery. Falling out of the tree left the bird *dazed* for several minutes.
   4. (weather); windy, especially in bursts
   5. They thought they could buy food along the trail; ideas
   6. the noise the prospectors made; Sue *clattered* down the street carrying empty soda cans to be recycled.

Reading Warm-up B, p. 104

Sample Answers

   1. the sky grew darker; A typical activity I might be doing at *dusk* is helping my mom prepare dinner.
   2. Losing this game would end the Sharks' season; In *desperation*, Cindy dove across the floor and tried to catch the falling vase.
   3. (playoffs); prevent.
   4. (ball); The finches flew in an *arc* from the bird feeder to the tree branches.
   5. (baseball mitt); A lion's mane might be described as *tawny*.
   6. (shower, water, poured); I might see a *cascade* of water from a faucet.

Writing About the Big Question, p. 105

A. 1. communicate
   2. express
   3. speak
   4. contribute

B. Sample Answers

   1. Hello, my name is Mia Simon. I sit behind you in class, and I noticed that you have a soccer sticker on your backpack. I hope you might want to join our soccer team.
   2. I'd like to **inform** a new person that I am friendly and **express** that I'd like to help the person make friends and feel comfortable.

C. Sample Answer

   Facial expressions or body language can be more expressive than words.

Literary Analysis: Comparing Narrative Poems, p. 106

Sample Answers

"The Highwayman": Plot and conflict—The highwayman visits his sweetheart before going off to commit a robbery. Tim, who loves Bess, overhears their conversation and reports it to the redcoats. The soldiers bind Bess up with a musket pointed at her chest. The conflict occurs when Bess hears the highwayman coming and shoots herself to warn him of the danger he is in. *Poetic devices*—The poem contains metaphors ("The moon was a ghostly galleon," "the road was a ribbon"), similes ("his hair like moldy hay," "Down like a dog on the highway"), rhythm, and rhyme.

"How I Learned English": Plot and conflict—The narrator, newly arrived in the United States, is playing baseball with neighborhood boys but has little idea of the game. Daydreaming, he is hit in the head and mistakenly calls his head his shin. The conflict occurs when the other boys laugh. The narrator joins in the laughter, is accepted by the others, and goes back to the game, imitating the motions of the others and therefore learning to fit in. *Poetic devices*—There is no regular rhyme or rhythm and no metaphors or personification; there is a simile ("dusting me off with hands like swatters").

Vocabulary Builder, p. 107

A. Sample Answers

1. F; *bound* means "tied up," so the dog would not be free to roam.

2. F; *writhing* means "squirming," so the person would not be lying still.

3. T; a torrent is a flood and would likely cause a river to overflow its banks.

4. F; to whimper is to moan, and people are unlikely to moan when they are content.

5. F; *transfixed* means "standing still," so the person would not be running.

6. F; to *strive* is to struggle, and people who struggle are not likely to be lazy.

B. 1. A *torrential* rain can cause a small waterfall to turn into a torrent.

2. People's fear and excitement can *transfix* them when they watch a scary movie.

3. Binding a wound can help keep it clean and prevent it from getting infected.

Open-Book Test, p. 109

Short Answer

1. Since the highwayman is a robber, he is preparing to commit a robbery. He tells Bess that he is "after a prize tonight" and that he will "be back with the yellow gold."
   Difficulty: *Easy*   **Objective:** *Interpretation*

2. *Bound* means "tied." Since Bess is tied to the foot of her bed, she cannot move to warn the highwayman that English soldiers are going to kill him.
   Difficulty: *Average*   **Objective:** *Vocabulary*

3. The highwayman rushes back to the inn to take revenge for the death of his love. He rides "like a madman, shouting a curse" and has his "rapier brandished high."
   Difficulty: *Average*   **Objective:** *Interpretation*

4. *Transfixed* means "rooted to the spot." If a deer were rooted to the spot in a road, it might get hit by the oncoming car.
   Difficulty: *Challenging*   **Objective:** *Vocabulary*

5. By laughing at his situation, the narrator shows that he does not take himself seriously. When Joe helps him up, it shows that the boys accept the speaker as one of their group.
   Difficulty: *Challenging*   **Objective:** *Interpretation*

6. Even though he still has no skill at the game, the narrator says he is doing all right because he has been accepted as one of the boys. For now, tugging at his cap the right way, crouching low, and saying "Hum baby" are enough to make him feel part of the group.
   Difficulty: *Average*   **Objective:** *Interpretation*

7. "The Highwayman" rhymes. In the first two lines, *trees* rhymes with *seas*.
   Difficulty: *Easy*   **Objective:** *Literary Analysis*

8. They combine elements of fiction and poetry to tell a story.
   Difficulty: *Average*   **Objective:** *Literary Analysis*

9. "The Highwayman" has a third-person narrator not involved in the action. The first-person narrator of "How I Learned English" is the boy who just arrived in the United States.
   The narrator of "The Highwayman" is not a character in the poem, while the narrator of "How I Learned English" is.
   Difficulty: *Average*   **Objective:** *Literary Analysis*

10. "The Highwayman" is suspenseful because the reader knows that the redcoats are waiting to capture the highwayman, and Bess seems powerless to stop it. "How I Learned English" is suspenseful because the reader is not sure if the narrator will be accepted by the boys.
    Difficulty: *Challenging*   **Objective:** *Literary Analysis*

Essay

11. Students should correctly identify the setting of "The Highwayman" as England in the time of highwaymen and redcoats, and the setting of "How I Learned English" as Williamsport, Pennsylvania, in the present. They should recognize that the setting of "The Highwayman" is important because it takes place at a time when robbers might have been seen as romantic characters. The setting of "How I Learned English" is important because to the narrator it is a foreign place. Students will probably say that the setting of "How I Learned English" could more easily change since it could take place almost anywhere in the United States, while it would be hard to place the events in "The Highwayman" in another place and time.
    Difficulty: *Easy*   **Objective:** *Essay*

12. Students should note that the conflict in "The Highwayman" occurs when Bess is held captive by the soldiers, and that the conflict reaches a climax when Bess shoots herself to warn her love of the danger that awaits him. Students should recognize that the conflict in "How I Learned English" occurs when the narrator, newly arrived in the United States, finds himself on a baseball field trying to fit in with the American boys. The conflict is resolved when the ball hits him in the forehead and he mistakenly calls it his shin. All the boys laugh, including the narrator, and the ice is broken; he is accepted as one of the boys. Students will probably find the boy's conflict more realistic because everyone feels out of place at some point and yearns to

fit in. The drama and heroism in "The Highwayman" is rarer, and thus the conflict might seem less realistic.

Difficulty: *Average* **Objective:** *Essay*

13. Students might note that the poetic version has remained popular because the elements of poetry work well for such a romantic poem. Images presented through metaphor, such as "The road was a ribbon of moonlight over the purple moor," paint dramatic pictures in the reader's mind. The rhythm of the poem also helps add to the drama and suspense, as does the repetition of lines and words, such as *moonlight*. Students might note that the story would lose some of its dramatic flavor if it were in prose. However, they might indicate that telling the story in prose would allow for more character development and detail.

Difficulty: *Challenging* **Objective:** *Essay*

14. Students may note that in "The Highwayman" the lovers communicate their feelings through action rather than words. Bess sacrifices her own life to save her beloved's life. Thinking only of revenging his lost love, the highwayman rides back to the inn and is himself killed. By these events, the poem suggests that the best way to communicate is through deeds. Students might indicate that communication in "How I Learned English" also has more to do with actions than with words. The narrator speaks little English, so he cannot communicate his feelings to the other boys. However, words seem barely necessary after the ball hits him on the forehead. Groaning about his shin, the boy inadvertently causes the other boys to laugh. When he laughs too, he becomes accepted into the group. As a result, the poem also suggests that a person's actions speak louder than words.

Difficulty: *Average* **Objective:** *Essay*

Oral Response

15. Oral responses should be clear, well organized, and well supported by appropriate examples from the poems.

   4. **Difficulty:** *Average* **Objective:** *Oral Interpretation*

Selection Test A, p. 112

Critical Reading

1. ANS: A	DIF: Easy	OBJ: Comprehension
2. ANS: B	DIF: Easy	OBJ: Interpretation
3. ANS: A	DIF: Easy	OBJ: Interpretation
4. ANS: C	DIF: Easy	OBJ: Interpretation
5. ANS: A	DIF: Easy	OBJ: Literary Analysis
6. ANS: A	DIF: Easy	OBJ: Comprehension
7. ANS: D	DIF: Easy	OBJ: Interpretation
8. ANS: A	DIF: Easy	OBJ: Literary Analysis
9. ANS: D	DIF: Easy	OBJ: Literary Analysis

Vocabulary

10. ANS: B	DIF: Easy	OBJ: Vocabulary

11. ANS: A	DIF: Easy	OBJ: Vocabulary
12. ANS: D	DIF: Easy	OBJ: Vocabulary

Essay

13. Students should recognize that Bess is memorable because she shoots herself in an attempt to save the highwayman's life and that the narrator of "How I Learned English" is memorable because, by laughing with his teammates at his mistake, he gained acceptance. They should support their opinion of the more memorable character with at least two details from the relevant poem.

Difficulty: *Easy*

Objective: *Essay*

14. Students should correctly identify the setting of the two poems (England in the time of highwaymen and red-coats for "The Highwayman," and Williamsport, Pennsylvania, in the present for "How I Learned English"). They should recognize that the setting of "The Highwayman" is important because it takes place at a time when highway robbers might have been seen as romantic characters; the setting of "How I Learned English" is important because, to the narrator, it is a foreign place. Students should support their choice of the more interesting setting by citing at least two details from the poem whose setting they find more interesting.

Difficulty: *Easy*

Objective: *Essay*

15. Students may note that in "The Highwayman," the lovers communicate their feelings through action rather than words. Bess gives up her own life to save her beloved's life. The highwayman wants to revenge his lost love. So he rides back to the inn and is himself killed. Likewise, students might argue that the communication in "How I Learned English" also has more to do with actions than with words. Even though the narrator does not speak much English, words seem unnecessary after the ball hits him. When he and the boys laugh together about the injury to his "shin" he becomes accepted into the group. The poem therefore suggests that actions speak louder than words.

Difficulty: *Average*

Objective: *Essay*

Selection Test B, p. 115

Critical Reading

1. ANS: D	DIF: Average	OBJ: Interpretation
2. ANS: B	DIF: Average	OBJ: Interpretation
3. ANS: C	DIF: Challenging	OBJ: Literary Analysis
4. ANS: D	DIF: Average	OBJ: Interpretation
5. ANS: A	DIF: Challenging	OBJ: Interpretation
6. ANS: B	DIF: Average	OBJ: Interpretation
7. ANS: C	DIF: Average	OBJ: Comprehension
8. ANS: D	DIF: Average	OBJ: Literary Analysis
9. ANS: D	DIF: Average	OBJ: Comprehension

10. ANS: A	DIF: Challenging	OBJ: Interpretation
11. ANS: B	DIF: Average	OBJ: Interpretation
12. ANS: B	DIF: Challenging	OBJ: Literary Analysis
13. ANS: D	DIF: Average	OBJ: Literary Analysis
14. ANS: C	DIF: Average	OBJ: Literary Analysis

Vocabulary

15. ANS: A	DIF: Average	OBJ: Vocabulary
16. ANS: C	DIF: Average	OBJ: Vocabulary
17. ANS: D	DIF: Challenging	OBJ: Vocabulary
18. ANS: A	DIF: Average	OBJ: Vocabulary

Essay

19. Students should recognize that the highwayman memorably returns to the inn to avenge Bess's death, although he knows that doing so puts him in danger. He, therefore, is inclined to take risks and acts heroically. Students should recognize that the narrator, in "How I Learned English," is memorable in the way that he gained acceptance and felt part of the team; this came as a result of his laughing at his mistaken use of *shin*. Some students may note that although the narrator did nothing very heroic, he seems to have felt extraordinary by the end of the game.

    Difficulty: *Average*

    Objective: *Essay*

20. Students should recognize that the setting on the moor, the darkness, and the moonlight provide many images that give the poem a mysterious tone. They may give examples such as "She writhed her hands till her fingers were wet with sweat or blood!/ They stretched and strained in the darkness," and "for the road lay bare in the moonlight;/ Blank and bare in the moonlight." The setting of Williamsport, Pennsylvania, affects the speaker because it is unfamiliar to him and the other characters speak in a language unfamiliar to him. The setting places the story in small-town America, a setting familiar to American readers.

    Difficulty: *Average*

    Objective: *Essay*

21. Students should compare the conflicts in the two poems. They should recognize that the conflict in "The Highwayman" occurs when Bess is held captive by the soldiers, that suspense mounts when Bess hears the highwayman approach before the soldiers do, and that the conflict reaches a climax when Bess shoots herself to warn her beloved of the danger that awaits him. Students should recognize that the conflict in "How I Learned English" occurs as the narrator plays a game of baseball while not understanding the rules of the game or the language of the other players, that suspense mounts when the narrator is hit in the head with a baseball, and that the conflict is resolved when the boys help the narrator up and treat him like one of their own. Students should express an opinion of the more

realistic and the more enjoyable conflict and should defend their opinions with well-reasoned explanations.

Difficulty: *Challenging*

Objective: *Essay*

22. Students may note that in "The Highwayman," the lovers communicate their feelings through actions rather than words. Bess sacrifices her own life to save her beloved's life. Thinking only of avenging his lost love, the highwayman rides back to the inn and is himself killed. By these events, the poem suggests that the best way to communicate is through deeds. Students might indicate that communication in "How I Learned English" also has more to do with actions than with words. The narrator speaks little English, so he cannot communicate his feelings to the other boys. However, words seem barely necessary after the ball hits him on the forehead. Groaning about his shin, the boy inadvertently causes the other boys to laugh. When he laughs too, he becomes accepted into the group. As a result, the poem also suggests that a person's actions speak louder than words.

Difficulty: *Average*

Objective: *Essay*

Writing Workshop

Writing for Assessment: Integrating Grammar Skills, p. 119

A. 1. talented, modifies poet
   2. Standing in front of the students, modifies she
   3. stirring, modifies voice
   4. fascinated by her performance, modifies students

B. Sentences may vary slightly.

   1. A visiting speaker told us all about Robert Frost.
   2. Born in San Francisco, Frost grew up in New England.
   3. Traveling to England, he published his first book of poetry there.
   4. The talented poet became very famous.

Unit 4 Answers

Benchmark Test 7, p. 120

MULTIPLE CHOICE

1. ANS: B
2. ANS: C
3. ANS: A
4. ANS: B
5. ANS: D
6. ANS: B
7. ANS: D
8. ANS: D
9. ANS: A
10. ANS: B
11. ANS: A

12. ANS: B
13. ANS: C
14. ANS: B
15. ANS: D
16. ANS: A
17. ANS: C
18. ANS: A
19. ANS: C
20. ANS: D
21. ANS: C
22. ANS: D
23. ANS: D
24. ANS: A
25. ANS: C
26. ANS: D
27. ANS: B
28. ANS: A
29. ANS: C
30. ANS: C
31. ANS: C
32. ANS: A
33. ANS: B
34. ANS: B
35. ANS: D

ESSAY

36. Students should list details that clearly address the writing prompt and seem like key elements of their response. Among the things they might mention are the world of information to which computers provide access, the online friendships that can be formed, the uses of computers on the job, and the health problems sometimes resulting from spending too much time indoors at a computer.

37. Students will choose various topics of interest. Student work should be evaluated on how well he or she understands the poetic forms. Appropriate rhyme scheme, number of lines, and subject matter, where applicable, should be considered, in addition to spelling, grammer, and punctuation.

38. Writing should be evaluated on correct use of figurative language. Students may write that the use of simile and metaphor makes the subject come alive, or gives the reader a visual image.

Poetry Collection: Shel Silverstein, James Berry, Eve Merriam

Vocabulary Warm-up Exercises, p. 128

A. 1. simply
2. wait
3. expectancy
4. mimic

5. remember
6. multiplied

B. Sample Answers

1. T; A *windowpane* is the glass in a window; it could be broken if a baseball hit it.
2. F; *Dry* means lacking moisture, and pudding is usually very moist because it is made from milk. So, if it is dry, it will not taste right.
3. F; A *rumble* is a heavy, deep sound that usually can be heard from far away.
4. T; The texture of fresh potato chips is dry and crisp, not *soggy*, which means soaked with moisture.
5. T; A *splatter* is a splash, and if you're mixing the batter very hard that could cause it to splash.
6. T; A *puddle* is a pool of water, and people usually do not want to get their feet wet while walking in the house.

Reading Warm-up A, p. 129

Sample Answers

1. (for him to join them); *Expectancy* means "a waiting for something to happen, an expectation."
2. he quickly set his guitar down; If I asked someone to *wait* for me, I might want to finish combing my hair or doing my homework.
3. the others to like him; *Simply* means "absolutely or completely."
4. their love of the game; In the story, it means that Marc decides to imitate his friends' fondness for the game.
5. (how to play all those notes); Do you *remember* the day we went to the beach?
6. (the number of friends he had); An antonym for *multiplied* is *decreased*.

Reading Warm-up B, p. 130

Sample Answers

1. glass; smooth surface; We could not even see out the grimy *windowpane* of the bus.
2. (falls heavily) (hits the ground) (drenches the Earth); *Splatter* means "a splash or spatter."
3. (after a rainfall); A *puddle* could be formed by a leaking water pipe, spilled cake batter, or oil leaking from a car.
4. moist; *Soggy* means "soaked with water or another liquid."
5. (When this happens, the water in the puddle *evaporates*, which means it dries up and turns into a gas called water vapor.); Cake or bread might dry out in the dry air, or a wet towel might become *dry* if left out in *dry* conditions.
6. When a flash of lightning lights the sky; *Rumble* means "a deep, heavy, rolling sound."

Writing About the Big Question, p. 131

A. 1. Technology
2. transmit
3. speak
4. react

B. Sample Answers

1. I sent a text message to a friend criticizing her outfit. She was very hurt and upset.

2. If I had spoken directly to my friend, I would have seen that she was getting upset. I might not have been as critical.

C. Sample Answer

The use of musical language can **produce** a strong rhythmic feeling in a poem, or the feelings that the poem is like a song.

Reading: Read Aloud According to Punctuation in Order to Paraphrase, p. 132

Sample Answers

1. "Dot a dot dot dot a dot dot"—that is the sound of raindrops as they hit the window.

2. No one can wear my clothes for me or feel the way I feel when I fall or go running for me. In addition, no one hears what I hear when listening to the music I listen to.

3. Something awful happened to poor Sarah, but I cannot tell you about it now because it is late. But when it is time to do your chores, think of Sarah, and "always take the garbage out!"

Literary Analysis: Sound Devices, p. 133

1. alliteration
2. alliteration
3. onomatopoeia, alliteration
4. alliteration
5. repetition, alliteration
6. alliteration
7. onomatopoeia, repetition, alliteration

Vocabulary Builder, p. 134

A. Sample Answers

1. No; the flowers were dried out, so they would not have been brightly colored.

2. They would have thrown it out because spoiled food is not good to eat.

3. Yes, he was probably nervous. People often stutter when they are nervous.

4. No, *curdled* milk has gone bad and would taste awful.

5. She was probably waiting for someone or something.

6. Yes, she put on a lot of sunscreen, which would help keep her from getting sunburned.

B. Sample Answers

1. T; *Infancy* is the state of being an infant.

2. F; Someone who shows *hesitancy* is showing unsureness.

3. T; A diamond is a very shiny, brilliant stone.

Enrichment: Alliteration, p. 135

Letters that students are to circle appear in parentheses. (Only sounds at the beginnings of words should be considered.) Sample answers follow the circled sounds:

1. Crusts of (b)lack (b)urned (b)uttered toast, / Gristly (b)its of (b)eefy roasts—In the first line, the *b* sounds stress how the toast looks by putting emphasis on the words *black* and *burned*. In that line, the *b* sounds also force the reader to speak slowly, again emphasizing the condition of the toast. In the second line, the *b* sounds add emphasis to the idea of a "beefy" roast.

2. (M)oldy (m)elons, dried up (m)ustard, / Eggshells (m)ixed with lemon custard—The *m* sounds make these foods seem less disgusting than some of the others because the *m* is a softer sound. It might remind readers of the sound a satisfied diner makes: *mmmmm.*

3. Note that in this example, the *f* in *freckling* does not count as part of the alliteration if the repeated sound is considered to be *fl*: (Sp)ack a (sp)ack (sp)eck (fl)ick a (fl)ack (fl)eck / Freckling the windowpane—These sounds are short, clear-cut, and harsh, like the sound of individual drops of sleet hitting a window.

4. Note that here, too, the *g* in *galosh* and the *gl* in *glide* are not good examples of alliteration; one could argue that the initial sounds are not the same. (Sl)osh a galosh (sl)osh a galosh / (Sl)ither and (sl)ather a glide—The *sl* sounds emphasize the sound of sloshing water.

5. And (m)irrors can show (m)e (m)ultiplied / (m)any times— The *m* sound emphasizes the speaker, or the idea that the poem is about *me, myself.*

Open-Book Test, p. 136

Short Answer

1. Sample answer: "Sarah Cynthia Sylvia Stout" is an example of alliteration because all the words start with an "s" sound. Lines 2 and 6 repeat the phrase "would not take the garbage out."

   Difficulty: *Easy*   **Objective:** *Literary Analysis*

2. The word *rancid* means "spoiled and smelling bad." The poem is about the girl's unwillingness to take out the garbage, so it makes sense that the meat has rotted.

   Difficulty: *Average*   **Objective:** *Vocabulary*

3. Sample answer: The speaker seems to be giving a warning ("But children, remember Sarah Stout") but with humor. Saying that Sarah met a fate that cannot be told "because the hour is much too late" follows the exaggerated humor of the rest of the poem.

   Difficulty: *Challenging*   **Objective:** *Interpretation*

4. Line 1; Dot a dot dot dot a dot dot; Repetition; Line 3: flick a flack fleck; Alliteration; Line 5: spatter; Onomatopoeia

   "Dot a dot dot dot a dot dot" repeats words; "flick a flack fleck" repeats a sound at the beginning of each word; "spatter" makes a sound that suggests its meaning.

Difficulty: *Average*   **Objective:** *Literary Analysis*

5. Sample answer: The first two lines show that small dots of raindrops are creating spots on the window. The second two lines show that other shapes of raindrops are adding freckles—more spots in more places. It seems that the rainstorm is becoming stronger.

Difficulty: *Average*   **Objective:** *Interpretation*

6. Sample answer: With my galoshes on, I splash around. I jump in and out of puddles. I jump into and slide through a mud puddle.

Difficulty: *Challenging*   **Objective:** *Reading*

7. Sample answer: The poet repeats the words "nobody" and "my." He uses repetition of these words to emphasize that the poem is about him and how he is unique.

Difficulty: *Challenging*   **Objective:** *Literary Analysis*

8. Sample answer: He seems to feel that those are not important qualities about him—anybody can do them. He does seem to recognize that he would be embarrassed by his "howl."

Difficulty: *Average*   **Objective:** *Interpretation*

9. Sample answer: There is only one me, and I am special. This is my body, these are my actions, and these are my words. Nobody can do or feel any of this but me.

Difficulty: *Average*   **Objective:** *Reading*

10. The speaker might *stutter*, or speak in a hesitant way, because his anger is so great that he can't really control how he is speaking.

Difficulty: *Easy*   **Objective:** *Vocabulary*

Essay

11. Sample answer: The poet uses images such as "coffee grounds, potato peelings, rotten peas" and "it filled the can, it covered the floor" to show not only the disgusting variety of what was building up in the trash, but also how much room it was taking up as it spread. It gave me a very good (and ugly and gross) picture of what the poem is about.

Difficulty: *Easy*   **Objective:** *Essay*

12. Sample answer: Young children might enjoy hearing the poem read to them because the sounds are so interesting. The poet uses nonsense phrases such as "A juddle a pump a luddle a dump" and nonsense words like "puddmuddle" to support the fun mood of the poem. They can also relate to the fun of playing in puddles.

Difficulty: *Average*   **Objective:** *Essay*

13. Sample answer: By going back and forth between what "nobody" can do and what "anybody" can do, the poet emphasizes what the speaker finds to be unique and important about himself. The things that "nobody" can do are crucial to the speaker's idea of himself. The things that "anybody" can do are not real—they are copies, echoes, and images from mirrors. I found the

technique to be effective because it made me think about what is "real" about a person.

Difficulty: *Challenging*   **Objective:** *Essay*

14. Sample answer: The message of "One" communicated strongly to me because it is a subject anyone can relate to. We all want to feel different and special and be "only one of me." Also, we all don't like being made fun of ("anybody can howl how I sing") or even thought of as just one person in the crowd ("mirrors can show me multiplied").

Difficulty: *Average*   **Objective:** *Essay*

Oral Response

15. Oral responses should be clear, well organized, and well supported by appropriate examples from the poems.

Difficulty: *Average*   **Objective:** *Oral Interpretation*

Selection Test A, p. 139

Critical Reading

1. ANS: A	DIF: Easy	OBJ: Literary Analysis
2. ANS: C	DIF: Easy	OBJ: Reading
3. ANS: D	DIF: Easy	OBJ: Comprehension
4. ANS: A	DIF: Easy	OBJ: Interpretation
5. ANS: C	DIF: Easy	OBJ: Literary Analysis
6. ANS: B	DIF: Easy	OBJ: Interpretation
7. ANS: B	DIF: Easy	OBJ: Interpretation
8. ANS: D	DIF: Easy	OBJ: Literary Analysis
9. ANS: A	DIF: Easy	OBJ: Comprehension

Vocabulary and Grammar

10. ANS: C	DIF: Easy	OBJ: Vocabulary
11. ANS: D	DIF: Easy	OBJ: Vocabulary
12. ANS: C	DIF: Easy	OBJ: Grammar

Essay

13. Students should cite any two lines from the poem that contain alliteration, successfully identify the repeated sound, and suggest how the alliteration contributes to the poem's humor. They might note, for example, that the *gl* in "Gloppy glumps of cold oatmeal" is a funny sound and helps the reader picture the congealed oatmeal. In "The garbage rolled on down the hall, / It raised the roof, it broke the wall," students might say that the *r* sound emphasizes the sense of movement as the garbage builds and takes on a life of its own.

Difficulty: *Easy*

Objective: *Essay*

14. Students should correctly identify onomatopoeic words in the poem (such as *spack, flick,* and *slosh*) and suggest how those words contribute to the mood of the poem. For example, the opening line of the poem, "Dot a dot dot

a dot dot," suggests the sound of rain as it is just starting. The third line, "Spack a spack speck flick a flack fleck," suggests a heavier rainfall. Students might recognize that the *slosh, slither,* and *splosh* of the fifth verse suggest the sounds that are made as someone—perhaps a child—walks through the rain.

Difficulty: *Easy*
Objective: *Essay*

15. Sample answer: The message of "One" communicated strongly to me because it is a subject anyone can relate to. We all want to feel different and special and be "only one of me." We also all don't like being made fun of ("anybody can howl how I sing") or even thought of as just one person in the crowd ("mirrors can show me multiplied").

Difficulty: *Average*
Objective: *Essay*

Selection Test B, p. 142

Critical Reading

1. ANS: C	DIF: Average	OBJ: Literary Analysis
2. ANS: D	DIF: Average	OBJ: Interpretation
3. ANS: D	DIF: Average	OBJ: Reading
4. ANS: B	DIF: Challenging	OBJ: Interpretation
5. ANS: B	DIF: Average	OBJ: Interpretation
6. ANS: C	DIF: Average	OBJ: Interpretation
7. ANS: D	DIF: Average	OBJ: Interpretation
8. ANS: C	DIF: Challenging	OBJ: Interpretation
9. ANS: C	DIF: Average	OBJ: Literary Analysis
10. ANS: B	DIF: Challenging	OBJ: Reading
11. ANS: B	DIF: Challenging	OBJ: Reading
12. ANS: B	DIF: Average	OBJ: Literary Analysis

Vocabulary and Grammar

13. ANS: B	DIF: Average	OBJ: Vocabulary
14. ANS: A	DIF: Average	OBJ: Vocabulary
15. ANS: C	DIF: Average	OBJ: Grammar
16. ANS: B	DIF: Average	OBJ: Grammar

Essay

17. Students should correctly identify an instance of exaggeration and tell what it adds to the poem. Students might realize, for example, that "And so it piled up to the ceilings" introduces the idea that the speaker cannot be trusted. "The garbage rolled on down the hall, / It raised the roof, it broke the wall" suggests that the garbage is alive and capable of movement. In general, students should recognize that the exaggeration heightens the poem's humor.

Difficulty: *Average*
Objective: *Essay*

18. Students might recognize that all three poems are playful. They should recognize that "Sarah Cynthia Sylvia Stout Would Not Take the Garbage Out" both entertains and

teaches a lesson, "One" expresses the speaker's feelings, and "Weather" entertains and perhaps teaches something about the sounds of words and the playfulness of language. In their comparisons, students should point to two examples in each poem to support their points.

Difficulty: *Challenging*
Objective: *Essay*

19. Sample answer: The message of "One" communicated strongly to me because it is a subject anyone can relate to. We all want to feel different and special and be "only one of me." We also all don't like being made fun of ("anybody can howl how I sing") or even thought of as just one person in the crowd ("mirrors can show me multiplied").

Difficulty: *Average*
Objective: *Essay*

Poetry Collection: William Shakespeare, Louise Bogan, Eve Merriam

Vocabulary Warm-up Exercises, p. 146

A. 1. rushes
   2. clearing
   3. distance
   4. hours
   5. plains
   6. hear

B. Sample Answers

1. No, it is not likely you will find a piece of *coral* in the woods because coral is a sea creature, not one found on dry land in the woods.
2. No, he or she would not have *clear* vision, because the water that *splashes,* meaning it spatters, from the mud puddle would have made the window dirty and clouded, which is the opposite of *clear.*
3. Yes, it might seem *strange* to sleep in a different room than usual, because *strange* means "unfamiliar, different, or unusual."
4. Yes, it is likely that people live *below* Jean because she is on the top floor, which implies there are other floors under, or *below,* her, where others might live.
5. No, a *sea* breeze probably does not propel the sailboat because the sea has to do with the ocean, and the boat is being sailed away from the sea on a mountain pond.

Reading Warm-up A, p. 147

Sample Answers

1. (one long railroad); When Mary visits her aunt, she will take a plane to cover the *distance* between their homes.
2. countless; Other units of time are minutes, seconds, weeks.
3. wide, open; *Plains* are "flat, open areas of land."
4. if trees stood in their path; A *clearing* is "an area of land that is cleared of trees."

5. (each train); Amy loves her singing lesson so much that she *rushes* to get to her teacher's house.

6. (the whistles of two trains riding the new rails); Some things I might *hear* every day are my dog barking, cars riding past the house, and the voices of people in my family.

Reading Warm-up B, p. 148

Sample Answers

1. there is a strange and wonderful world; An antonym for *below* is *above*.

2. (It is the world of the coral reef.); *Strange* means "different, unusual, or of another place."

3. (the outer layer of the reef); *Coral* is a living thing composed of a lot of calcium.

4. (creatures); A synonym for *sea* is *ocean*.

5. The sparkling water makes it easy to see the sea life of the coral reef.; Other things that might look *clear* are glass or plastic wrap.

6. in the water around the atoll; The baby has fun as he *splashes* in the bathtub.

Writing About the Big Question, p. 149

A. 1. express

2. listen

3. enrich

B. Sample Answers

1. Once, I **informed** a friend that I thought he was being really mean to someone else. Another time, I tried to **speak** to a friend about her lateness when we had plans.

2. When I told my friend he was being mean, he was really surprised. He hadn't realized it. He wasn't mad at all, and he changed the way he was acting. I think the discussion made our friendship stronger.

C. Sample Answer

When you really **listen**, you can not only hear but understand more fully.

Reading: Read Aloud According to Punctuation in Order to Paraphrase, p. 150

Sample Answers

1. A stream of water gushes from the faucet. At last the water is no longer coming out in jerky motions, and then it makes a sudden splashing sound, and then it comes forth full blast, and it is clear it is no longer rusty.

2. The train seems to beat out a rhythm that sounds something like these lines. At the same time, the train is traveling through lightning storms, cities, and a starlit sky while time passes.

3. The speaker imagines that beautiful maidens said to live in the sea ring a bell every hour to mourn the father's death. "Ding-dong" is the sound the bell makes. The

speaker imagines hearing the nymphs ringing the bell. He hears the "ding-dong" sound.

Literary Analysis: Sound Devices, p. 151

1. alliteration

2. alliteration, onomatopoeia

3. repetition, alliteration

4. onomatopoeia; alliteration (Note that the initial *s* sound is repeated in these lines, but one could argue that there is no alliteration because the initial sounds are *st*, *sp*, and *spl*.)

5. alliteration, repetition

Vocabulary Builder, p. 152

A. Sample Answers

1. No, that would be a plug. You should purchase a faucet, the device that water flows through to reach the sink.

2. No, someone who sputters is not speaking calmly. She is probably excited or nervous.

3. Yes, groves are small groups of trees, so if you have orange groves on your property, you definitely have trees.

4. Yes, a *fathom* is six feet of water.

5. No, a *smattering* is just a few and wouldn't soak your clothes.

6. Yes, *garlands* are made of flowers or fir branches and would smell good.

B. 1. F; A *careless* person would not take care of a precious possession.

2. T; An *endless* movie would seem to go on forever because it was long or boring.

3. F; Someone who is *joyless* is not happy at all.

Enrichment: Onomatopoeia, p. 153

A. Sample Answers

Water Sounds: gurgle, slosh, whoosh

Animal Sounds: bark, bow-wow, buzz, caw, cluck, coo, cuckoo, gobble, oink, peep, purr, ribbit, woof

Loud Sounds: kaboom, kerplunk, wham

Other Sounds: bong, cackle, clang, crackle, gong, honk, hush, pop, swish, twitter, whirr

B. Students should use these or other onomatopoeic words in a short poem. The words should logically relate to the subject of the poem.

Poetry Collections: Shel Silverstein, James Berry, Eve Merriam; William Shakespeare, Louise Bogan, Eve Merriam

Integrated Language Skills: Grammar, p. 154

A. 1. Eve Merriam's lifelong love was poetry even though she wrote fiction, nonfiction, and drama.

2. Because language and its sound gave Eve Merriam great joy, she tried to communicate her enjoyment by writing poetry for children.
3. Berry moved to the United States when he was seventeen.
4. If Berry had not lost his job as a telegraph operator, he might not have become a writer.
5. Because he did not play ball or dance when he was young, Shel Silverstein began to draw and write.
6. Silverstein began to draw cartoons after he served in the military.

B. Sample Answers
1. Sarah Stout was a stubborn young woman, although she did finally agree to take out the garbage.
2. The rain spotted the windowpane as it hit the side of the house.
3. Anyone can dance like me once he or she gets the hang of it.
4. Before anyone had discovered the body, the drowned man's bones had turned to coral.

Poetry Collection: William Shakespeare, Louise Bogan, Eve Merriam

Open-Book Test, p. 157

Short Answer

1. The listener's father is dead in the sea. He lies "full fathom five," or in water about 30 feet deep. His body is changing to coral and pearls, and sea nymphs ring the funeral bell.
   Difficulty: *Easy* **Objective:** *Interpretation*
2. Sample answer: Your father's bones, like his body, are now part of the sea.
   Difficulty: *Average* **Objective:** *Reading*
3. Line 1 uses alliteration of the letter "f": "Full fathom five." The end of the poem uses onomatopoeia to make the "ding-dong" sound of a bell.
   Difficulty: *Average* **Objective:** *Literary Analysis*
4. Sample answer: Lines 4–7 indicate that the listener's father did not "fade" as a person might in death. Instead, he went through a "sea change" to become something more interesting, or at least "rich and strange." The speaker feels sadness but also a sense of wonder.
   Difficulty: *Challenging* **Objective:** *Interpretation*
5. Onomatopoeia: sputters; plash; Other Sound Device: (Alliteration): spigot sputters; slash, splatters, scatters, spurts
   The sound devices help the reader imagine the sound and movement of the water.

Difficulty: *Average* **Objective:** *Literary Analysis*
6. Sample answer: A faucet might *sputter*—make spitting sounds—when it is first turned on, especially if it hasn't been used for awhile.
   Difficulty: *Easy* **Objective:** *Vocabulary*
7. The poet wants to show that the water is flowing in an irregular way before it finally comes out in a steady stream. It "splutters," "splatters," "scatters," and finally "gushes."
   Difficulty: *Average* **Objective:** *Interpretation*
8. "Back through" is repetition; it appears in both lines. "Clouds" and "clearing" are alliteration.
   Difficulty: *Average* **Objective:** *Literary Analysis*
9. *Groves* are groups of trees. The train is traveling through the countryside.
   Difficulty: *Easy* **Objective:** *Vocabulary*
10. Sample answer: The lack of punctuation emphasizes the poet's message that the train is in constant motion. If the poet had used punctuation, the reader would get more of an interrupted feeling, such as when a train makes stops.
   Difficulty: *Challenging* **Objective:** *Interpretation*

Essay

11. Sample answer: The poet introduces sea nymphs who ring a knell, or funeral bell, every hour. The speaker is emphasizing the fact that the king is dead. The sea nymphs use the bell to mourn the king.
   Difficulty: *Easy* **Objective:** *Essay*
12. Sample answer: An old spigot, covered in rust, gets turned on. A few drops come out. Then, a few more come out. The water starts and stops. Finally, it comes rushing out and runs clear.
   I think the poem is more effective in capturing the sound and the movement of water as it struggles to come out of an old faucet. The poet's use of sound devices makes the experience more lively.
   Difficulty: *Average* **Objective:** *Essay*
13. Sample answer: The poet's use of the word *back* is unusual because trains go forward. She is using the contrast of these two movements to create the impression that life is not a one-way journey forward. We go back through things many times: days, places, emotions.
   Difficulty: *Challenging* **Objective:** *Essay*
14. Sample answer: In "Train Tune," the rhythm of the phrase "back through," with its repetition, lets the reader feel the chugging of a train as it moves along a track. In "Full Fathom Five," the poet notes the rhythm of an hourly death knell, which the reader feels as a continuous presence. The rhythm in "Train Tune"

seems more effective in communicating because the words are repeated throughout the entire poem.

Difficulty: *Average*   **Objective:** *Essay*

Oral Response

15. Oral responses should be clear, well organized, and well supported by appropriate examples from the poems.

    Difficulty: *Average*   **Objective:** *Oral Interpretation*

16. Sample answer: In "Train Tune," the rhythm of the use of the phrase "back through" lets the reader feel the chugging of a train as it moves along a track. In "Full Fathom Five," the poet notes the rhythm of an hourly death knell. The rhythm in "Train Tune" seems more effective because the words are repeated throughout the entire poem.

    Difficulty: *Average*

    Objective: *Essay*

Selection Test A, p. 160

Critical Reading

1. ANS: C	DIF: Easy	OBJ: Reading Skill
2. ANS: A	DIF: Easy	OBJ: Literary Analysis
3. ANS: B	DIF: Easy	OBJ: Literary Analysis
4. ANS: D	DIF: Easy	OBJ: Interpretation
5. ANS: C	DIF: Easy	OBJ: Literary Analysis
6. ANS: D	DIF: Easy	OBJ: Interpretation
7. ANS: D	DIF: Easy	OBJ: Comprehension
8. ANS: B	DIF: Easy	OBJ: Interpretation
9. ANS: C	DIF: Easy	OBJ: Reading
10. ANS: A	DIF: Easy	OBJ: Interpretation

Vocabulary and Grammar

11. ANS: A	DIF: Easy	OBJ: Vocabulary
12. ANS: B	DIF: Easy	OBJ: Grammar
13. ANS: D	DIF: Easy	OBJ: Grammar

Essay

14. Students should recognize that in Merriam's poem the onomatopoeic words are *sputters, splutter, spatters, slash, splatters, scatters, spurts, sputtering, plash, gushes, rushes,* and *splashes.* They might say, for example, that *sputters* sounds as if it is uncertain, unsure of how to get started, just as water might sound as it begins to flow through a rusty faucet.

    Difficulty: *Easy*

    Objective: *Essay*

15. Students should name one of the poems in the collection as their favorite and refer to at least two words or phrases from the poem to support their choice. Students who choose "Full Fathom Five" might be attracted to the poem's strangeness; they might cite lines such as "Those are pearls that were his eyes" and "Sea nymphs hourly ring his knell" to illustrate its eerie quality. Students who choose "Onomatopoeia" will probably explain that they like the use of onomatopoeia in words like *sputter, spurts,* and *plash.* Students who choose "Train Tune" may say that the repetition reminds them of the rhythm that is established by a moving vehicle traveling over a long distance.

    Difficulty: *Easy*

    Objective: *Essay*

Selection Test B, p. 163

Critical Reading

1. ANS: B	DIF: Average	OBJ: Reading
2. ANS: C	DIF: Average	OBJ: Interpretation
3. ANS: A	DIF: Challenging	OBJ: Interpretation
4. ANS: D	DIF: Challenging	OBJ: Comprehension
5. ANS: B	DIF: Average	OBJ: Reading
6. ANS: C	DIF: Average	OBJ: Literary Analysis
7. ANS: D	DIF: Average	OBJ: Interpretation
8. ANS: A	DIF: Average	OBJ: Literary Analysis
9. ANS: A	DIF: Challenging	OBJ: Comprehension
10. ANS: C	DIF: Average	OBJ: Literary Analysis
11. ANS: D	DIF: Average	OBJ: Interpretation
12. ANS: B	DIF: Challenging	OBJ: Interpretation
13. ANS: D	DIF: Challenging	OBJ: Reading

Vocabulary and Grammar

14. ANS: B	DIF: Average	OBJ: Vocabulary
15. ANS: D	DIF: Average	OBJ: Vocabulary
16. ANS: C	DIF: Average	OBJ: Grammar
17. ANS: B	DIF: Challenging	OBJ: Grammar

Essay

18. Students should describe the variation in line lengths (lines contain one word, two words, three words, and at most, five words) and recognize that the variation suggests the stop-and-start character of water making its way through a rusty spigot.

    Difficulty: *Average*

    Objective: *Essay*

19. Students should cite two instances of alliteration in "Full Fathom Five" and explain how they help establish the atmosphere. For example, they may suggest that the *f* sound in the first line, "Full fathom five thy father lies," emphasizes the depth below the surface of the sea (five fathoms) at which the father's body lies. The *s* sound in lines 5–7 helps the reader hear the sounds of the sea and so helps the reader understand that the father has been transformed into an element of the sea.

    Difficulty: *Average*

    Objective: *Essay*

20. Students should offer a well-thought-out explanation of the meaning of the words. They may suggest, for example, that many of the words (the concrete nouns, such as "clouds," "clearing," "groves," "garlands," and "rivers") are the images seen by passengers on the train, whereas the others (the abstract nouns: "distance," "silence," "hours," "noon," and "midnight") have to do with the experience of being on a train as time passes. Alternatively, students may suggest that the words represent the point of view of the train as it travels through the country. The title of the poem suggests that the train is singing to itself, an interpretation that supports the idea that the images are seen from the train's point of view.

   Difficulty: *Challenging*

   Objective: *Essay*

21. Sample answer: In "Train Tune," the rhythm of the use of the phrase "back through," with its repetition, lets the reader feel the chugging of a train as it moves along a track. In "Full Fathom Five," the poet notes the rhythm of an hourly death knell, which the reader feels as a continuous presence. The rhythm in "Train Tune" seems more effective because the words are repeated throughout the entire poem.

   Difficulty: *Average*

   Objective: *Essay*

Poetry Collection: Edgar Allan Poe, Raymond Richard Patterson, Emily Dickinson

Vocabulary Warm-up Exercises, p. 167

A. 1. darling
   2. maiden
   3. dreary
   4. reason
   5. worth
   6. age

B. Sample Answers
   1. relative; The king invited all of his kinsmen to his wedding.
   2. enthusiasm; An enthusiasm for extreme sports can be dangerous.
   3. smarter; My mother is smarter than my sister.
   4. desiring; Picasso's talent is worth desiring.
   5. sideways; We stepped sideways to get past the crowd.

Reading Warm-up A, p. 168

Sample Answers
   1. Ordinary language cannot express the experience of deep love; One *reason* why writers write about love is because it is a beautiful feeling.
   2. (Annabel Lee); In the mid-1800s, Edgar Allan Poe wrote *Annabel Lee*, a poem about a lovely young *girl* who died.
   3. (beautiful); The old abandoned house was dark and *dreary*.

4. (her everlasting importance); I don't think you can put a price on a person's *worth* or value, like an article of clothing. The people we love are priceless.
5. (beloved); My baby brother is my little *darling*.
6. when Death was a popular subject in art and literature; A synonym for *age* as it is used in this passage is *time*.

Reading Warm-up B, p. 169

Sample Answers
   1. (justice); I have a *passion* for rock music.
   2. (tore communities apart); One *public* event I attended recently was a free concert in the park.
   3. non-violent protest; A synonym for *wiser* is *smarter*.
   4. riots and violent acts; We walked *into* the middle of the crowd.
   5. (his success); *Envying* means "wanting something that someone else has."
   6. The writer is probably referring to people of all colors who shared King's beliefs, when he is using the word *kinsmen*; (followers)

Writing About the Big Question, p. 170

A. 1. produce
   2. communicate
   3. express
   4. speak

B. Sample Answers
   1. I **argued** with the president of our Community Club over which charity should get the money raised by the club. I **expressed** the **opinion** that we should donate to the Brothers and Sisters organization, and I was able to **teach** her about the group.
   2. I used a very calm tone of voice, and I described the Brothers and Sisters as a great organization that helped a lot of kids.

C. Sample Answer

   Words can be used to **produce** strong feelings and emotions in the reader.

   The way people **react** can be different from what the poet intended.

Reading: Reread in Order to Paraphrase, p. 171

Sample Answers
   1. A wind blew on a cloudy night, causing the speaker's dear Annabel Lee to die of a chill; her wealthy relatives arrived and carried away her body, burying it in a tomb in this seaside kingdom.
   2. He was part of a time that was full of sorrow and anger, but he was so full of love that he faced the troubles and tried to make things better.
   3. How depressing it would be to be famous. How exposed to the public—as a Frog is—you would be if you were telling your name all the time to a crowd of admirers.

Literary Analysis: Rhythm, Meter, and Rhyme, p. 172

A. Stressed syllables are indicated by capital letters; unstressed syllables are indicated by lowercase letters:

1. But our LOVE it was STRONG-er by FAR than the LOVE / Of THOSE who were OLD-er than WE

2. His PAS-sion, SO pro-FOUND, / He WOULD not TURN a-ROUND.

B. Words that students are to circle appear in parentheses:

1. Students should connect *ago* and *know*; *sea, Lee,* and *me*: (ago) (sea) (know) (Lee) thought (me)

2. Students should connect the three rhyming words: child (sea) love (Lee) Heaven (me)

3. Students should connect the four rhyming words: ago (sea) night (Lee) came (me) sepulcher (sea)

4. Students should connect the three rhyming words: Heaven (me) know (sea) chilling (Lee)

5. Students should connect *love* and *above*; *we, we, sea,* and *Lee*: (love) (we) (we) (above) (sea) soul (Lee)

6. Students should connect *Lee, Lee, sea,* and *sea; side* and *bride*: dreams (Lee) (Lee) (side) (bride) (sea) (sea)

7. Students should connect the rhyming words in each line: (age) (rage) / (wide) (aside) / (profound) (around)/ (Earth) (worth) / (be) (free)

Vocabulary Builder, p. 173

A. Sample Answers

1. No; *coveted* means "were jealous"; the angels wanted a love like the love between the speaker and Annabel Lee.

2. Yes; *profound* means "deeply or intensely felt," so King was very passionate, according to the speaker in the poem.

3. No; *banish* means "send away," so "they" will exile the speaker from their social circle.

4. Yes; when you envy something, you want it for yourself.

5. Yes; someone's kin is that person's relative.

6. No; King felt love—passion is strong love.

B. 1. The person would have a new tooth placed, or planted, in his or her mouth.

2. The picture would appear printed on the T-shirt.

3. It has been taken to a place where cars are held, a car pound.

Enrichment: Art, p. 174

Students should create a collage that consists of ten to fifteen words from one of the poems in this collection cut from different kinds of paper and attached to a single sheet of paper.

Open-Book Test, p. 175

Short Answer

1. In the first group are *ago* and *know*. In the second group are *sea, Lee,* and *me*.

Difficulty: *Easy*   **Objective:** *Literary Analysis*

2. Annabel Lee was taken away from her love by a "cold, chilling wind" that killed her. The wind was sent by the angels in Heaven, who envied their love.

Difficulty: *Average*   **Objective:** *Interpretation*

3. Sample answer: Every night I see Annabel Lee. The moon brings me dreams of her, and I see her eyes in the stars.

Difficulty: *Average*   **Objective:** *Reading*

4. The three stressed syllables are *tomb, side, sea*. The three stressed syllables show the location of where the speaker meets his love.

Difficulty: *Challenging*   **Objective:** *Literary Analysis*

5. GO: age/rage; wide/aside; profound/around; earth/ worth; slain/again (circle this pair)

   The poet might have chosen a not-perfect rhyme to emphasize the last line of the poem.

Difficulty: *Average*   **Objective:** *Literary Analysis*

6. Sample answer: The word *profound* means "deeply felt." A deeply felt passion is one that a person would not give up; King would have stayed committed to civil rights if he had lived longer.

Difficulty: *Average*   **Objective:** *Vocabulary*

7. Sample answer: The poet may mean that King's spirit is alive in others or that another person with these same qualities will emerge as a new leader to carry on King's work.

Difficulty: *Average*   **Objective:** *Interpretation*

8. The rhythm of "I'm Nobody" is irregular. The dashes in the middle of the lines cause breaks in the rhythm. Lines 1 and 2 would have a regular and repeated rhythm without the dash in line 2.

Difficulty: *Challenging*   **Objective:** *Literary Analysis*

9. Sample answer: To banish someone is to send him or her away. The speaker fears being sent away by the "Somebodies."

Difficulty: *Easy*   **Objective:** *Vocabulary*

10. Sample answer: The poet chooses a frog to be a "Somebody" because frogs announce their presence with their croaking all the time. But frogs are not really important "somebodies." They are not particularly special or important.

Difficulty: *Challenging*   **Objective:** *Interpretation*

Essay

11. Sample answer: The main idea of this poem is that King was committed to his work to bring peace to a *suffering earth*. His *love* for the world was so strong that he wanted to save people by getting them to work together during *an age, / Beset by grief, by rage*.

Difficulty: *Easy*   **Objective:** *Essay*

12. Sample answer: The poem is somewhat depressing because the speaker has lost his true love. However, there is also a note of triumph because the speaker says

he dreams of his lost love each night. He feels that he has outsmarted the angels, who did not realize that his love for Annabel Lee would outlast her death.

Difficulty: *Average* **Objective:** *Essay*

13. Sample answer: The speaker much prefers being a nobody because she thinks it is "dreary" to be a somebody. She would not want to live her life in "public," having to deal with others knowing all of her business and being admired by a "bog" of unworthy people.

Difficulty: *Challenging* **Objective:** *Essay*

14. Sample answer: In "I'm Nobody," there are several big ideas presented about how it is to live life as a nobody or a somebody. The poet elegantly explores certain ideas—popularity, fame, shyness, and phoniness—in a very short space, and I don't think they could be presented better in prose form.

Difficulty: *Average* **Objective:** *Essay*

Oral Response

15. Oral responses should be clear, well organized, and well supported by appropriate examples from the poems.

Difficulty: *Average* **Objective:** *Oral Interpretation*

Selection Test A, p. 178

Critical Reading

1. ANS: B	DIF: Easy	OBJ: Literary Analysis
2. ANS: D	DIF: Easy	OBJ: Comprehension
3. ANS: B	DIF: Easy	OBJ: Reading
4. ANS: B	DIF: Easy	OBJ: Literary Analysis
5. ANS: B	DIF: Easy	OBJ: Literary Analysis
6. ANS: D	DIF: Easy	OBJ: Interpretation
7. ANS: C	DIF: Easy	OBJ: Interpretation
8. ANS: B	DIF: Easy	OBJ: Comprehension
9. ANS: B	DIF: Easy	OBJ: Reading
10. ANS: A	DIF: Easy	OBJ: Interpretation

Vocabulary and Grammar

11. ANS: A	DIF: Easy	OBJ: Vocabulary
12. ANS: B	DIF: Easy	OBJ: Vocabulary
13. ANS: D	DIF: Easy	OBJ: Grammar
14. ANS: A	DIF: Easy	OBJ: Grammar

Essay

15. Students should state the poem they prefer, offer a paraphrase of the poem's main idea, and tell what they like about the poem. For example, they may point to the rhymes, rhythm, and love story in "Annabel Lee" or the way in which "Martin Luther King" celebrates King's achievements.

Difficulty: *Easy*

Objective: *Essay*

16. Students should refer to two details in the poem in explaining their reasons for agreeing or disagreeing with Dickinson's premise. For example, students may claim that it is not "dreary" to be well known and that having "an admiring Bog" can be a satisfying experience. Students who agree with Dickinson may stress the value of privacy.

Difficulty: *Easy*

Objective: *Essay*

17. Students should pick one poem and explain why it would work better or not as well in prose format. Students should focus on key ideas and images from the poem of their choice and explain how or why they might or might not work better in another format. Their answers should be supported by specific examples from the text.

Difficulty: *Average*

Objective: *Essay*

Selection Test B, p. 181

Critical Reading

1. ANS: C	DIF: Average	OBJ: Literary Analysis
2. ANS: C	DIF: Challenging	OBJ: Literary Analysis
3. ANS: B	DIF: Average	OBJ: Comprehension
4. ANS: B	DIF: Challenging	OBJ: Interpretation
5. ANS: A	DIF: Average	OBJ: Interpretation
6. ANS: B	DIF: Challenging	OBJ: Literary Analysis
7. ANS: A	DIF: Challenging	OBJ: Reading
8. ANS: D	DIF: Challenging	OBJ: Interpretation
9. ANS: D	DIF: Average	OBJ: Interpretation
10. ANS: A	DIF: Average	OBJ: Literary Analysis
11. ANS: C	DIF: Average	OBJ: Interpretation
12. ANS: B	DIF: Challenging	OBJ: Reading
13. ANS: C	DIF: Average	OBJ: Interpretation

Vocabulary and Grammar

14. ANS: A	DIF: Average	OBJ: Vocabulary
15. ANS: C	DIF: Average	OBJ: Vocabulary
16. ANS: C	DIF: Average	OBJ: Grammar
17. ANS: A	DIF: Average	OBJ: Grammar

Essay

18. Students should state their opinion and then cite three details in the poem in support of their argument. Students who say that the poem tells a story may cite references to the two lovers' having known each other since childhood and growing up to love each other, to Annabel Lee's death, and to her family's burial of the corpse. They may note that the speaker vows that he will not forget her. Students who say that the poem conveys a mood may refer to the speaker's seeing his beloved in his dreams. They may cite

the jealous angels and the make-believe home for Annabel Lee "in a kingdom by the sea."

Difficulty: *Average*

Objective: *Essay*

19. Students should cite elements of the poem in describing Dickinson. For example, they might say that she thought about issues, such as the value of celebrity and privacy. They might note her sense of humor, evidenced by the image of the Frog telling his name "to an admiring Bog." They might also note that she seems to want to talk to her audience, for she directs her questions to "you." Students might say that Dickinson would have been relieved to know that she would not have to deal with the fame she eventually achieved. They might say that her shyness kept her from seeking fame in her lifetime, but she would have been pleased to know that her work would win literary acclaim.

Difficulty: *Easy*

Objective: *Essay*

20. Students should recognize that both poems have a regular rhythm and rhyme scheme. They may recognize that the meter of the two poems differs. They may also recognize that "Annabel Lee" makes more complex use of poetic devices, and they may point to other devices, such as the alliteration in "Annabel Lee" and the repetition in both poems.

Difficulty: *Challenging*

Objective: *Essay*

21. Sample answer: In "I'm Nobody," there are several big ideas presented about how it is to live life as a nobody or a somebody. The poet elegantly explores certain ideas—popularity, fame, shyness, and phoniness—in a very short space, and I don't think they could be presented better in prose form.

Difficulty: *Average*

Objective: *Essay*

Poetry Collection: Lewis Carroll, Robert Frost, Gwendolyn Brooks

Vocabulary Warm-up Exercises, p. 185

A. 1. suppose
2. replied
3. hardly
4. enough
5. steady
6. awfully

B. Sample Answers

1. The teacher was very happy with the student's <u>clever</u> answers.
2. Because the two friends disagreed about everything, they <u>argued</u> constantly.
3. The <u>ointment</u> helped to clear up the man's skin problems.

4. People who keep their <u>promises</u> are usually very trustworthy.
5. The patient took her <u>medicine</u> to get well.

Reading Warm-up A, p. 186

Sample Answers

1. (money); *Enough* means, "all that is necessary."
2. (company); Sometimes my friends would call, but I <u>rarely</u> ever had company except for Bobby Standish.
3. "<u>I don't think so</u>"; (told)
4. <u>guess</u>; I <u>suppose</u> we'll take a family vacation again this year.
5. (very); I think sky-diving must be <u>awfully</u> dangerous, but great fun, too.
6. (legs); I need to get up, but my legs feel <u>shaky</u>.

Reading Warm-up B, p. 187

Sample Answers

1. (old age); We spend a lot time in school during our <u>childhood</u>.
2. <u>If you live long you will grow old</u>; Two <u>promises</u> I have made to myself are that I will graduate from school and get my driver's license.
3. <u>a short life</u>; *Medicine* means "a substance for treating illness."
4. <u>to ease many ailments</u>; I used an <u>ointment</u> to get rid of my pimples.
5. (quick); My friend Dan has a <u>clever</u> mind and always makes up great jokes!
6. <u>that elderly minds offer something of value</u>; *Argued* means "to present reasons in order to prove something."

Writing About the Big Question, p. 188

A. 1. entertain
2. express
3. learn; listen

B. Sample Answers

1. I listened to a recording of Robert Frost reading his poem "Stopping by Woods on a Snowy Evening." I was moved by listening to the poet himself read his poem.
2. I learned that you can understand a poet's words differently by **listening** than by reading. The poet's voice **enriched** my listening experience.

C. Sample Answer

Messages that **entertain** as well as **inform** can make a very strong impression on the listener or reader.

Reading: Reread in Order to Paraphrase, p. 189

Sample Answers

1. The sun should reward him in the greatest way it can.
2. "When I was young," said the wise man as he shook his gray curls, "I kept my arms and legs elastic by using

this lotion. A box of it costs one shilling. May I sell you a couple of boxes?"

3. The horse shakes the bells on his gear to ask if I have stopped by accident. Besides the sound of the bells, I hear only the sweeping motion of the effortless wind and the soft, fluffy snowflakes.

Literary Analysis: Rhythm, Meter, and Rhyme, p. 190

A. Stressed syllables are indicated by capital letters; unstressed syllables are indicated by lowercase letters:

1. "You are OLD," | said the YOUTH, | "as I MEN- | tioned be-FORE, | / And have GROWN | most un-COM- | mon | ly FAT." |

2. He GIVES | his HAR- | ness BELLS | a SHAKE | / To ASK | if THERE is SOME | mis-TAKE. | / The ON- | ly OTH- | er SOUND'S | the SWEEP | / Of EAS- | y WIND | and DOWN- | y FLAKE. |

B. Words that students are to circle appear in parentheses.

1. Students should connect the two rhyming words in each line: boy (Jim) gold (him) / sick (in) bread (medicine) / room (see) baseball (Terribly)

2. Students should connect the two rhyming words in every other line: (said) (white) (head) (right) / (son) (brain) (none) (again) (before) (fat) (door) (that)

3. Students should connect the two rhyming words in every other line: (locks) (supple) (box) (couple) / (weak) (suet) (beak) (do it) (law) (wife) (jaw) (life)

4. Students should connect the two rhyming words in every other line: (suppose) (ever) (nose) (clever) / (enough) (airs) (stuff) (downstairs)

5. Students should connect the first, second, and fourth word in each line: (know) (though) here (snow) / (queer) (near) lake (year)

6. Students should connect the first, second, and fourth word in the first line and every word in the second line: (shake) (mistake) sweep (flake) / (deep) (keep) (sleep) (sleep)

Vocabulary Builder, p. 191

A. Sample Answers

1. No; *incessantly* means "without stopping," so Father William does not take breaks when he is standing on his head.

2. Yes; a *sage* is a wise person, so Father William would probably do well on a quiz show.

3. No; *supple* means "flexible," so Father William probably had no trouble bending down to tie his shoes.

4. No; something that is *downy* is light and fluffy.

5. No; the *harness* is used so a person can control the horse's movements.

6. No; someone who is *uncommonly* fat is unusually fat.

B. 1. If you were *unprepared* for a test, you would not do well.

2. No, most fantasies have *unrealistic*, imaginary characters such as wizards or elves.

3. No, it is usually hard to sleep if a bed is *uncomfortable*.

Enrichment: Healthy Living, p. 192

1. Answers will depend on the date on which students answer the question. As of this writing, the oldest living man is Emiliano Mercado Del Toro of Puerto Rico. He was born in 1891 and served in the U.S. Army in 1918.

2. Answers will depend on the date on which students answer the question. As of this writing, the oldest living woman is Hendrijke Van Andel-Schipper of the Netherlands. She was born in 1890 and has been an avid soccer fan for eighty years.

3. The oldest man to complete a marathon was Dimitrion Yordanidis of Greece. He completed the Athens Marathon in 1976 at the age of ninety-eight.

4. The oldest woman to complete a marathon was Jenny Wood-Allen of Dundee, Scotland. She completed the London Marathon in 2002 at the age of ninety.

5. The oldest man to climb Mount Everest was Min Bahadur Sherchan of Nepal. He scaled the mountain in 2008 at the age of seventy-six.

6. The oldest woman to win an Academy Award for Best Actress was Jessica Tandy. She won the award for her role in *Driving Miss Daisy* in 1990 at the age of eighty.

7. Students should write about an active older person whom they know personally or have read about, explaining what is admirable about him or her and what remarkable things the person does, given his or her age.

Poetry Collections: Edgar Allan Poe, Raymond Richard Patterson, Emily Dickinson; Lewis Carroll, Robert Frost, Gwendolyn Brooks

Integrated Language Skills: Grammar, p. 193

A. 1. compound
2. complex
3. simple
4. simple
5. compound

B. Students should write a coherent, grammatically correct paragraph about one of the poems in these collections. They should use and correctly identify at least one simple sentence, one compound sentence, and one complex sentence.

Poetry Collection: Lewis Carroll, Robert Frost, Gwendolyn Brooks

Open Book Test, p. 196

Short Answer

1. The poet rhymes the word *terribly* with *see*. It works as a rhyme because *terribly* ends with the long "e" vowel sound.
   Difficulty: *Easy*   **Objective:** *Literary Analysis*

2. Sample answer: When his mother was sick, Jim took care of her. He brought her food and medicine.
   Difficulty: *Average*   **Objective:** *Reading*

3. Sample answer: The speaker's high opinion of Jim is deserved. He takes care of his mother when he would much rather be out playing baseball.
   Difficulty: *Average*   **Objective:** *Interpretation*

4. Sample answer: *Incessantly* means "without stopping." Therefore, Father William is clearly different from most seniors, who do not stand on their heads all of the time.
   Difficulty: *Average*   **Objective:** *Vocabulary*

5. Father William needs to be supple, or very flexible, so that he can turn back-somersaults.
   Difficulty: *Easy*   **Objective:** *Vocabulary*

6. *weak/beak*, 1 syllable; *suet/do it*, 2 syllables; *law/jaw*, 1 syllable; *wife/life*, 1 syllable
   The lines that end with *suet* and *do it* end on unstressed syllables. The other lines end on stressed syllables.
   Difficulty: *Average*   **Objective:** *Literary Analysis*

7. His explanation is that by arguing law cases with his wife, he made his jaw incredibly strong. It is a humorous explanation because it suggests arguing with his wife was harder than arguing with anybody else.
   Difficulty: *Challenging*   **Objective:** *Interpretation*

8. Sample answer: The speaker seems to be stopping to enjoy the snow and the woods. He is in the middle of a journey and wants to pause for a few quiet moments. He knows he must go on.
   Difficulty: *Average*   **Objective:** *Interpretation*

9. In the other stanzas, the 1st, 2nd, and 4th lines rhyme. In the last stanza, all four lines rhyme. The poet might have done this to emphasize the last stanza.
   Difficulty: *Challenging*   **Objective:** *Literary Analysis*

10. Sample answer: The speaker has enjoyed being in the woods, because they are "lovely, dark, and deep." However, he has to leave, although he doesn't want to, because he has obligations, or "promises to keep." His journey through life is not over, so he has to keep going.
    Difficulty: *Challenging*   **Objective:** *Interpretation*

Essay

11. Sample answer: Jim does not let his mother see how much he would rather be playing baseball because he understands that his mother needs him. She is sick and needs care. He is a good son who loves his

"Mother-dear." Jim seems to be a loving person who puts the needs of others first.
Difficulty: *Easy*   **Objective:** *Essay*

12. Sample answer: The speaker is not just talking about tasks that he has to do in any one day. He is talking about all of the responsibilities he has in his life. "Miles to go before I sleep" is repeated to emphasize that he is talking about his entire life, after which will finally come his "sleep."
    Difficulty: *Average*   **Objective:** *Essay*

13. Sample answer: The message of the poem is that older people can do much more than they are ordinarily given credit for. Each of the three questions is also answered in a very clever way, showing that older people are very aware. Even though Father William says he "has no brain," he clearly is saying just the reverse—that the things he thought were true in his youth have turned out to be assumptions rather than truths.
    Difficulty: *Challenging*   **Objective:** *Essay*

14. Sample answer: In "Jim," we meet a devoted son who does what he needs to do instead of what he wants to do. In "Father William," we meet an old man who is surprising in his attitude and abilities. In "Stopping by Woods. . ." we meet a person who is taking a short break from his life. "Jim" seems to best explore how the character feels because we learn the most about how he feels—he intensely misses playing baseball.
    Difficulty: *Average*   **Objective:** *Essay*

Oral Response

15. Oral responses should be clear, well organized, and well supported by appropriate examples from the poems.
    Difficulty: *Average*   **Objective:** *Oral Interpretation*

Selection Test A, p. 199

Critical Reading

1. ANS: B	DIF: Easy	OBJ: Interpretation
2. ANS: B	DIF: Easy	OBJ: Literary Analysis
3. ANS: D	DIF: Easy	OBJ: Reading
4. ANS: D	DIF: Easy	OBJ: Literary Analysis
5. ANS: C	DIF: Easy	OBJ: Literary Analysis
6. ANS: B	DIF: Easy	OBJ: Interpretation
7. ANS: C	DIF: Easy	OBJ: Interpretation
8. ANS: B	DIF: Easy	OBJ: Literary Analysis
9. ANS: D	DIF: Easy	OBJ: Comprehension
10. ANS: B	DIF: Easy	OBJ: Reading Skill

Vocabulary and Grammar

11. ANS: A	DIF: Easy	OBJ: Vocabulary
12. ANS: D	DIF: Easy	OBJ: Grammar
13. ANS: C	DIF: Easy	OBJ: Grammar

Essay

14. Students may point out that the basic situations in the two poems are so different as to be opposites—in "Jim" the parent is ill; in "Father William" the parent is youthful and vigorous. Jim is appropriately subdued, therefore, whereas Father William's son is lively. Students will probably note that Jim is respectful and selfless, whereas Father William's son is disrespectful and insensitive.

Difficulty: *Easy*

Objective: *Essay*

15. Students are likely to say that Frost had a deep love for the natural world. They may suggest that the speaker in the poem, most likely Frost himself, is drawn to the beauty of the woods, even on a cold winter night. He stops his horse to watch the snow and seems to move on reluctantly, reminding himself of his responsibilities. Students might point to phrases such as "easy wind and downy flake" and the statement that "The woods are lovely, dark, and deep" to support their argument.

Difficulty: *Easy*

Objective: *Essay*

16. Students should pick the character that they responded to more than the others, and explain why that poem communicated more effectively to them. Their answers should be supported by specific examples from the text.

Difficulty: *Average*

Objective: *Essay*

Selection Test B, p. 202

Critical Reading

1. ANS: C	DIF: Average	OBJ: Literary Analysis
2. ANS: B	DIF: Average	OBJ: Literary Analysis
3. ANS: D	DIF: Average	OBJ: Interpretation
4. ANS: D	DIF: Average	OBJ: Reading
5. ANS: D	DIF: Average	OBJ: Literary Analysis
6. ANS: C	DIF: Average	OBJ: Comprehension
7. ANS: C	DIF: Average	OBJ: Interpretation
8. ANS: C	DIF: Challenging	OBJ: Literary Analysis
9. ANS: D	DIF: Average	OBJ: Comprehension
10. ANS: C	DIF: Average	OBJ: Interpretation
11. ANS: A	DIF: Average	OBJ: Reading
12. ANS: B	DIF: Challenging	OBJ: Interpretation

Vocabulary and Grammar

13. ANS: A	DIF: Average	OBJ: Vocabulary
14. ANS: C	DIF: Average	OBJ: Vocabulary
15. ANS: C	DIF: Average	OBJ: Grammar
16. ANS: D	DIF: Average	OBJ: Grammar
17. ANS: B	DIF: Challenging	OBJ: Grammar

Essay

18. Students should name one of the characters and cite three details from the poem to support their reasons for finding the character interesting. For example, students who choose Jim may admire the selflessness and generosity he shows at a young age. Those who choose Father William may admire his spunk and his ability to defend himself. Those who choose Father William's son may cite his audaciousness and his sass. Students who choose Frost's poem may admire his willingness to put aside his responsibilities to admire the beauty of nature.

Difficulty: *Average*

Objective: *Essay*

19. Students should make a statement about youth and old age that logically relates to the poem, and they should support that point with three details from the poem. They might say, for example, that society tends to underestimate the abilities of older people. They might point to the father's somersaults, his appetite for goose, his ability to balance an eel on his nose, and his ready answers to his son's prying questions.

Difficulty: *Average*

Objective: *Essay*

20. Students should demonstrate an understanding of the difference between a literal interpretation and a figurative interpretation. In the last paragraph, for example, they should understand that on a literal level the speaker says that although the woods are beautiful, he must not stay because he must keep promises he has made (perhaps he promised someone he would be home by midnight), and he has a long way to go before he gets home; on a symbolic level, he might mean that there is a great deal he wants to accomplish before he dies.

Difficulty: *Challenging*

Objective: *Essay*

21. Sample answer: In "Jim," we meet a devoted son who does what he needs to do instead of what he wants to do. In "Father William," we meet an old man who is surprising in his attitude and abilities. In "Stopping by Woods. . . ," we meet a person who is taking a short break from his life. "Jim" seems to best explore how the character feels because we learn the most about how he feels—he intensely misses playing baseball.

Difficulty: *Average*

Objective: *Essay*

Poetry by Walt Whitman and E.E. Cummings

Vocabulary Warm-up Exercises, p. 206

A. 1. Manhattan

2. balloonman

3. sight

4. motion

5. lame

6. delicate

B. Sample Answers

1. Most people do not enjoy being bitten by <u>insects</u>, such as flies.

2. If someone <u>whistles</u>, he uses his lips and breath to make a noise.

3. It will be easier to find the lost ring in the <u>light</u> of day.

4. It was a <u>miracle</u> that Dean passed the test when he studied so little for it.

5. This <u>spring</u> the flowers will be pretty colors.

Reading Warm-up A, p. 207

Sample Answers

1. (one of the most exciting parts of New York City); If I lived in or visited *Manhattan*, I would like to see the museums, the shops, the plays.

2. <u>activity</u>; The *motion* of the boat on the waves made Ed seasick.

3. <u>lines of her sketches</u>; *Delicate* means "beautifully fine in texture, quality, or appearance."

4. <u>selling his wares</u>; Other places a *balloonman* might be seen are at a party or at the circus.

5. (a little old lady lovingly feeding a lame pigeon); *Sight* means "the act of seeing with one's eyes."

6. (pigeon); If someone's leg is hurt and *lame*, a crutch may help him or her to walk.

Reading Warm-up B, p. 208

Sample Answers

1. <u>after winter and before summer.</u>; Linda loved the *spring* best of all because she didn't have to wear a heavy winter coat any more.

2. (birds), (Their chirping); *Whistles* means "makes a note or tune by blowing through the lips."

3. (This season of new life); *Miracle* means "a marvel or a remarkable, unexplained event."

4. (never-ending journey); Other things that are *continual* are sunrises and sunsets each day or the buzzing sound of a computer that is turned on.

5. <u>Earth receives the sun's rays more directly at this time</u>; *Light* means "the daylight hours."

6. <u>ants</u>; Other kinds of *insects* include flies, beetles, termites.

Writing About the Big Question, p. 209

A. 1. communicate

2. learn

3. enrich

B. Sample Answers

1. I like to **communicate** with others through music. I use music to **entertain** when I play my violin. I also like to mix CDs with special songs on them for my friends.

2. When people listen to me play music, they can understand what I feel. When they hear my CDs,

they can learn about me through the words of the songs.

C. Sample Answer

Descriptive words can enrich a piece of writing because they can help the reader make a picture in his or her mind.

Literary Analysis: Comparing Imagery, p. 210

Sample Answers

1. sight, touch

2. sight

3. sight, touch

4. hearing

5. sight, touch, smell, taste

6. sight

7. sight, hearing

8. sight

9. sight

10. sight

11. sight, hearing

12. sight

13. sight

14. sight, touch

15. sight

16. sight, touch

17. sight, hearing

18. sight, hearing

19. sight, touch, hearing

20. sight, touch

21. sight, hearing

22. sight

23. sight, touch, hearing

Vocabulary Builder, p. 211

A. Sample Answers

exquisite: Synonyms—superior, superb; *Antonyms*—flawed, faulty, imperfect; *Example sentence*—The exquisite flowers were perfect in every way.

distinct: Synonyms—different, separate, notable; *Antonyms*—identical, similar; *Example sentence*—Charles has such a distinct way of looking at life that no one ever agrees with him.

B. 1. D; 2. B

Open-Book Test, p. 213

Short Answer

1. *Exquisite* means "beautiful in a delicate way." Line 13 describes the sundown and stars shining, both of which could be described as exquisite.

Difficulty: *Challenging* **Objective:** *Vocabulary*

2. *Distinct* means "separate and different." If your umbrella were different from the others, it would stand out and be easy to find.
   Difficulty: *Average*   **Objective:** *Vocabulary*

3. Sample answers: stand under trees in the woods; sit at table at dinner; the sea
   All of life is miraculous, even the most commonplace things.
   Difficulty: *Average*   **Objective:** *Interpretation*

4. The speaker is saying that spring is rainy, leaving puddles on the ground and making mud. He finds the weather wonderful and luscious.
   Difficulty: *Easy*   **Objective:** *Interpretation*

5. The children are happy that both have arrived. The first pair "come running"; the second pair "come dancing."
   Difficulty: *Average*   **Objective:** *Interpretation*

6. The balloonman stands for the coming of spring. The references to spring—his association with the forest, fields, and wild animals—support this idea.
   Difficulty: *Challenging*   **Objective:** *Interpretation*

7. Both appeal strongly to the sense of sight. In "Miracles," the speaker sees the roofs, watches animals, and views phenomena like the sunset, the moon and stars, and the sea. In "in Just—" the "lame balloonman" and the children running and dancing are important sight images.
   Difficulty: *Easy*   **Objective:** *Literary Analysis*

8. The image of talking to a loved one appeals to the sense of hearing. An image that appeals to the sense of hearing in "in Just—" is "whistles far and wee."
   Difficulty: *Average*   **Objective:** *Literary Analysis*

9. In "Miracles," the images of everyday occurrences that the speaker finds miraculous give the reader a feeling of wonder and awe. The images of spring and playing children in "in Just—," create a feeling of joy and playfulness.
   Difficulty: *Challenging*   **Objective:** *Literary Analysis*

10. The images in "Miracles" deal with the whole world, whereas those in "in Just—" describe only a single park scene.
    Difficulty: *Average*   **Objective:** *Literary Analysis*

Essay

11. Students should recognize that Whitman focuses on sight in "Miracles" because this is the main sense through which we experience nature. The meaning of the poem is that we should find wonder in all that the world presents to us. The speaker darts his sight over the roofs of houses and looks into the faces of strangers; he watches honeybees, animals feeding, and birds and insects; he views the sundown, stars shining, and the delicate thin curve of the new moon. All of these sight images are of common objects and events. The idea is that the commonplace is wonderful and miraculous.
    Difficulty: *Easy*   **Objective:** *Essay*

12. Students should give examples of images appealing to sight (for example, "the streets of Manhattan" in "Miracles" and "the little lame balloonman" in "in Just—"), sound ("talk by day" in "Miracles" and the balloonman's whistle in "in Just—"), and touch (wading barefoot in "Miracles" and "mud-luscious" in "in Just—"). In citing differences between the two poems, students might point out that Whitman presents conventional pictures of the world, while Cummings mixes imaginative, unexpected images with everyday images. Students might say that the images are the same in that they both present positive views of nature.
    Difficulty: *Average*   **Objective:** *Essay*

13. Students should recognize that Whitman says that all everyday scenes and occurrences (a beach, a woods, honeybees at a hive, animals feeding in field, and so on) are miracles. He treasures the world for all of the miracles it presents and is thus in awe of nature. Students should recognize that Cummings presents nature from the point of view of children greeting the arrival of spring, using playful images like "mud-luscious," "puddle-wonderful," and "the balloonman whistles far and wee." Instead of using a solemn tone as in "Miracles," the poet appears to be saying that in nature one can be happy and carefree.
    Difficulty: *Challenging*   **Objective:** *Essay*

14. Students may note that in "Miracles" the speaker finds wonder in everyday events. This wonder is communicated to him through his senses as he views the world. As a result, he might say that the best form of communication is being in touch with the natural world through all of our senses. Students should note that the speaker of "in Just—" takes joy in the coming of spring. Again, this joy is communicated through his senses as he finds the world "mud-luscious" and "puddle-wonderful." He views the coming of spring as a balloonman who "whistles far and wee." In this way, the playful nature of spring is communicated through the senses. Consequently, this speaker would agree with the speaker of "Miracles" that the best form of communication is using your senses to keep in touch with the world around you.
    Difficulty: *Average*   **Objective:** *Essay*

Oral Response

15. Oral responses should be clear, well organized, and well supported by appropriate examples from the poems.
    Difficulty: *Average*   **Objective:** *Oral Interpretation*

Selection Test A, p. 216
Critical Reading

1. ANS: C   DIF: Easy   OBJ: Literary Analysis
2. ANS: B   DIF: Easy   OBJ: Literary Analysis
3. ANS: D   DIF: Easy   OBJ: Comprehension
4. ANS: A   DIF: Easy   OBJ: Comprehension

5. ANS: A   DIF: Easy   OBJ: Literary Analysis

6. ANS: C   DIF: Easy   OBJ: Comprehension

7. ANS: D   DIF: Easy   OBJ: Comprehension

8. ANS: B   DIF: Easy   OBJ: Interpretation

9. ANS: A   DIF: Easy   OBJ: Literary Analysis

10. ANS: C   DIF: Easy   OBJ: Literary Analysis

11. ANS: D   DIF: Easy   OBJ: Literary Analysis

Vocabulary

12. ANS: D   DIF: Easy   OBJ: Vocabulary

13. ANS: B   DIF: Easy   OBJ: Vocabulary

Essay

14. Students should recognize that "Miracles" is all about nature; the entire poem is devoted to praising nature, which Whitman considers a series of miracles. He sees these miracles (and, therefore, nature) everywhere—when walking on city streets, wading on a beach, dining with friends or family, sitting with strangers—and in everything—in bees at their hive, stars shining at night, and so on. Students should also recognize that Cummings focuses on an aspect of nature: the arrival of spring ("when the world is mud-luscious" and "puddle-wonderful"). Unlike Whitman, Cummings does not celebrate nature as a thing in itself. Instead, it is the background against which children play and the balloonman arrives. It is a happy, carefree time, but the poet does not call it a miracle.

    Difficulty: *Easy*

    Objective: *Essay*

15. Students should give examples of images appealing to sight (for example, "the streets of Manhattan" in "Miracles," "the little lame balloonman" in "in Just—"), sound (the balloonman's whistle in "in Just—"), and touch (wading barefoot at the beach in "Miracles"). In citing differences between the two poems' images, students might point out that Whitman presents conventional pictures of the world as we are used to seeing it whereas Cummings mixes imaginative, unexpected images ("mud-luscious" and "puddle-wonderful") with everyday images (boys playing with marbles, girls playing hopscotch). Students should defend their choice of their preferred images with well-reasoned explanations.

    Difficulty: *Easy*

    Objective: *Essay*

16. Students might note that "Miracles" shows that the best form of communication is being in touch with nature through all of our senses. Students might note that the speaker of "in Just—" takes joy in the coming of spring. This speaker would agree with the speaker of "Miracles" that the best form of communication is using your senses to keep in touch with the world around you.

    Difficulty: *Average*

    Objective: *Essay*

Selection Test B, p. 219

Critical Reading

1. ANS: D   DIF: Challenging   OBJ: Interpretation

2. ANS: B   DIF: Average   OBJ: Literary Analysis

3. ANS: C   DIF: Average   OBJ: Literary Analysis

4. ANS: C   DIF: Challenging   OBJ: Interpretation

5. ANS: C   DIF: Average   OBJ: Interpretation

6. ANS: D   DIF: Average   OBJ: Interpretation

7. ANS: A   DIF: Challenging   OBJ: Interpretation

8. ANS: D   DIF: Challenging   OBJ: Interpretation

9. ANS: D   DIF: Average   OBJ: Literary Analysis

10. ANS: A   DIF: Challenging   OBJ: Interpretation

11. ANS: B   DIF: Average   OBJ: Comprehension

12. ANS: C   DIF: Average   OBJ: Interpretation

13. ANS: B   DIF: Average   OBJ: Literary Analysis

14. ANS: C   DIF: Average   OBJ: Literary Analysis

15. ANS: D   DIF: Average   OBJ: Literary Analysis

16. ANS: C   DIF: Average   OBJ: Literary Analysis

Vocabulary

17. ANS: A   DIF: Average   OBJ: Vocabulary

18. ANS: B   DIF: Challenging   OBJ: Vocabulary

Essay

19. Students should identify two images of nature from "Miracles" (a beach, a woods, honeybees at a hive, animals feeding in a field, and so on) and one from "in Just—" (the world as "mud-luscious" or "puddle-wonderful"). They should recognize that Whitman says that all of those everyday scenes and occurrences, as well as those involving human beings, are miracles; he treasures the world for its miraculousness. They should recognize that Cummings presents the world from the point of view of children on the arrival of spring. The poet appears to be saying that in nature one can be happy and carefree.

    Difficulty: *Average*

    Objective: *Essay*

20. Students should point to at least two images from each poem and correctly identify the sense or senses to which they appeal. They should name the poem whose images they prefer and present logical reasons in support of their choice.

    Difficulty: *Average*

    Objective: *Essay*

21. Students may note that, in "Miracles," the speaker finds wonder in everyday events. This wonder is communicated to him through his senses as he views the world. As a result, he might say that the best form of communication is being in touch with the natural world through all of our senses. Students should note that the speaker of "in Just—" takes joy in the coming of spring.

Again, this joy is communicated through his senses, as he finds the world "mud-luscious" and "puddle-wonderful." He views the coming of spring as a balloonman who "whistles far and wee." In this way, the playful nature of spring is communicated through the senses. Consequently, this speaker would agree with the speaker of "Miracles" that the best form of communication is using your senses to keep in touch with the world around you.

Difficulty: *Average*

Objective: *Essay*

Writing Workshop

Persuasive Essay: Integrating Grammar Skills, p. 223

A. 1. R; 2. R; 3. F; 4. S

B. Rewritten sentences, especially corrected fragments, may vary.

1. The school bus usually arrives at seven, but sometimes it is late.
2. I am usually waiting on the corner with my sister and brother.
3. My brother takes one bus; my sister and I take another.
4. I arrive at school by seven-thirty.

Vocabulary Workshops, pp. 224–225

Sample Answers

A. 1. clever: positive; sly: negative
2. boastful: negative; proud: positive
3. reckless: negative; brave: positive; heroic: positive
4. large: neutral; hearty: positive; fat: negative
5. immature: negative; youthful: positive
6. alone: neutral; lonely: negative; independent: positive

B. Sentences will vary. Possible responses are shown.

1. Positive: challenging; She knew the contest would be challenging, so she tried her hardest.

   Negative: confusing; The students had difficulty understanding the confusing directions.
2. Positive: discipline; Every small child benefits from guidance, love, and discipline.

   Negative: punishment; As punishment, John was forced to clean the basement.
3. Positive: curious; Hal was curious about hawks and eagles, so he researched the facts.

   Negative: nosy; Our nosy neighbor often stands in her window and watches us.
4. Positive: tiptoeing; Not wanting to disturb the baby, the girls were tiptoeing down the stairs.

   Negative: sneaking; Not wanting to be detected, the girls were sneaking off with the cookies.

5. Positive: requested; She politely requested another serving of pie.

   Negative: demanded; She loudly demanded another serving of pie.

Benchmark Test 8, p. 227

MULTIPLE CHOICE

1. ANS: A
2. ANS: B
3. ANS: A
4. ANS: D
5. ANS: B
6. ANS: D
7. ANS: C
8. ANS: B
9. ANS: D
10. ANS: B
11. ANS: C
12. ANS: A
13. ANS: B
14. ANS: D
15. ANS: A
16. ANS: C
17. ANS: D
18. ANS: B
19. ANS: D
20. ANS: A
21. ANS: B
22. ANS: C
23. ANS: A
24. ANS: D
25. ANS: B
26. ANS: A
27. ANS: C
28. ANS: D
29. ANS: D
30. ANS: A
31. ANS: B
32. ANS: B
33. ANS: D
34. ANS: D
35. ANS: A
36. ANS: C

ESSAY

37. Students' poems should demonstrate an understanding of sound devices and how they are used.

38. Students' paraphrases should demonstrate their understanding of paraphrasing.

39. Students should identify possible concerns, such as cost, congestion, noise, dirt, and/or crime, and give reasons why these concerns are unwarranted or why the benefits of the stadium outweigh the drawbacks.

Vocabulary in Context, p. 232

MULTIPLE CHOICE

1. ANS: D
2. ANS: A
3. ANS: D
4. ANS: B
5. ANS: C
6. ANS: A
7. ANS: A
8. ANS: D
9. ANS: C
10. ANS: B
11. ANS: D
12. ANS: C
13. ANS: B
14. ANS: B
15. ANS: B
16. ANS: C
17. ANS: B
18. ANS: C
19. ANS: C
20. ANS: C